The Other Side of Assimilation

D1615888

The Other Side of Assimilation

HOW IMMIGRANTS ARE CHANGING AMERICAN LIFE

Tomás R. Jiménez

UNIVERSITY OF CALIFORNIA PRESS

University of California Press, one of the most distinguished university presses in the United States, enriches lives around the world by advancing scholarship in the humanities, social sciences, and natural sciences. Its activities are supported by the UC Press Foundation and by philanthropic contributions from individuals and institutions. For more information, visit www.ucpress.edu.

University of California Press
Oakland, California

Library of Congress Cataloging-in-Publication Data

Names: Jiménez, Tomás R. (Tomás Roberto), author.
Title: The other side of assimilation : how immigrants are changing American life / Tomás R. Jiménez.
Description: Oakland, California : University of California Press, [2017] | Includes bibliographical references and index.
Identifiers: LCCN 2017004043 | ISBN 9780520295698 (cloth : alk. paper) | ISBN 9780520295704 (pbk : alk. paper) | ISBN 9780520968370 (ebook)
Subjects: LCSH: Assimilation (Sociology)—California—Santa Clara Valley (Santa Clara County) | Immigrants—California—Santa Clara Valley (Santa Clara County) | City dwellers—Cultural assimilation—California—Santa Clara Valley (Santa Clara County)
Classification: LCC HM843.J56 2017 | DDC 303.48/20979473—dc23
LC record available at https://lccn.loc.gov/2017004043

26 25 24 23 22 21 20 19 18 17
10 9 8 7 6 5 4 3 2 1

For Nova Diana Jiménez

Contents

Illustrations and Table

Preface

The idea for this book came from a long walk with my wife, Nova. It was the summer of 2008, and we were about to move back to Silicon Valley after having been away for ten years. We both grew up in the Valley—she in San Jose, and I in Santa Clara—during the 1980s and 90s. Our impending return to the region where we had grown up sparked a conversation about what things were like during our childhood, and how much they had changed since last we lived there. During our youth, Silicon Valley was coming into its own as a global hub of technological innovation. It was also during that time that the Valley emerged as a popular landing spot for immigrants from Asia, Latin America, and beyond. We knew many of these immigrants and their children. Nova, having grown up in the eastern part of San Jose, played and went to school with the children of immigrants from Mexico, the Philippines, and Vietnam. Santa Clara, where I grew up, had large Filipino, Vietnamese, Mexican, and Portuguese populations that were a mix of U.S.- and foreign-born individuals. Some of the immigrants and their children were my friends, my classmates, and my teammates in soccer, baseball, and basketball.

When we had returned to visit family during our decade away, we had noticed our hometowns were changing. Many immigrant Chinese and

Indian families had settled in the neighborhoods of my youth. The east San Jose neighborhoods where Nova had spent her childhood were bustling with new Latino and Asian arrivals. Our informal observations squared with what often-cited demographic data showed about the region: by the turn of the twenty-first century, it had become one of the largest per capita immigrant destinations in the nation, and a majority of the population was made up of people of color.

As Nova and I continued our walk that summer evening, our recollections turned to our immigrant and second-generation childhood friends, and what had become of them. Many seemed to have followed the story of assimilation portrayed in academic research. We noted that they all spoke English, that many were enthusiastic consumers of American popular culture, that they had found different paths into the middle class, and that many had dated and eventually married people from ethnic backgrounds different from their own. That view of their assimilation fit with the model of American immigration I had learned from my own study of immigration in the United States. Throughout graduate school and into my early career as an academic sociologist, I had been deeply engaged with debates about immigrant assimilation. What I read about assimilation treated it as a process that found each new generation born in the United States becoming more similar to the populations that were already there. In my own early research, I looked at how ongoing immigration shaped the experiences of the later-generation descendants of the early twentieth-century Mexican immigration wave. As I conducted that research, I occasionally wrestled with the question of who was assimilating to whom, and the book that resulted *(Replenished Ethnicity: Mexican Americans, Immigration, and Identity)* documented the various ways that ongoing Mexican immigration had a significant influence on the lives of Mexican Americans whose families had lived in the United States for generations. But the conclusions I drew in that book, as well as my other research and writing, nonetheless followed the conventional thinking about assimilation.

As our walk wore on, Nova began reflecting more about what it was like for her to come of age around so many people living in immigrant households. She spoke of the normalcy that came with growing up around people whose parents came from another country. She talked about encounters with other ethnic traditions. She had enjoyed them and came to feel as though some, like Chinese New Year and Cinco de Mayo, were somehow American. She spoke of not being able to understand some of her friends' parents because they spoke languages other than English. But she also picked up a few words of those languages—enough to joke with her friends. And she talked about her mixed Mexican and Irish ancestry leading her to be seen as the "white" girl in some contexts, but the "Mexican" girl in others. Her own identity, how she saw herself, seemed to depend on whether she was around mostly Asians, mostly Mexicans, or a mixed group of peers.

As she went on, I interrupted, asking, "So, was it like you were adjusting to all of the immigration?" "Exactly!" she quickly replied.

Our conversation during that long summer walk, along with a catalogue of my own informal observations, prompted me to begin to study assimilation in a different light. It spurred me to think about assimilation in a way that reflected Nova's and my recollections of a childhood full of interactions with immigrants and their children. It led me to turn assimilation on its head in order to consider how immigration might shape the experiences of the most established people in the United States: the people who are not immigrants or the children of immigrants.

Nova and I were not alone in noticing how much things had changed in our respective hometowns because of immigration. Close observers have marveled at the ways that immigrants to America have transformed virtually every aspect of our national life. In spite of that commonly articulated observation, however, scholars interested in understanding assimilation have focused almost exclusively on how immigrants and their children—"newcomers" as I call them in this book—adjust to the new racial, class, and political contexts in the United States. The observation about the abundant changes resulting from immigration raises an obvious, but important question: How do people whose families have been in the United States for several generations adjust to all of these changes?

This book documents what I learned as I tried to answer that question, using Silicon Valley as a laboratory. Over a period of two years, two Stanford University graduate students and I interviewed residents who were born in the United States to U.S.-born parents—"established individuals," as I call them throughout the book. The people we interviewed came from a spectrum of racial and social class backgrounds. Their neighbors, friends, coworkers, schoolmates, and even family members included large numbers of newcomers. I wanted to learn how the established individuals we interviewed made sense of navigating daily life around so many newcomers. After dozens of interviews, I learned that established individuals saw their lives and the lives of newcomers as deeply enmeshed. That closeness meant that the intentional and incidental ways that newcomers attempted to belong were forcing established individuals to make significant and often uncomfortable adjustments of their own. Their stories showed them coming to terms with changing demographic and cultural norms, with reshuffled conceptions of racial and ethnic identity, and with an American national identity that newcomers seemed to make clearer in some respects, but more opaque in others.

As I stepped back to consider the vast research literature about newcomer assimilation, combined with what I learned about the adjustment process that established individuals undergo, I began to conclude that assimilation no longer looks like a process where newcomers, over time, become more similar to established individuals. Instead, assimilation appears to be a more relational process—a back-and-forth set of adjustments and readjustments in which both newcomers and established individuals work out, through interactions with one another, what it means to belong. That process, which plays out in everyday life in both obvious and subtle ways, is remaking America. Newcomers are changing, yes. But they are not the only ones. Ultimately, I learned, America is being remade because newcomers are shaping how America's most established individuals understand the world around them.

Acknowledgments

It takes a proverbial village to do a lot of things, including to write a book. Indeed, putting this book together took a rather large village to which I owe a tremendous debt of gratitude. First and foremost, I thank the individuals who allowed us to interview them for this book. They were generous with their time, and thoughtful in answering our questions. Some people were especially generous in helping us get to know the three communities from which we drew the respondents. In East Palo Alto, Larry Moody, Bob Hoover, and Will Brown were invaluably helpful. In Cupertino, Viviana Montoya-Hernandez, Bill Wilson, and Laura Domondon Lee provided vital guidance. And in Berryessa, Greg Boyd and Marc Liebman were valued sources of information and help.

I was fortunate to have lots of financial help in carrying out this project. I thank the following organizations for their generous financial support: the National Science Foundation (SES-1121281), the American Sociological Association Fund for the Advancement of the Discipline, the Institute for Research in the Social Sciences at Stanford, the United Parcel Service Endowment Fund at Stanford, Stanford's department of sociology, and the Russell Sage Foundation. I am especially grateful to Stanford for providing a sabbatical while I was still an assistant professor. It gave me the time I needed to get this book off the ground. I spent that sabbatical at the Center for Advanced Studies in the Behavioral and Social Sciences at Stanford, where I had the joy of talking through ideas big and small with some really smart and interesting people.

Several colleagues and friends helped me hone my analysis, ideas, and writing. Natasha Warikoo deserves special thanks for offering input as the project developed and for her feedback on the entire manuscript. John Skrentny, Jennifer Lee, David FitzGerald, and Mario Small were extremely helpful in figuring out the project's design, and they have been supportive throughout. Other colleagues read portions of the book and offered sage advice at different stages: Paolo Parigi, Monica McDermott, Corey Fields, Cristobal Young, Michelle Jackson, Irene Bloemraad, Deborah Schildkraut, and Aliya Saperstein. The data collection, analyses, and writing were possible only because I worked with talented and committed Stanford graduate students. Many of them now have professional careers of their own. Adam Horowitz and Maneka Brooks helped me gather the interviews. I cannot thank them enough for their time and talent. Patricia Seo, Ariela Schachter, Lorena Castro, Anna Boch, and Priya Fielding-Singh also assisted with the research at different stages. Several undergraduates also made important contributions. From Stanford, Amy Xu, Sean Podesta, and Nikesh Patel pitched in with research assistance. Felipe Huicochea from UCLA and Alex Ornelas from UC Santa Barbara also provided valuable assistance. Special thanks go to Cherrie Potts and Pat Steffens for so ably transcribing all of the interviews. Isabella Furth offered amazing editorial input. I am deeply grateful for her help in translating my ideas into clear writing. I am also grateful to Caroline Knapp for helping me ready the manuscript for publication. Naomi Schneider from University of California Press deserves special thanks for supporting the project and its publication.

Lots of friends and colleagues also helped in myriad ways as the project developed: Al Camarillo, Cecilia Ridgeway, Cybelle Fox, David Grusky, Dowell Myers, Frank Bean, Frank Samson, Gary Segura, Helen Marrow, Jack Dovidio, Jessica Vasquez, Jody Agius-Vallejo, Juan Pedroza, Julie Park, Karen Cook, Mary Waters, Matt Snipp, Mia Tuan, Michael Rosenfeld, Min Zhou, Philip Kasinitz, Richard Alba, Robb Willer, Robert Smith, Roger Waldinger, Ruben Hernández-Leon, Seth Hannah, Shelley Correll, Susan

Brown, Susan Olzak, Taeku Lee, Tristan Ivory, Van Tran, Wendy Roth, and Yuen Huo.

My family has, as with just about everything in my life, been an unwavering source of support. My parents, Francisco and Laura, offered editorial and intellectual input, as well as much-needed child care that freed up my time to get the writing done. I am extremely grateful that my best friends also happen to be my brothers, Pancho and Miguel. I thank them for their constant encouragement. My sisters-in-law, Lori and Susie; my nephews, Carlo and Dario, and my niece, Camille: thank you for being a source of joy. I started the research for this book when my wife, Nova, was pregnant with our first son, Orlando. At about the conclusion of the data collection, we welcomed our second son, Marcel. All three of them bring me pure joy, showing me always what really matters. They are the light of my life. I want especially to thank Nova. She helped me come up with the idea for this book, and she was my strongest supporter at every step of the way. She is everything I could ask for in a life partner. I dedicate this book to her.

Introduction

It would seem like a cliché to say that immigration is changing America if it were not so true. As immigrants have streamed into the country from Latin America, Asia, the Caribbean, Africa, and the Middle East over the last four decades, that change is apparent in the ways people dress, eat, pray, debate, speak, travel, shop, dance, and identify. In the past, the imprint of America's immigrant population was most visible in coastal urban areas and Chicago. But that too has changed. Today, virtually every space on the American national map—coast to coast, North, Midwest, and South—has a notable immigrant presence.

In places with large immigrant populations the ethnic and racial landscape has experienced seismic shifts in the last four decades. Immigration is moving the entire United States toward a country defined more and more by nonwhites, if not a "majority-minority" nation (Frey 2014; Alba 2016). More than one out of ten people in the United States was born in another country, and one in four has at least one parent who was born in another country. Those numbers have also changed American politics. Whether politicians try to earn the approval and votes of people connected to an immigrant population by presenting accommodating views, or take a more restrictive stance to curry favor with people who would rather see immigration limited, the politics of immigration is simply too big to ignore (Barreto and Segura 2014; Wong et al. 2011). The politics of immigration is closely connected to the economic impact of America's foreign-born population. Orange orchards in Florida, beef-packing plants in Nebraska, corporate boardrooms in New York, labs at research universities, and technology start-ups all have significant immigrant representation. Indeed, some would argue that just about every sector of the economy depends on a foreign-born workforce (Frey 2014; Wadhwa, Saxenian, and Siciliano 2012). The influence of the large immigrant population appears in the changed sights, smells, tastes, and sounds found throughout the United States. "Ethnic" food is abundantly available just about everywhere, including large supermarket chains. In some metropolitan areas, Latin American and Asian hot sauces compete with ketchup for a place on hamburgers and hotdogs. And, of course, there is an apparent linguistic effect. Pressing "1" for English is routinely the first choice callers have to make on most phone trees, and Latin beats and Indian vocals regularly punctuate pop tunes bumping from stereo speakers and headphones across the United States.

What these changes mean has inspired much debate about the assimilation of the "post-1965" wave of immigration, named for the year immigration laws were liberalized and immigration rates began to climb dramatically. Are the immigrants of this wave assimilating? And if they are, what form does that assimilation take? While the full story remains to be seen, scholars and pundits offer reasons for optimism and for pessimism. For some, the supposedly divided political loyalties of today's immigrants, as well as their purported lack of desire to learn English and adherence to an ethnic identity, are eroding the national fabric (Buchanan 2006; Coulter 2015; Krikorian 2008). Others see a failure to assimilate, especially for poor Latino and Caribbean immigrants, that stems not from a lack of desire to fit in, but instead from persistent discrimination that blocks opportunity for social integration and economic mobility (Haller, Portes, and Lynch 2011; Portes and Rumbaut 2001; Rumbaut 2005; Telles and Ortiz 2008). Other observers are much more sanguine, noting that assimilation appears to be following a pattern similar to that seen in previous immigration waves, whose members, by most accounts, made it successfully into the American mainstream (National Academies of Science,

Engineering, and Medicine 2015). These more optimistic accounts note that some immigrants, like those from India and China, outpace the average American in education and earnings. And even those who arrive poor have second-generation children who fare better in their social and economic outcomes; in fact, some in the second generation are said to have an advantage because of their ability to navigate between cultures (Alba, Kasinitz, and Waters 2011; Alba and Nee 2003a; Kasinitz et al. 2008; Park and Myers 2010).

However the post-1965 immigrant assimilation fully plays out, which is likely to take a couple more generations, the story that close observers have offered so far is only a partial account. The other part of that story is unfolding not among immigrants or their children. It is taking place among individuals whose roots in the United States extend back at least three generations—people who were born in the United States to U.S.-born parents. These "established" individuals, as I refer to them throughout the book, have no ancestral ties to the post-1965 wave of immigrants. Yet they are undergoing an adjustment process that bears resemblance to the one so closely associated with immigrants and their second-generation children. The land itself may not be new to established individuals, whose familial experience of immigration, if it exists at all, is relegated to a distant past. But the settlement of immigrants has changed the ethnic, racial, political, economic, and cultural terrain to such a degree that it forces America's most established individuals to undergo an assimilation of their own.

This book tells the story of the established population's important, but not-so-well documented assimilation to a context heavily defined by individuals who are immigrants or the second-generation children of immigrants. I call these individuals "newcomers" because their lives are so deeply characterized by having come from another country or, in the case of the second-generation children of immigrants, having parents who were born in another country (Portes and Rumbaut 2001; Kasinitz et. al 2008). My account comes from interviews and observations conducted in California's Silicon Valley, a region known not only for its technology industry, but also for its large and diverse immigrant population. Like the United States as a whole, Silicon Valley is divided into racial and class segments.[1] Rather than examining whether immigrants and their children are assimilating into these racial and class segments (which has been the thrust of studies of "segmented assimilation," a highly influential perspective in social science since the early 1990s [Portes and Zhou 1993; Portes and Rumbaut 2001]), I examine how the individuals who already occupy these segments make sense of life in contexts with a large immigrant population. Those racial and class segments are represented in this study by residents of three different areas in Silicon Valley: East Palo Alto, a poor city that was once black majority and is now Latino majority; Cupertino, an upper-middle-class city, where whites have been replaced by Asians as the majority population; and Berryessa, a middle-class neighborhood of San Jose that has always been ethnically mixed, but that now has an Asian majority, mostly as a result of a large settlement of Vietnamese immigrants. Much of this book focuses on life in these three cities, but the racial and class segments described here extend beyond the physical places where they are found. They are also social positions. The findings I report, then, also cover how established individuals make sense of their experience in immigrant-rich environments at work, in school, in public interactions, romantic life, and leisure activities.

The established individuals among the interview respondents were of various ages, class backgrounds, and racial origins—including whites, blacks, Latinos, Asians, and people of multiple ethnic and racial backgrounds. What they shared in common was that their family roots in the United States extended back three generations or more. For most established individuals, the specific number of generations since immigration was almost irrelevant because their family had been in the United States for so long. Even the people who knew that their ancestors—whether from Europe, Latin America, or Asia—came as immigrants scarcely knew details beyond the existence of an immigrant history. Among established African Americans, details about the forced migration of their forebearers as slaves were almost entirely unknown.

The established individuals I interviewed also all shared in common a great deal of contact with newcomers. This contact profoundly shaped their experience in daily life and their worldviews. The interviews showed that, much as immigrants and their children adapt to their new environment, established individuals make often uncomfortable adjustments to new contexts as those contexts are changed by immigration. Those adjustments come as result of contact with newcomers that is extensive enough for aspects of the immigrant experience to be braided into the lives of the established individuals—so that the immigrant experience and the culture that immigrants bring with them become a familiar part of the lives of these established individuals. The established population does not necessarily adopt the music, food, celebrations, and language that immigrants bring with them. Nonetheless, they see cultural vibrancy resulting from mass immigration as a normal part of the world around them.

All of that familiarity does not entirely breed comfort for established individuals. For one, immigration unsettles the racial categories with which established individuals identify. While immigration inflects what it means to be black, white, Latino, and Asian differently into different people's lives, a large immigrant presence leads many established individuals to express greater discomfort about what it means to identify with these categories. As their experience of immigration challenges their concept of American identity, they respond to that challenge by tightening some notions of what it means to be American, but also by coming to more expansive ideas than those offered up in federal immigration policy or popular political rhetoric—ideas that draw far more on personal experience. In sum, how established Americans make sense of their experiences amounts to the flip side of the process of adjustment that immigrants undergo: much as immigrants feel a sense of mingled gain and loss resulting from their adjustment, so too do established individuals view the immigration-driven changes around them through ambivalent lenses.

WHO ASSIMILATES TO WHOM?

Together, these interview findings revealed a process of assimilation that is much more expansive than is popularly understood. The interviews showed that assimilation is a *relational process*. Newcomers and established individuals start off as strangers to each other. But over time and through regular contact, these populations become more familiar and often similar to each other through a set of back-and-forth, reciprocal adjustments. Perhaps surprisingly the relational view of assimilation that emerged among the established populations in Silicon Valley has much in common with the earliest thinking about assimilation. Chief among these early thinkers was the sociologist Robert Park, a founding father of the "Chicago School" of sociology, so named for his academic institution (the University of Chicago), but also because Park and his colleagues used the city of Chicago as a laboratory to understand urban dynamics—including those resulting from the arrival of thousands of mostly Southern and Eastern European immigrants in the early twentieth century. The well-traveled sociologist noted growing contact between people of different "races" in Chicago, the United States, and abroad, and he concluded that this contact would inevitably initiate an irreversible "race relations cycle" that would proceed from contact, to conflict, to accommodation and, finally, to assimilation (Park 1950). Studying that cycle, Park argued, required understanding the experiences of the individuals involved and examining "how the transactions looked through the eyes of individuals seeing it from opposing points of view" (1950: 152). The call to understand race relations from the perspective of multiple actors revealed an understanding of assimilation that had an almost twenty-first century multicultural sensibility. Park's assumptions regarding the inevitability of assimilation were flawed to be sure.[2] But he ultimately defined assimilation as a process that potentially changes all of the groups involved. Park, along with his University of Chicago colleague Ernest Burgess, developed the following definition of assimilation for their influential textbook on sociology: "Assimilation is a process of interpenetration and fusion in which persons and groups acquire the memories, sentiments, and attitudes of other persons or groups, and, by sharing their experience and history, are incorporated with them in a common cultural life" (1969 [1921]: 735). Park and Burgess's definition did not specify whether any particular group would change to become more like the other. Instead, assimilation could, according to their definition, involve mutual change among multiple groups of individuals.

The study of assimilation thereafter developed in a direction subtly different from that implied by Park and Burgess's definition. Rather than examining the mutual adaptation of the settled population *and* new arrivals, social scientists focused squarely on how immigrants and subsequent U.S.-born generations fit into a homogenous established population. This concept of assimilation held that the process proceeded in a straight line:

over the course of generations, the political, ethnic, racial, and religious strangeness of foreigners gave way to descendants whose comportment and stations in life resembled those of a largely white, Protestant, and middle-class mainstream. Scholars of European-origin assimilation argued that the pace of this assimilation could vary depending on minority-group attributes, like skin color and social class (Warner and Srole 1945). But the consensus was that assimilation was an inevitable and irreversible, and that it ran in one direction only (Gordon 1964; Warner and Srole 1945).

Writing in the early 1960s, just as the third-generation descendants of the early twentieth-century European immigrants were coming of age, sociologist Milton Gordon (1964) offered what many regard as the most complete theoretical statement on assimilation up to that point. Gordon posited an assimilation model made up of interrelated stages, through which foreign groups grew progressively more similar to the native one. The two most important sets of stages were *structural assimilation*—"the entrance of [a minority group] into primary group relationships with [a majority group]"—and *identificational assimilation*—"the taking on of a sense of [majority group] peoplehood" (Gordon 1964: 70). A less-noted but still important component of Gordon's treatise was his consideration of different paradigms for assimilation. Writing in the midst of the civil rights movement, Gordon was keenly aware of the aspirational models of cultural maintenance articulated in the burgeoning black, Chicano, Asian, and Native pride movements. Gordon considered a range of models, from "the melting pot" to "cultural pluralism" to its ideological and empirical antonym, "Anglo conformity." Ultimately, he concluded that "Anglo conformity," which involves "the complete renunciation of the immigrant's ancestral culture in favor of the behavior and values of the Anglo-Saxon core group" (Gordon 1964: 85), best described what had played out in the United States, at least among groups of European origin. Gordon's claim that immigrant cultures "scarcely obscured [American culture's] essential English outlines and content" (1964: 110) captures the essence of canonical assimilation theory for much of the twentieth century. Such arguments were more empirical assessment than ideological endorsement. But later scholarship critiqued them as providing the normative underpinning for a decidedly antiminority ideology of Americanization. The popularity of this critique led assimilation theory to fall out of favor in the decades after the civil rights movement, when multiculturalism and an accompanying value of diversity gained popularity (Alba and Nee 2003; Skrentny 2002).

The 1965 immigration reform all but forced scholars to reconsider assimilation. As both immigrant and long-established populations became more diverse, many scholars turned away from the idea that assimilation proceeds in a straight line, with formerly despised minorities ultimately being absorbed into a monolithic mainstream. Instead, some scholars treated assimilation as a "segmented" process: immigrants and their descendants (particularly the second generation) assimilate into one of many segments of a U.S. society that is divided by race and class (Portes and Rumbaut 2001; Portes and Zhou 1993; also see Gans 1992b). The segment of society into which the second generation assimilates depends on their immigrant parents' human capital, which determines the racial and class profile of the neighborhoods in which they settle on arrival; the type of reception and support (positive, negative, or neutral) they receive from established populations and polices; and the strength of their ties to a co-ethnic community that can enable the second generation to hang on to an immigrant-oriented identity while resisting American-style racial identities that are deleterious to socioeconomic mobility (Portes and Rumbaut 2001; Portes and Zhou 1993; Waters 1999; Zhou and Bankston 1998). Yet this segmented perspective, like the straight-line version that preceded it, is still a story of immigrant absorption—in the straight-line account, a monolithic host population absorbs minorities; in the segmented account, immigrants and their descendants are absorbed into various racial and class segments of a host population.

The established population has not been entirely missing from theories of assimilation. But assimilation scholarship relegates these more fully established generations to the role of a *gatekeeper* to full belonging for newcomers or a *benchmark* that sets the standard for social and economic attainment. The idea of the established population as gatekeeper flows from assimilation perspectives old and new, which suggest that the more newcomers can conform to the established population's expectations, the more receptive the established population will be, and the easier it will be for these newcomers to assimilate. While this view is mostly tacit in research on attitudes about immigrants and immigration (see Hainmueller and Hopkins 2014 for an overview), the segmented assimilation perspec-

tive makes that role explicit. According to this perspective, reigning attitudes among individuals in the established population are a "mode of
incorporation" that, along with policies that shape the terms of immigrant
entrance, act as a gatekeeper to full belonging in U.S. society (Portes and
Rumbaut 2001). The established population plays a more passive role in
assimilation research that aims to gauge the socioeconomic advancement
of immigrants, which treats the established population as a benchmark. In
this line of research, "native-born whites," whose socioeconomic progress is
least impaired by the discrimination and the low class status associated
with many of today's immigrants, are the standard against which to compare the progress of immigrant groups across generations. Only rarely,
though, do these models treat native-born whites as a population that is
itself subject to change (see Park, Myers, and Jiménez 2014; Park and
Myers 2010).

And so in spite of Park and Burgess's foundational definition of assimilation, which made clear that assimilation may entail mutual adjustment,
nearly a century of subsequent assimilation research and theorizing
scarcely entertained that possibility. It has only been more recently that a
number of scholars have offered definitions that allow for the possibility
that assimilation changes multiple groups of individuals, not just minority
groups (Alba and Nee 2003; Bean, Brown, and Bachmeier 2015; Massey
and Sánchez 2010; National Academies of Science, Engineering, and
Medicine 2015). Richard Alba and Victor Nee's (2003) "new assimilation
theory" stands as the most full-throated modern reconceptualization of
assimilation. Alba and Nee, like Park and Burgess, provide a definition
that is neutral about the direction of change that assimilation produces:
"[Assimilation is] the decline of an ethnic distinction and its corollary
cultural and social differences . . . . Individuals' ethnic origins become less
and less relevant in relation to members of another ethnic group (typically, but not necessarily, the ethnic majority group), and individuals on
both sides of the boundary see themselves more and more as alike, assum-
ing they are similar in terms of some other critical factors such as social
class" (2003: 11). Alba and Nee contend that as assimilation unfolds,
groups may contribute to the character of the "mainstream," which they
defined as "that part of the society *within* (emphasis in origin) which ethnic and racial origins have at most minor impacts on life chances or

opportunities" (2003: 12). Over time, Alba and Nee argue, elements of culture lose their association with an ethnic origin and become part of the mainstream's composite culture. Alba and Nee's theory asserts explicitly that the society into which immigrants assimilate changes. But even when scholars like Alba and Nee have offered versions of assimilation that allow for the influence of immigrant groups on established populations, the studies that have followed are still largely concerned with the process by which immigrant groups change. Still, Alba and Nee's version was the first modern account to emphasize relational change as a central feature of assimilation.

RELATIONAL ASSIMILATION

To the degree that change shows up in Alba and Nee's theory, it is only after several generations, when the mainstream is altered as a result of new groups being added. But if the receiving society changes as a result of immigration, that change must be happening on an individual level to the people who are living in it. The question is: How does that change unfold?

The answer begins with the premise that immigrant-origin and established individuals start off as strangers to each other. Assimilation is, in essence, the process by which they become more familiar (Brubaker 2001). As Alba and Nee suggest, that process involves changes among multiple parties, not for the newcomers alone. The process by which the established population and newcomers become familiar involves individuals from various backgrounds, newcomer and established alike, interpreting the details of daily living—the very aspects of life that might eventually alter a mainstream. Indeed, every version of assimilation theory—from Park and Burgess to Alba and Nee—implicitly or explicitly foregrounds individual interpretations of others' appearance and actions, usually in relation to notions of ethnic and racial similarity. Such interpretation is important for assimilation among newcomers because migration places them or their parents in contexts different from the ones they left, requiring them to make sense of these contexts in order to get along. But it is also important among established individuals because migrants can change the contexts in which established individuals are living. Social scientists have focused almost entirely on migrants' processes of interpretation, while virtually ignoring the simultaneous adjustments of long-established populations. The research that this book reports breaks from the orthodoxy of assimilation research by taking a close look at how established individuals interpret living, working, playing, finding romance, and forming families in a context that is heavily defined by immigration.

My examination of that process leads to the conclusion that assimilation is *relational:* it involves back-and-forth adjustments in daily life by both newcomers and established individuals as they come into contact with one another. This volley of back-and-forth adjustments starts off with rapid-fire intensity as new arrivals and established individuals first meet, and it gradually moderates over time (often across generations), as a working consensus around ethnic, racial, and national belonging develops. When considered side by side, the processes of established and newcomer adjustment are mirror images: both parties feel a tremendous sense of loss, often longing for the way things were; both also feel a sense of gain because of the dynamism that migration can produce. But the deliberate and incidental adjustments that established and newcomer individuals make are more than just mirror images—they implicate each other. As the following chapters show, newcomers' efforts to maintain a cultural connection to their country of origin through language, food, and religious customs led established individuals to conceive of a more expansive notion of cultural norms and their own relationship to those norms. The way newcomers interpreted the American racial landscape informed how they approached school and work, and this in turn radically shaped how established individuals experienced the meaning and status of their own racial and ethnic identities. The collective strategies that newcomers employed to make it in the labor market meant that established individuals felt pressure to compete and, in some cases, felt excluded from the market altogether. These local experiences affected people's views of belonging at a national scale too. And as newcomers continued to speak in their native languages or figured out ways to cope with precarious legal statuses, established individuals adjusted their own views about what it means to be American.

Assimilation is relational, but it is not necessarily symmetrical. The findings from Silicon Valley suggest that the symmetry of relational assimilation varies according to the relative power of the participants, which stems from group size, group status, and existing institutional arrangements. Individuals attached to large groups with high status, and who have a foothold in mainstream institutions, are best positioned to exert influence on notions of ethnic, racial, and national belonging. However, as the following chapters show, the individuals with the most influence are not necessarily native-born whites, as most assimilation perspectives predict. Indeed, there are instances in which newcomers have tremendous power to shape how notions of belonging play out in important realms of life, like neighborhoods and schools. But there are other instances in which established individuals articulate unbending views of belonging, especially when it comes to the importance of English-language use as a marker of national belonging. Institutional arrangements, like immigration and citizenship laws, can also tilt the balance of influence toward one group. As the subsequent chapters show, legal status can mark a hard boundary defining insiders and outsiders. And yet those who benefit most from such institutional arrangements may also push back against those arrangements, as this study saw among respondents who believed that immigration laws should be changed to allow more people access to citizenship. The overall picture of assimilation that emerges from this study, considered alongside voluminous studies of newcomer assimilation, is of a give-and-take process among individuals that requires everyone to adjust to some degree as they become less strange, and more familiar to each other.

Even as relational assimilation is taking place at the individual level, the composition of the established population is likewise changing significantly. Today's newcomers, who are mostly Latino and Asian, will give way to future generations that will be part of an established population that is much less white in character. That more diverse established population will likely have to adjust to the arrival of future waves of immigrants, much as the respondents in this book have done. That adjustment is part of American history, its contemporary landscape, and likely its future. It is the story of how the United States has been and will continue to be remade.

THE ESTABLISHED POPULATION

Given the heavy emphasis in contemporary social science on understanding minority populations, it is perhaps no surprise that assimilation research has focused overwhelmingly on immigrants and their second-generation children—the newcomers. This is even less surprising considering that so many of these first- and second-generation immigrants are not white. That focus on newcomers results in part from parsing majority and minority groupings of individuals along racial lines. But as close observers of assimilation have always pointed out, differences by generation-since-immigration, or "generation," are an important marker of time in the assimilation process (see, for example, Hansen 1952; Jiménez 2010a; Telles and Ortiz 2008; Warner and Srole 1945). Of course, the ethnic, racial, and generational lines that demarcate the groups are potentially blurry. As others have shown, where there are large numbers of newcomers of different racial and ethnic origins, there may be an assimilation taking place that does not include any notable presence of established individuals, including white established individuals (Kasinitz et al. 2008; Lee and Zhou 2015; Warikoo 2004). But in contemporary American society, not enough time has passed for there to be a large, adult established population that is descended from the post-1965 immigration wave.[3] As a result, the post-1965 immigration wave is currently overwhelmingly defined by first- and second-generation individuals. The generational line distinguishing these newcomers from established individuals is especially salient, for it delineates two fundamentally different experiences of what it is like to live in America. Newcomers, whether they or their parents were the ones who immigrated, live or grow up in immigrant-headed households. As an entire body of research literature has made clear, living in an immigrant family can shape a set of experiences that is altogether different from those of individuals who do not live in such families (see, for example, Kasinitz et al. 2008; Portes and Rumbaut 2001; Waters 1999). In this regard, there is much more differentiating newcomers from established individuals than there is distinguishing different generations of established individuals from each other.

Figure 1 shows the generational breakdown of individuals living in the United States at each decennial U.S. Census since 1970. The established

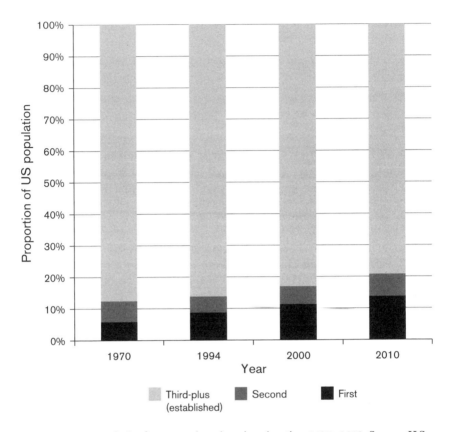

Figure 1. U.S. population by generation-since-immigration, 1970–2010. Source: U.S. Census 1994, 2000, 2010, March Current Population Survey. Note: Data for 1980 are unavailable, and thus not reported.

population—those who were born in the United States to U.S.-born parents—still constitutes a large majority of the U.S. population, at more than 75 percent. But that share is much lower than it was a few decades ago, prior to the growth of the post-1965 immigration wave. Though specific racial groups tend to cluster in particular immigrant generations, individuals from different racial groups can be found across the generational spectrum. Whites, blacks, Latinos, and Asians include both recent immigrants, as well as those who came to the United States many decades ago. Figure 2 takes a closer look at the established population, breaking it down by racial origin.

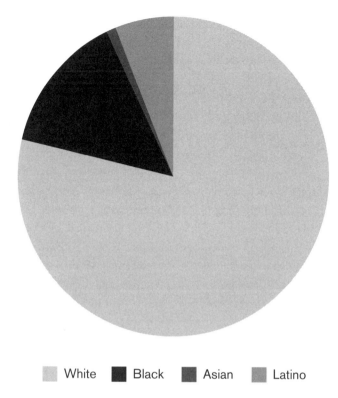

White   Black   Asian   Latino

Figure 2. Established population (U.S.-born of U.S.-born
parents) in the United States by racial background, 2010.
Source: U.S. Census 2010, March Current Population Survey.

If today's immigrants are moving the color line beyond black and white
(Lee and Bean 2010), the established population is still mostly defined
in by those groups. Whites make up the overwhelming share of the
established population, at roughly 77 percent. But more than one out
of five established individuals identifies as nonwhite, with blacks
(14 percent) making up the largest segment, Latinos representing about
6 percent of established individuals, and Asians making up about 1 percent. However, these national figures mask the prominence of the established *within* racial groups (see Jiménez, Fields, and Schachter 2015).
Among Latinos, 27 percent are established individuals, as are 8 percent of
Asians.

These figures are illustrative of the fact that the established society in the United States is far from monolithic, in terms of either race or social class. As multiple studies have made clear, class divisions, whether measured by income, wealth, education, or occupation, are correlated with race (Massey 2007). Race colors this class hierarchy throughout, with whites and Asians doing quite well, while Latinos and especially blacks lag far behind. There are, to be sure, significant internal class differences at work in all of these groups, differences that the broad racial labels mask (Jiménez, Fields, and Schachter 2015). But these broad categories nonetheless depict a U.S. society that is still highly stratified by race and class (Grusky and Kricheli-Katz 2012; Massey 2007). Contact between newcomers and established individuals—whether at work, school, or in neighborhoods—is shaped by this segmentation. It is mostly within these class segments that there is a crossing of racial lines. Whites are most likely to have contact with Asian newcomers and, to some degree, Latinos. Blacks are most likely to have significant contact with Latinos but also have contact with certain Asian subgroups (Frey 2014; Logan and Zhang 2011).

My exploration of how established individuals make sense of immigration-driven change started from a recognition of this segmentation. Rather than conceiving of the established population as including only U.S.-born whites, as has been the convention, I tried to capture how a racially and class-diverse set of individuals make sense of living amid so many newcomers. I also wanted to study how established individuals interpret newcomer-driven changes when those changes are significant—when there are lots of newcomers. Those conditions offer the best chance of observing how the process of adjustment among established individuals unfolds.

A VALLEY OF IMMIGRANTS

These criteria led me to my own backyard: the Silicon Valley.[4] The term "Silicon Valley" has come to refer to the entire San Francisco Bay Area and the technology industry that thrives there. But it originally referred to Santa Clara Valley, which encompasses most of Santa Clara County and includes San Jose and a number of other medium-sized cities in the South

Table 1 Selected Characteristics of Research Locales, Santa Clara County ("Silicon Valley") and the United States, 2010

Selected Population Characteristics	East Palo Alto	Cupertino	Berryessa	Silicon Valley	United States
Total Population	28,597	59,080	34,056	1,812,208	311,536,594
Race/Ethnicity (%)*					
White (non-Hispanic)	8.2	28.6	17.2	34.7	63.3
Black/African American	15.3	0.2	2.7	2.6	12.6
Hispanic/Latino	61.0	5.3	14.7	26.8	16.6
Asian/Pacific Islander	13.6	63.8	61.6	32.9	5.1
Two or more races	2.3	2.4	2.9	4.6	2.8
Foreign-born (%)	40.2	50.0	48.5	37.1	12.9
Ratio of high- to low-skilled foreign-born**	–	–	–	1.93:1	1.06:1
Unauthorized Immigrants*** (% of total foreign-born)	–	–	–	21.0	27.0
Unauthorized Immigrants (% of total population)	–	–	–	7.6	3.5
Top three locales of birth of foreign-born	Mexico El Salvador Oceania	China (incl. Taiwan) India Korea	Vietnam Philippines China	Mexico Vietnam India	Mexico China India
Median household income (in 2013 $)	50,142	129,976	94,500	91,702	53,046
Bachelor's degree or more (age 25 and over) (%)	16.3	74.6	39.2	46.5	28.8
In managerial or professional occupations (employed, age 16 and over) (%)	20.1	77.0	48.3	49.8	36.2
Median value of owner-occupied housing (in 2013 $)	378,800	1,000,000+	550,282	645,600	176,700

SOURCES: U.S. Census Bureau 2013, unless otherwise noted.

* Columns may add to more than 100 due to rounding.

** Source: Hall et al. 2011; high-skilled immigrants have a college degree or more; low-skilled immigrants lack a high school diploma.

*** Source: Passel and Cohn 2011, data unavailable for individual cities.

Bay Area.[5] A remarkable, but perhaps less noted feature of Silicon Valley is the presence of a tremendously large and diverse foreign-born population that has created an intensified form of the immigration-driven trends unfolding in the rest of the United States—especially those related to immigrant population size, legal status, class, and race.

To begin with, Silicon Valley has a very large immigrant population. As table 1 shows, Silicon Valley's immigrants make up a share of the region's total population (37 percent) that is almost three times the share of immigrants in the U.S. population (13 percent). The context is also shaped by the numeric dominance of the newcomers relative to the established population. Nationwide, first- and second-generation immigrants comprise roughly a quarter of the total population. In the largest ten U.S. metro areas by population size, these individuals make up 43 percent of the population.[6] The newcomers in Silicon Valley, by comparison, comprise 54 percent of the total population, making the U.S.-born-of-U.S.-born parent established population a numerical minority.

The established population in Silicon Valley is adjusting not only to the size of the immigrant population, but also to an immigrant population that is highly stratified by class. Indeed, a key characteristic of today's immigrants across the United States is that they are segmented by class; Silicon Valley's immigrant population exhibits an exaggerated form of that segmentation. Much as popular perception would suggest, high-skilled immigrants are overrepresented in Silicon Valley. Roughly 29 percent of the nation's adult immigrants have a college degree or more, but in Silicon Valley, that share is roughly 47 percent, with high-skilled immigrants outnumbering low-skilled (defined as having less than a high-school degree) by nearly two to one (Hall et al. 2011). While high-skilled immigrants are overrepresented in the region, there is still a large immigrant population that is low-skilled: 21 percent of Silicon Valley immigrants lack a high-school degree (compared to 28 percent of the nation's foreign-born).

Silicon Valley's immigrant population also exhibits a more pronounced form of nationwide patterns with respect to legal status. A defining feature of today's immigrant population is the relatively large number who are unauthorized either because they entered the United States without proper documentation or because they overstayed a visa. In Silicon Valley, the percentage of immigrants who are unauthorized is slightly lower than in the rest of the United States (21 percent versus 27 percent of the foreign-born population). But because this book tells the story of the established population, it is also important to consider the size of the unauthorized population relative to the region's entire population. Unauthorized immigrants make up twice as large a slice of the population in the region as they do in the United States as a whole (8 percent compared to 4 percent). But a nontrivial percentage of immigrants in Silicon Valley are U.S. citizens: more than half (53 percent) of the foreign-born are naturalized, compared to slightly less than half (46 percent) of the nation's foreign-born population. Taking the region as a whole, 19 percent of the total population are naturalized citizens, compared to 6 percent of the nation's total population. As these figures begin to suggest, the established population in the region is adjusting to a context defined by immigrants with a range of legal statuses.

The contours of that adjustment, as later chapters show, are shaped by the regional origins of the immigrant population. Like immigrants to the United States as a whole, the overwhelming majority of Silicon Valley's immigrants come from Asia and Latin America. Silicon Valley stands out, however, because its immigrant population has a rather different distribution in terms of regional origin. Immigrants from Asia are overrepresented in the Valley. According to 2010 U.S. Census figures, 27 percent of the region's immigrants come from Latin America, 61 percent from Asia, and 8 percent from Europe. By comparison, in the United States as a whole, 53 percent of immigrants come from Latin America, 28 percent from Asia, and 13 percent from Europe. While nationwide, 9 percent of the foreign-born come from the Caribbean, those immigrants account for less than 1 percent in Silicon Valley.

Silicon Valley may stand out because of the size and characteristics of its immigrant population, but the effect of the large immigrant population on the racial composition of the region puts Silicon Valley at the forefront of some demographic trends now unfolding in many other parts of the country. Since 1999, the majority of Silicon Valley residents have been nonwhite, a milestone that the rest of the United States is projected to reach in 2043 (U.S. Census Bureau 2012). This projection should be read with some caution, since it is based on the arguably problematic way the U.S. Census assigns identification to the growing population of people who have both white and nonwhite ancestry (Alba 2016). Nonetheless,

Silicon Valley's palpably large and growing nonwhite population is a depiction of a likely future for the rest of the country. And yet the region diverges significantly from the rest of the country in the composition of its nonwhite population. As table 1 shows, non-Hispanic whites make up just 35 percent of the population, while Latinos comprise 27 percent and Asians make up nearly one in three Silicon Valley residents. African Americans make up a very small share of the region's population, at just 3 percent, which is well below the national share (13 percent in 2011). The 3.5 percent of Silicon Valley's population that claim more than one racial identity hints at a diversity created by racial mixing in the region. The Census Bureau–defined metro area that encompasses most of Silicon Valley has the highest intermarriage rate in the nation: 21.5 percent of all current marriages involve spouses from different racial groups (Lee and Bean 2010: table 4.4).[7]

These immigration-driven demographic trends are set against a suburban backdrop that is more the rule than the exception for post-1965 immigrants. Whereas the suburbs were once a bastion of the white middle class, and home to more assimilated, later-generation descendants of European immigrants, today's immigrants are heading straight for suburbs (Alba et al. 1999; Singer, Hardwick, and Brettell 2008). Silicon Valley is a series of "ethnoburbs"—suburban areas with large clusters of ethnic minorities and ethnically themed businesses (Li 2009). The degree to which the region is ethnoburban is palpable in a drive down any of Silicon Valley's main thoroughfares. There are no Lower East Side-like ethnic storefronts or fruit and vegetable carts, but rather ethnically themed strip malls that house restaurants, grocery stores, bakeries, and tutoring centers. Whereas Catholic and Protestant churches once dominated the religious topography of the region, mosques and Hindu, Sikh, and Buddhist temples now feature prominently in the area's religious landscape (Eck 2001).

Nationwide demographic dynamics that are more exaggerated in Silicon Valley set the stage for a relational form of assimilation that, for established individuals, is marked by a profound ambivalence over what they think they have gained, and what they believe they have lost. As the ensuing chapters make clear, the sheer magnitude of immigration-driven class, racial, ethnic, legal status, and linguistic diversity structures that ambivalence.

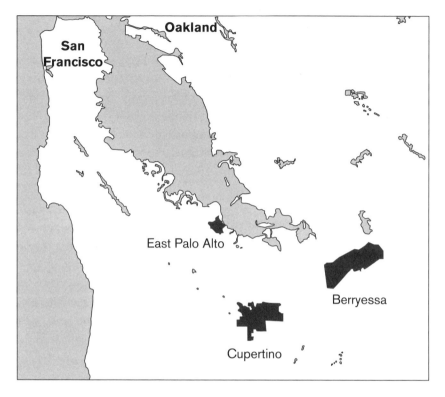

Figure 3. Map of Silicon Valley and study locales. Source: Map by Felipe Huicochea.

This immigration-driven diversity is not distributed evenly across the region. The racial and class segmentation that defines U.S. society in general, and today's immigrants in particular, also exists within the region. East Palo Alto, Cupertino, and Berryessa, the three places that I studied, offer a glimpse into three prototypical versions of that racial and class segmentation (see figure 3).

East Palo Alto: From White, to Black, to Brown

Located in the southernmost portion of San Mateo County and adjacent to the western banks of the San Francisco Bay, East Palo Alto is home to Silicon Valley's largest African American population. The city borders its wealthy and much better-known neighbor to the west, Palo Alto. Highway

101 and San Francisquito Creek separate East Palo Alto and Palo Alto. It takes roughly fifteen seconds by car to cross the freeway overpass (or "the ramp," as East Palo Alto residents call it) separating the two cities. But to cross to the other side of the ramp is to pass into another world entirely. As East Palo Alto interview respondents told us repeatedly, the city's reputation is well known to anyone who lives in Silicon Valley: black, blighted, and dangerous. That reputation was established in the 1970s, when "East Palo Alto" appeared in local news headlines almost exclusively in reference to violent and drug-related crime. Subsequent decades solidified the city's standing.

For much of the twentieth century, East Palo Alto was defined by small-scale farming (Berman 2002). The city's initial population growth was driven by the first significant migration of minorities to the area. In the 1950s and 1960s, African Americans who had gained an economic foothold in the San Francisco Bay Area looked for the sort of suburban life that was quickly defining the region. East Palo Alto's suburban environs fit the bill. The housing was relatively cheap, the weather idyllic, and, most importantly, it was one of the only communities on the Peninsula that did not have covenants forbidding African Americans from purchasing homes. Even so, the settlement of African Americans met resistance from East Palo Alto's existing and predominantly white residents. The process of white flight took hold in East Palo Alto just as it had in many other urban areas (Massey and Denton 1993). Real estate agents employed blockbusting techniques and banks practiced redlining. Efforts by some established white residents to intimidate their new black neighbors gave way to residential white flight as the city's black population grew. According to U.S. Census data, the white population plummeted from 10,170 (67.7 percent of the city's total population) in 1960 to just 5,574 (31.2 percent) in 1970, while the number of black residents grew from 2,291 (15.2 percent) to 10,846 (60.8 percent) during the same time span.

By the late 1960s, East Palo Alto was *the* black community on the Bay Area Peninsula, and self-consciously so. It was a hotbed of Afrocentrism. In 1968, for example, East Palo Alto was nearly renamed "Little Nairobi," and the Nairobi Day School and Nairobi College were founded as community-controlled schools with curricula centered on developing young black leaders with an active political and social consciousness (Hoover 1992; Cutler

2015). In the late 1960s, the University Village Shopping Center was renamed the Nairobi Village Shopping Center. But by the early 1970s, crime and drug use took hold in East Palo Alto. In 1976, for example, the city's crime rate was four times that of San Mateo County as a whole. In that same year, East Palo Alto's only high school, a point of pride and hub of civic life for local residents, shuttered. A voluntary bussing program, which transported white and black students in and out of East Palo Alto, became compulsory when the high school shut down (Robitaille 1989). Blacks who were bussed to nearby high schools were greeted mostly with subtle but palpable scorn, but sometimes local white students and residents reacted with violent backlash. East Palo Alto's institutional hollowing out continued into the 1980s, when all four of the city's banks left. Even the Nairobi Village Shopping Center was boarded up and eventually demolished in 1989 (Berman 2002). In spite of the growing blight and the city's solidified reputation for being a dangerous area, city leaders pushed for East Palo Alto to officially incorporate as an independent city and successfully did so in 1983 (Robitaille 1989).

By the mid-1980s, the crack epidemic and a corresponding wave of deadly violence cast a shadow over the city. A community activist and longtime resident whom I interviewed described East Palo Alto at that time as an "open-air drug market," whose patrons came primarily from outside the city limits. The worst effects of drug dealing fell squarely within East Palo Alto. Respondents who lived in the area during the time reported hearing gunshots on a nightly basis. Some even said that they slept on the floor in the back rooms of their home to avoid being hit by stray bullets. In 1992, there were 42 murders in the city of only 24,322 people, earning East Palo Alto the dubious distinction of being the per-capita murder capital of the United States (Warren 1993).

It was also during this time that East Palo Alto was undergoing another major demographic shift, this time spurred by the settlement of Latino (and especially Mexican) immigrants. The Bay Area's relatively stable job market made the region as a whole attractive, but it was also expensive for low-skilled immigrants. East Palo Alto was home to some of the only affordable housing in the area, and it was thus an appealing landing spot for poor Latino immigrants. As Latinos moved in, blacks began leaving the city in large numbers. From 1990 to 2010, East Palo Alto's total population grew by roughly 4,704 (to 28,155), but the Latino population

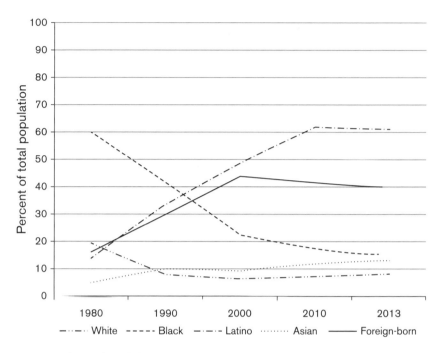

Figure 4. Change in racial and foreign-born composition in East Palo Alto, 1980
2013. Source: U.S. Census, Current Population Survey 2009–13, five-year estimates.

grew by 9,620, while the black population shrank by 5,629. Along with
Latinos, a sizeable Pacific Islander (mostly Tongan and Samoan) population moved in, and Asian/Pacific Islanders represented nearly 10 percent
of the total population by the year 2010. As recently as 1990, a plurality of
East Palo Alto residents were black: 30 percent of residents were foreign-
born; 42 percent were black, 36 percent were Hispanic, 9 percent were
Asian or Pacific Islander, and 12 percent were non-Hispanic white. By
2013, the picture had changed dramatically 40 percent of East Palo Alto
residents were foreign-born; 15 percent were black, 61 percent were
Hispanic, 14 percent were Asian/Pacific Islander, and 6 percent were non-
Hispanic white.[8]

Although the late 1950s and early 1960s were a period of mass white
flight, and the 1990s and early 2000s were a period of mass black flight,
the reasons that whites and blacks fled the city in the two time periods
differ markedly. It is clear that many white residents left East Palo Alto in

the 1950s and 60s *because* of the influx of African Americans; African Americans, however, do not appear to have left because of the arrival of Latinos. Though it is difficult to know for certain why the black population shrank, respondents said that African Americans left for financial and work-related opportunities. In particular, an unprecedented rise in housing prices enticed longtime black residents to sell their homes for many multiples of the original purchase price and use the equity to purchase larger and newer homes in California's Central Valley, the East Bay Area, and the southern United States. Others left under less fortunate circumstances. Some lost their homes entirely during the foreclosure crisis that began in 2008 and lasted well into 2012. To a lesser degree, the crackdown on drug dealing and violence that ultimately reduced the city's crime rate also led the incarceration of large numbers of the city's black male population. According to key informants, many of those convicted remain in prison or, if released, never returned to the city.[9]

Paralleling these demographic shifts have been massive economic changes in the city that, according to residents, have been a mixed blessing. The run-up in housing prices attracted middle- and upper-middle class homebuyers and spurred the development of several small tracts of new housing and commercial properties. These changes have grown the tax base, which funds important city services. However, according to some respondents the changes have threatened to take the city further away from its black roots as gentrification becomes a looming threat.

East Palo Alto remains a "city of color" (Camarillo 2007), and it remains something of a social, economic, and crime island amid neighboring communities whose fortunes have largely improved over the last decades. Though the city's crime rate has declined considerably since its peak in the early 1990s, it is still more than double the California average (there were eight homicides in 2011 and the number has fluctuated from a high of sixteen to a low of one since the 1992 peak) and remains well above the regional and state average (Lawrence and Shapiro 2010). In spite of significant economic development, residents remain poor. More than a third of residents lack a high school diploma, and just 16 percent have graduated from college (see table 1). At $50,142, the median household income in East Palo Alto might not seem all that low, but relative to other incomes in the area and to the regional cost of living, it is indeed modest.

The East Palo Alto median household income is slightly less than half the regional median and, when adjusted for the cost of living, is roughly $32,000.[10]

Cupertino: High-Tech Hub, High-Skilled Magnet

Just a little more than thirteen miles of freeway separate East Palo Alto from Cupertino, but the two cities are worlds apart. Cupertino is an upper-middle-class city located at the western edge of the Santa Clara Valley. It sits near the wealthy cities of Saratoga, Los Altos, and Los Altos Hills, as well as more middle-class Sunnyvale, Santa Clara, and west San Jose. Like East Palo Alto, and most of Silicon Valley, Cupertino has agricultural origins that seem a far cry from its present day status.

In 1955, still very much a small farming community, Cupertino incorporated as a city, partly in response to fears of annexation by neighboring cities, whose orchards were giving way to rapidly expanding housing developments (Stocklmeir 1975). Drawn by the city's new housing stock, large plots of land, and quiet environs, aerospace and computer engineers, college professors, and entrepreneurs flocked to the newly incorporated city. The relatively high class status of the city's growing residential population helped establish a strong reputation for its public schools. Cupertino also saw the settlement of Japanese and Chinese families following World War II. A small population of Chinese and Japanese flower growers had lived in Cupertino prior to the war, and Asian growers were able to buy land and start nurseries in Cupertino and other neighboring cities after the war (Handley 1997: 15). Still, the city was overwhelmingly comprised of whites, who, according to U.S. Census data, made up more than 95 percent of city residents in 1960.

In the 1970s Cupertino and the Santa Clara Valley's local economy shifted from prunes to silicon wafers. In hindsight, nothing defined the shift in Cupertino more than the founding of Apple Computer in 1976. From that point forward, Cupertino would be a locus of the technology industry, regionally and internationally. Shortly after Apple's founding, other technology giants established headquarters in the city. Much of Cupertino's modern development was financed by the success of Apple, especially during the company's phenomenal growth in the 1980s. But

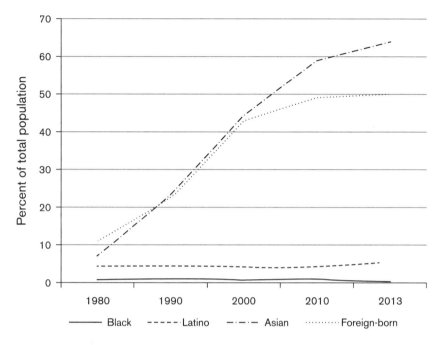

Figure 5. Change in racial and foreign-born composition in Cupertino, 1980–2013. Source: U.S. Census, Current Population Survey 2009–13, five-year estimates.

even during Apple's period of market share decline in the 1990s, Cupertino attracted other large high-tech companies.

The establishment of these companies burnished the already sterling reputation of the city's public schools. As Silicon Valley's technology sector boomed, and the region's technology workforce went global, Cupertino became an attractive residential landing spot for foreign-born, high-skilled immigrants, in large part because of its excellent public schools. Eight of the state's top twenty-five elementary schools as measured by California's Academic Performance Index are in the Cupertino Union Elementary School District (California Department of Education 2013). The Fremont Union High School District, which serves Cupertino residents, has two high schools ranked in the state's top fifteen based on average SAT scores (*Los Angeles Times* 2013). The allure of Cupertino's public schools to high-skilled East and South Asian immigrants is widely acknowledged among the city's residents.[11] Cupertino's popularity among high-skilled Asian immigrants can be seen in the city's demographic makeup, which in recent decades has changed at a dizzying pace. In 1990, just 22 percent of Cupertino residents were born in another country, 74 percent were white, and 23 percent were Asian. In 2013, half of Cupertino residents were for-eign-born, whites made up just 29 percent of the total population and Asians/Pacific Islanders comprised 64 percent (see table 1). Blacks and Latinos have always made up a small share of Cupertino's population—in 2010 they comprised less than 1 percent and 5 percent of residents, respec-tively. The large Asian population is even more apparent among Cupertino's younger residents. Asians (including South Asians) represent 70 percent of the students in Cupertino's elementary schools, whites comprise 23 per-cent, and Latinos make up just 5 percent. The decline in the number and percentage of whites in Cupertino does not owe to a classic form of "white flight," in which whites flee the neighborhoods into which minorities move (Massey and Denton 1993). By all accounts, the overwhelming majority of whites who moved away from Cupertino were older couples selling their homes in order to cash in on large home equity gains.

Even by Silicon Valley's heady standards, Cupertino is an upper-middle-class city, as indicated by its high median household income ($129,976), large percentage of residents who have a bachelor's degree or higher (74.6 percent), high proportion of workers in managerial and professional jobs (77 percent), and high median home value ($1,000,000+). Politically, the city's Asian population, both U.S.- and foreign-born, has gained a strong foothold (Lai 2011; Li and Park 2006). In 2010–11, when the interviews with established Cupertino residents took place, a majority of Cupertino's city council, including its mayor, was Asian American.

The imprint of the Asian-immigrant population on the city's landscape is evident from a short drive down Stevens Creek Boulevard, the city's busiest street, which nearly bisects it. Stevens Creek Boulevard reveals an upper-middle class ethnoburb in full bloom (Li 2009). Gone are virtually all remnants of Cupertino's agricultural past. Asian markets and restau-rants sit alongside retail emblems of the upper middle class, like Whole Foods. Bubble tea shops compete for popularity with Starbucks. Financial institutions, like Chase Bank and Charles Schwab, advertise their services in both English and Chinese characters, and tutoring centers dot the city's various strip malls.

Berryessa: Mixed in the Middle

Berryessa sits in the socioeconomic middle relative to East Palo Alto and Cupertino. From the outside, this subsection of the city of San Jose appears to be a nondescript, middle-class suburban setting with rows of single-family homes, large apartment complexes, and a smattering of public parks. Though there is no downtown or central shopping district to mark the area's distinctiveness, the abundant phở restaurants, taquerias, and ethnic supermarkets in the area's strip malls hint that Berryessa does not conform to antiquated stereotypes about the "burbs."

More than many other Silicon Valley subregions, Berryessa reflects a Spanish colonial past, in name at least. This neighborhood, which is the size of some small cities, is named for the family who received a Spanish land grant giving them ownership of the land.[12] In the early 1900s, there were just a few homes sprinkled among the various orchards that blanketed Berryessa, and Berryessa remained very much a rural setting well into the middle of the century. Though Mexican immigrants worked in Berryessa, they did not live there, and the area just south of the neighborhood, known to San Jose locals today as "the East Side," was a veritable Mexican *barrio*. Its largely first- and second-generation residents were poor, and their very modest homes lined dirt roads with no sidewalks (Pitti 2003: 90). The East Side retained its Mexican-immigrant character through the twentieth century, and because of the continual influx of Mexican immigrants, continues as such an enclave even today.

As the Santa Clara Valley headed toward its "silicon" days, Berryessa's development unfolded differently than did that of the East Side neighborhoods right next door. After World War II, when the transition from agriculture to technology was well under way, real estate developers began buying up land all over the valley, including in Berryessa. By the 1960s, new residential developments sat cheek by jowl with orchards that would be utterly overtaken by residential creep in the early 1970s (Cortese 2013). Because Berryessa is in the eastern portion of San Jose, an area of the city generally regarded as less "desirable" because of its large poor Mexican-origin population, the new, large homes were affordable and thus attractive to Silicon Valley's burgeoning young, professional class. Berryessa thus became home to mostly white, middle-class residents, but also to upwardly mobile Mexican Americans, African Americans, and Asian Americans (Filipino, Chinese, and Japanese). Two decades before the rest of Silicon Valley turned majority-minority, Berryessa already exhibited tremendous diversity. In 1980, roughly six in ten Berryessa residents were white, Latinos and Asian Americans each made up about 15 percent of the population, and blacks about 6 percent. In spite of its status as a residential neighborhood of San Jose, Berryessa developed a strong sense of political and civic distinctiveness. Though residents today lament its lack of a civic center, such as a downtown or shopping area, the area's social and political distinctiveness is marked by its own city council district, school district, county political district, little leagues, citizens council, and arts and wine festival.

The ethnic and racial mix in Berryessa began to change dramatically in the 1980s, when Berryessa became a popular settlement area for Vietnamese immigrants. There was already a Vietnamese presence in Berryessa prior to the 1980s (they made up roughly 1 percent of the Berryessa population in 1980). But by 1990, 9 percent of Berryessa's population was of Vietnamese origin. The area also saw a rise in its Chinese and Latino (largely Mexican) populations. Latino immigrants who had gained an economic foothold moved into the area, helping to maintain the Latino share of the Berryessa population at or near 15 percent for the last four decades. The imprint of the growing Asian and Latino immigrant populations was apparent. Mexican- and Vietnamese-owned restaurants and grocery stores began popping up in the neighborhood. As older, mostly white residents moved away, more Asian and Latino families began moving in.

The next two decades saw an acceleration of these demographic trends. By the end of the first decade of the new millennium, Asians made up a majority of Berryessa residents and among Asians, Vietnamese dominated. In 2013, just 17 percent of Berryessa residents were white, and 3 percent were black, while 15 percent were Latino and 61 percent were Asian. The demographic makeup of Berryessa schools is perhaps even more telling of the degree of immigration-driven change. According to data from the California Department of Education, in 2010 Asians made up 61 percent of students in the elementary school district, Latinos comprised 21 percent, African Americans constituted 3 percent, and whites made up just 6 percent.

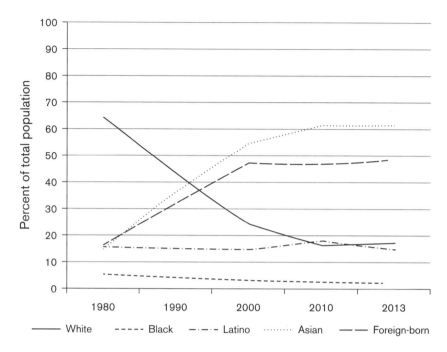

Figure 6. Change in racial and foreign-born composition in Berryessa, 1980–2013.
Source: U.S. Census, Current Population Survey 2009–13, five-year estimates.

As in Cupertino and East Palo Alto, remnants of Berryessa's agricultural past are hard to find. The neighborhood retains the middle-class suburban character that city planners originally foresaw (Santa Clara County Planning Department 1956). Its tree-lined streets are relatively peaceful and it is regarded as one of San Jose's safer neighborhoods.

STUDYING THE ESTABLISHED POPULATION

I wanted to understand how established-population individuals living in each of these racial and class segments experience and make sense of living amid such a large immigrant and second-generation population. With the help of two research assistants, I interviewed people living in these three cities who were U.S.-born of U.S.-born parents. We interviewed people who had lived in their respective cities for at least a decade because

I wanted to be sure that they had some familiarity with living, working, going to school, and socializing in the area. We sought out interview respondents who were fifteen years of age or older to hear from individuals who were young enough to have lived their entire lives amid a large immigrant population, but who were not so young that they might have a hard time articulating their interpretation of those experiences. We tried to interview a roughly even number of respondents from three different age cohorts: the "oldest" (55+), "middle" (35–54), and "youngest" (15–34). These individuals had experienced immigration-driven change at very different points in history and at different points in their life course, which potentially influenced how they made sense of the large immigrant presence (see Alba, Jiménez, and Marrow 2014).

Although I grew up in and am a resident of this region, I was not equally familiar with each of the three places. I thus used a variety of tactics to find interview respondents. In East Palo Alto, I began finding respondents though a college friend who grew up there and through professional contacts. Along with Maneka Brooks, then a doctoral student at Stanford's Graduate School of Education, I interviewed sixty residents of the city, ranging in age from fifteen to eighty. All but one of the respondents were African American. Based on their level of education and employment status, nearly all of the East Palo Alto respondents were poor or working class.

I found the first few respondents in Cupertino through the Cupertino Block Leaders Program, which includes more than two hundred people who serve as liaisons between the city government and neighborhoods (about a third of neighborhoods in Cupertino had a block leader at the time). The head of the program sent out an email on my behalf asking block leaders for help finding respondents for this project. Many contacted me to offer names of people in their neighborhood for me to interview. I then solicited referrals from this initial sample of respondents. Adam Horowitz, at the time a PhD student in sociology at Stanford, and I interviewed sixty-one established-generation Cupertino residents between the ages of fifteen and seventy-seven. Ten of the respondents had some Asian ancestry; the rest were white. Almost all had a least a college degree, and many had advanced degrees.

In Berryessa, I relied almost exclusively on personal contacts to identify an initial set of respondents, and these initial respondents referred me to others. I ended up with fifty-eight respondents in Berryessa between the ages of fifteen and eighty-one. Adam and I interviewed these individuals. Of these respondents, thirty-four were white, seven were Latino (all but one of Mexican ancestry), seven were African American, five were of Asian descent, and five were multiracial (most with some Mexican ancestry). Virtually all white respondents had a college degree or more. Those who lacked a college degree tended to be Latino. All except one of the adult African Americans we interviewed in Berryessa had a college degree or more.[13]

Much distinguishes the cities in which the respondents resided, and the people whom we interviewed tended to have a class standing, based on education and occupation, that reflected the place in which they lived. But these three locales, inasmuch as they depict different racial and class segments in the United States in general, and Silicon Valley in particular, also contain some class diversity within racial groups, as well as considerable racial diversity within class groups. In selecting interview respondents, we tried to talk to people who represented various aspects of intra-group diversity within the established population (Alba, Jiménez, and Marrow 2014; Jiménez, Fields, and Schachter 2015). Still, the racial and class composition of Silicon Valley meant that the interview sample lacked some of the diversity that might be found in other areas. In particular, Silicon Valley has a relatively small working-class white population. Indeed, while 77 percent of U.S. whites over age twenty-five lack a college degree, that figure is 60 percent among whites in Silicon Valley, and there is no geographic concentration of working-class whites in the area.[14] As a result, working-class whites were rare in the interview sample. There were five adult white respondents in Berryessa who lacked a college degree and two such respondents in Cupertino. Both of the Cupertino respondents without a college degree had spouses who had college degrees and who worked in professional jobs. As I discuss in the concluding chapter, working-class whites may have a rather different experience of relational assimilation than their more educated counterparts in Silicon Valley (see McDermott 2006; Hartigan 1999; Gest 2016).

Interviewing such a diverse set of individuals meant thinking seriously about how to present my own identity, and how to choose research assistants for the project. Before doing any of this research in earnest, I did preliminary interviews to test out my questions. I noticed that the pilot

respondents were hesitant to say too much about immigration, and especially about Latinos. I suspected that their cautiousness owed to their
knowledge of my own Latino ancestry and, in some cases, their awareness
that my father is a Mexican immigrant. My strong sense was that they
were afraid to offend me. So when I conducted the interviews for this
book, I decided to present myself to respondents as "TJ," a name that
downplayed my Mexican ancestry. Most respondents failed to make the
connection between TJ and my full, professional name printed on consent
forms. Some, in fact, assumed I was a graduate student helping a professor. That small change in how I presented my name, I think, made people
feel more comfortable speaking about immigration and their experiences
with immigrants without fear of insulting me.

While changing my name may have lessened my perceived outsider status, it certainly did not make me an insider, especially in East Palo Alto,
where almost all of the respondents were African American. And so I
hired Maneka, who is African American and Sri Lankan, and whom most
people perceive as black, to help with the interviews in East Palo Alto.
While the race of the interviewer never showed up clearly as an issue in
the interviews I conducted in East Palo Alto, some black respondents
made comments to Maneka suggesting a shared understanding of a particular experience based on race. In such instances, Maneka asked the
respondents to explain anyway.

In addition to these interviews with established respondents, we conducted thirty interviews with key informants, including teachers, school
counselors, clergy, city government officials, and civic leaders. These
interviews provided information about the larger context and an opportunity to check emerging findings against these informants' perceptions.
While the findings I report here are primarily based on the interviews, I
also draw on observational field notes we took at key events and when we
came to the cities to conduct interviews.

The interviews provide a rich picture of the experiences of established
populations living in three specific communities adjusting to a context of
heavy immigration. Interviews are a good tool for understanding how people make sense of their experiences and of their perceptions more generally—but the claims I make should not be read as representative of the
established population in the region, the state, or nationwide. Surveys of

randomly selected, representative groups of individuals are much better suited for that kind of analysis. What this book does capture is people's interpretations of living in a very particular area. Silicon Valley is no doubt a unique place for lots of reasons. Relative to the rest of the United States, its population has a much a larger share of immigrants and a much larger share of unauthorized immigrants; its immigrants tend to be more educated and more Asian; and the proportion of whites is much smaller. But I chose to do this research in Silicon Valley precisely because it is an "extreme" case in these respects. Studying extreme cases limits the degree to which the specific findings are easily generalizable to other contexts. But the value of this study is not that it allows the reader to generalize in a statistical sense, but rather that it reveals processes at play, to varying degrees, in other places where immigrants have settled. As sociologist Arthur Stinchcombe (2005: chapter 3) explained, examining an extreme case like Silicon Valley—one where the immigrant population is large and heavily skewed toward the extremes of the class distribution—throws social processes like relational assimilation into sharp relief, because the exaggerated nature of the context makes those processes jump out. Sociologist Marianne Cooper, who studied individuals' emotional responses to inequality in Silicon Valley, offered a similarly germane explanation for her selection of an extreme context of inequality: "in order to understand how high-level trends are playing out in people's everyday lives, it is helpful to examine an extreme case. In an extreme case, trends and social dynamics can be more visible and thus easier to spot and document" (Cooper 2014: 55). And so the interviews we conducted in Silicon Valley do more to reveal *how* an established population adjusts than they do to show the extent of that adjustment. The fundamental process of relational assimilation is likely to play out in other places where immigrants have settled in ways similar to Silicon Valley, if not to the same degree. Nonetheless, the situation in Silicon Valley hints at the factors that might shape the extent to which assimilation is relational. Those factors include relative group size, group status, and institutional arrangements. I discuss those factors more fully in the concluding chapter.

It is also important to bear in mind that the pages that follow detail established Silicon Valley residents' interpretations of their experiences. What they told us were not pure accounts of their actions (Jerolmack and

Khan 2014). Their words were instead recollections and interpretations of events and the meaning that people assigned to those events. Those recollections and interpretations are the building blocks of all social phenomena (Weber 1978 [1922]). Where appropriate, I provide context for their interpretations. But rarely, if ever, do I correct their accounts with my knowledge of the "facts." As much as possible, I attempt to offer an account of the world as they saw it.

If the reader would like to get a fuller sense of the interviews, the archived transcripts are available through the Inter-university Consortium for Political and Social Research (www.icpsr.umich.edu) and Stanford University Libraries (http://data.stanford.edu). Portions of the transcripts have been omitted to protect the respondents' anonymity, but they are otherwise intact. All names that appear in the book are pseudonyms that, as much as possible, match the origin of respondents' actual names.

CHAPTER OVERVIEW

Together, the chapters of this book tell the story of the established population's adjustment as seen through the eyes of the people undergoing that adjustment. It is important to note that there were ways in which the respondents' experience of relational assimilation differed significantly by race and class. But there were also remarkable similarities in their experiences in spite of racial and class differences. I note throughout the book when these differences matter and when they do not. The dimensions of relational assimilation highlighted in each chapter correspond to dimensions of life important to newcomer assimilation as established in existing research: intergroup contact, ethnic cultural practices, ethnic and racial identity, language, and national identity. As sociologists Frank Bean, Susan Brown and James Bachmeier (2015) argue, other aspects of newcomer assimilation—educational attainment, occupational status, income, language, residential mobility, and culture—are not nearly as interconnected in postindustrial societies that give lots of room for individual expression. Indeed, immigrant groups generally exhibit uneven integration from one of these dimensions to another. Much of the same can likely be said of the assimilation that the established population experiences.

Some of those dimensions, like cross-race romantic partnerships, educational attainment, and residential locale, have a hard, structural quality best captured in survey research. Others, like ethnic cultural practices, racial identity, social boundaries, and national identity, are more sociocultural in quality, and come to light more vividly in qualitative research. As much as possible, I try to contextualize my respondents' views with existing survey research. But whether dealing with structural or sociocultural dimensions of assimilation, this book is about how the people we interviewed rendered and interpreted those facts.

The book's chapters are organized thematically. Each chapter relates a different dimension of relational assimilation from the perspective of the established individuals we interviewed. Within each chapter, I highlight the contexts in which relational assimilation unfolds. Generally speaking, neighborhoods, work, schools, and family are the most relevant contexts, according to respondents. The chapters thus focus significantly on these contexts. Other institutional contexts, like religious institutions, clubs and organizations, and political parties came up as less salient contexts for contact between established and newcomer individuals. I thus discuss these contexts much less as sites of relational assimilation.

Chapter 1 looks at established individuals' contact with immigrants and their children and the way that this contact has shaped their familiarity with the immigrant experience. In contrast to the prevailing assumption that established populations treat immigrants as strangers in a strange land, the established population in Silicon Valley described the immigrant experience as a normal part of their everyday context. Respondents in all three locales described frequent and meaningful contact with first- and second-generation immigrants, which gave respondents intimate familiarity with various dimensions of the immigrant experience, including being unauthorized, the struggle of being U.S.-born in an immigrant household, and transnationalism. It turned out that the newcomers among them were not so strange at all.

Chapter 2 explores whether and how established individuals engage the ethnic cultures that large immigrant populations make so abundant. Whether at school, at work, in their neighborhoods, or during leisure activities, respondents described a wealth of opportunities to witness and nominally participate in the symbols and practices associated with other ethnic origins. As a result, respondents offered a conception of a local mainstream that contains ethnically connected ways of eating, dressing, dancing, worshipping, and (to some degree) speaking. For whites, the exposure to ethnic culture produced a feeling that they themselves were ethnically bland and a corresponding desire to have a more robust connection to their own ancestry. African Americans in East Palo Alto expressed a strong sense of individual black identity, but the growing importance of Latino ethnic culture there contributed to a view that black culture ought be a more prominent part of East Palo Alto's civic identity, as it had been in the past. Established Latinos in Berryessa and established Asians in Cupertino and Berryessa reported an externally imposed expectation that they display the kind of cultural know-how more often found among co-ethnics closer to the immigrant generation. These findings suggest the emergence of a local mainstream that is defined not in terms of specific ethnic symbols and practices, but rather by having a strong connection to an ethnic ancestry.

Chapter 3 examines how a large immigrant population shapes racial identity, with a particular focus on whiteness in Cupertino and Berryessa, and blackness in East Palo Alto. In Cupertino, and to a lesser degree in Berryessa, whiteness is a highly visible—indeed a marked—racial identity where educational achievement is concerned. Though whites are doing well by most standards, Asian immigration to these communities has introduced new, racially encoded standards that place whites in a subordinate position when it comes to academic achievement. In both communities high-achieving whites experienced whiteness as a deficit in honors courses where Asians predominate. In East Palo Alto, on the other hand, the large Latino immigrant presence and the declining black population have rendered blackness less salient in a place that was once widely regarded as *the* black community in Silicon Valley. Blacks' growing invisibility is notable in both symbolic and material ways—from declining public recognition of black identity, to a perception that there are fewer jobs and services for blacks. In all three communities, respondents drew on historically embedded notions of race and privilege to make sense of these changes. While whites never described the putative "Asian" approach to schooling as a norm to which they ought to aspire, some African American respondents held up Latinos as an example that highlighted blacks' perceived inability to promote collective advancement. These findings show that the presence of immigrants can serve as a foil against which established populations can reexamine the meaning and status of existing racial categories. This can lead to reordering of racial categories—as with whiteness in Cupertino and Berryessa—but it can also reaffirm those categories, as with blackness in East Palo Alto.

Chapter 4 looks at the symbolic boundaries—the everyday notions of "us" and "them"—that mattered to respondents in these contexts. In some respects, the way respondents saw symbolic boundaries reflected their fears about the negative effect of ethnic and racial differences on social cohesion, but these concerns surfaced in class-inflected ways. Cupertino and Berryessa respondents linked a declining sense of community to an immigrant-origin Asian approach to life, which they characterized as an amped-up work ethic that led to reduced newcomer investment in community building. Interviewees in East Palo Alto believed the heavy Latino presence had diminished the cohesiveness of a distinctly black community. They also saw shifting racial symbolic boundaries at work in the changing focus of public and private institutions that had once served the city's poor blacks, but that now addressed the challenges of being a poor (and possibly unauthorized) immigrant. In all three study locations racial difference was not the only factor in respondents' rendering of the boundaries that mattered to them: they also saw immigration introducing multiple kinds of difference. The longtime settlement of some immigrants and the large second generation created *within*-group differences that respondents readily recognized. Interviewees in all three cities identified ability to speak English and length of neighborhood residence as important markers defining insiders and outsiders.

Chapter 5 examines the notions of national identity that emerged from respondents' interpretation of immigration-driven change. In all three study locales, established respondents showed strong consensus about what it means to be a member of the American nation in both the "soft" cultural sense and the "hard" legal sense. Respondents applied "hard" notions of the nation in ways that were at times consistent with policies and elite rhetoric and at times discordant with it. For instance, many were firmly convinced, in part because of their interactions with newcomers, that the behavioral aspects of national belonging revolved primarily around speaking English. Still, no one said that English should entirely supplant immigrants' native tongues. They embraced the "hard" notion that unauthorized immigrants unfairly take advantage of public services, which are funded by Americans and therefore should be enjoyed only by Americans. At the same time, interviewees' interactions with immigrants smoothed the edges off these hard notions of citizenship. Becoming a national insider and being a good citizen, they said, was not strictly a matter of legal status. Instead, it involved behavioral components: working hard, playing by the rules, raising a family, and speaking English. Immigrants who follow these informal criteria for membership, according to respondents, should be entitled to the legal dimension of citizenship because they behave like good citizens.

The conclusion draws on these findings to illustrate the long-term impact of relational assimilation, as the constant back and forth of individual adjustment and readjustment over time results in a dramatically changed America. The book's findings suggest how combinations of group size, group status, and institutional arrangements tilt the balance of relational assimilation in favor of one group over another. While the findings are particular to Silicon Valley, they point to processes likely at play in the United States wherever immigration is rapidly changing a region's ethnic and racial composition. The relational assimilation at play in Silicon Valley is also likely a process that has been unfolding since immigrants began coming to the United States, and one that will continue to play out so long as immigrant newcomers arrive.

1 The (Not-So-Strange) Strangers in Their Midst

The established population's participation in relational assimilation begins with the contact they have with newcomers. To read about immigrants in history books, popular media, and in social science is also to read about an established population whose contact with newcomers highlights these newcomers' strangeness. Immigrants and their children are depicted as strangers in a strange land (Higham 1955): people who are "uprooted" (Handlin 1951) from the comfortable soil of their home country and "transplanted" (Bodnar 1985) to the unfamiliar land of the country that receives them. Portrayals of the post-1965 immigrants reinforce this narrative. Studies show first- and second-generation immigrants struggling to navigate between the distinctly immigrant households in which they grow up and a strange and often unwelcoming receiving society outside (Portes and Rumbaut 2001; Waters 1999; Zhou and Bankston 1998).

There is more than a kernel of truth to this portrait of the immigrant experience. But there is also good reason to question whether it reflects the full complexity of that experience. From the perspective of the second generation in large metro areas, the immigrant experience may not be all that strange. Studies of the second generation in major immigrant gateways like New York (Kasinitz et al. 2008) and Los Angeles (Lee and Zhou

2015) find that many of the markers that used to highlight the "in-betweenness" of immigrant families are increasingly seen as normal. Multilingual households with spicy aromas emanating from the kitchen, the ability to move back and forth between cultures, and sadly, being unauthorized, are fairly typical experiences across contexts of heavy immigrant settlement like Silicon Valley, where first- and second-generation immigrants combined constitute a majority of the total population.

Established individuals in East Palo Alto, Cupertino, and Berryessa also regarded the immigrant experience as a familiar part of the contexts they navigated. The numerical dominance of the newcomer population made the immigrant experience a central part of these individuals' concept of regional identity. This regional self-concept arose from significant contact with newcomer individuals that made established respondents firsthand witnesses to—and, in some instances, participants in—the trials, tribulations, promises, and hopes of immigrant life. In general respondents had more frequent and meaningful contact, and thus greater familiarity, with immigrants whose class status was similar to their own. It is not that they had no cross-class contact. But that cross-class contact tended to be more sporadic and fleeting than intra-class contact. Nonetheless, within these confines the net result was an immigrant population and an immigrant experience that was more familiar than strange to everyone living in Silicon Valley, including the most generationally established.

THE IMMIGRANT EXPERIENCE AS REGIONAL IDENTITY

Immigration does not just define the demographic landscape in which large numbers of newcomers settle; it also changes the regional self-understanding held by individuals already living in these contexts. The immigrant experience, both past and present, was part and parcel of the larger narrative that respondents told about what it means to live in Silicon Valley. If newcomer individuals feel a degree of comfort knowing that so many of their fellow metro dwellers share in their experience (Kasinitz et al. 2008), so too did established individuals in this study attach a sense of normalcy to living amid so many immigrant newcomers.

To be sure, that sense did not perfectly overlap with the feelings of complete comfort that came with operating on an ethnic home turf. As I report in later chapters, immigration-driven diversity shaped the racial and ethnic identities of respondents in new and often uncomfortable ways. It produced perceptions of dislocation and community fragmentation among the people we interviewed; it inspired ambivalence among respondents; and it forced a rethinking of what it meant to be American. Still, immigration and the diversity that it brings sat at the center of how established individuals defined what it meant to live in Silicon Valley.

The extent to which immigration-driven diversity was enmeshed in interviewees' lives emerged prominently from their responses to the question that opened each interview: "How would you characterize the city in which you live to someone who has never been here before?" Respondents were quick to note their city's class profile, its major economic drivers, and its level of crime (low in Berryessa and Cupertino; high in East Palo Alto). Almost all of their descriptions also featured the immigration-driven ethnic and racial character of their community. In fact, only two of the individuals in the entire interview sample failed to mention some aspect of immigration-driven diversity when asked to describe the city in which they lived. Among Cupertino respondents, the depiction provided by Donna Williams, a white thirty-nine-year-old homemaker, was typical:

> Well, it has a small town feel. The population of 65,000 people. It's got a high-tech business base and is known for its excellent public school system as well as K-14 for community college. It's a community that's changed quite a bunch in the past years. It's seen a major cultural shift in the population from the onset of Asian immigrants, both Chinese and East Indian, and we've seen how that's affected neighborhoods and communities and businesses in lots of different ways.

Diane Campbell, a white sixty-four-year-old grammar school teacher from Berryessa, noted in a rather upbeat assessment that the area had always had some diversity, but that immigration had increased that diversity in recent years.

> I would describe it as a district of San Jose, which is a large city. And it's on the outskirts of it, which makes it a very favorable location, a good part of San Jose. It's not right in the middle of the downtown. It's towards the hills.

It's a more peaceful, non-trafficky place to be. And it's certainly got a great mix of ethnicities . . . . When I first moved here in 1973 it was not as mixed as it is now. And so, many groups have come in. Basically, there were a lot of Hispanic people here. But there were other ethnicities, too, Asians. And so by the time my children were growing up, I thought it was a really great place for them to grow up because they were not living in just a white, Caucasian area. But even at that time they had friends of different cultures. And so they grew up with that feeling that, hopefully, that different culture mixes is an advantage to be living among. It was a good place to be. As they grew up and the ethnicity became even more diverse with Vietnamese families living here who weren't really here before, and there were a lot of Chinese, and there's a certain amount of Japanese, and now Filipino, and it's a wonderful place to be. And they grew up knowing friends, having friends from all different cultures and never seeing a mix of cultures as being a barrier in any way, for them or for other people.

Among East Palo Alto respondents, "diverse" was a common descriptor of the city. But in contrast to Cupertino (where immigration brought diversity that had not existed previously) and Berryessa (where immigration built upon existing diversity), East Palo Alto interviewees noted a change in the kind of diversity that immigration brought about. They were quick to contextualize their descriptions of the city in terms of its self-conscious identity as the only historically black community in Silicon Valley. The fact that East Palo Alto once had a black majority was more than a demographic fact to respondents who lived there. East Palo Alto was a cultural home base for its black residents and for Silicon Valley's small African American population more generally, replete with black churches, schools, retail stores, barber shops, cultural centers, and public celebrations. East Palo Alto respondents' descriptions of the city—which also referenced its levels of crime and poverty—spoke to how different East Palo Alto was from Cupertino and Berryessa. In spite of these differences, references to immigration-driven change were just as prominent. Karen Jackson, a black fifty-three-year-old day care provider, explained the situation in East Palo Alto in much the same way as other respondents there:

At one time, I was told, it was predominantly black. Most people migrated over here because of the low cost of living. And a lot of those houses, new houses, are being bought by people other than blacks—Latinos and Tongans—because they're cheaper. I just think that people are just going out to all kind of places. They're just . . . . It's just not like the old way, where it used to be you had your two races. It's just a melting pot everywhere you go, now. People are just migrating all over the place.

There was thus a high degree of recognition among interviewees from all three cities that immigration had played a major role in defining the character of their respective cities.

The neighborhoods in which respondents lived were microcosms of their respective cities, and respondents often used their neighborhoods as more tangible instances of the dynamics in their cities and the region. To illustrate the high degree of diversity in their particular neighborhoods, respondents in all three locales often provided a verbal mapping of their own street, pointing in the direction of specific houses and reporting the occupants' ethnic backgrounds. Ben Braur, a retired, seventy-seven-year-old white engineer in Cupertino, had lived in his home for more than three decades. He was thus well positioned to explain the demographics of his neighborhood, both past and present:

> But just in our littie circle: Caucasian woman married to an Asian kid, who we've watched group up since [he was young]; two Caucasians next door. Next door to them is a family that just came from India. Next door to them is a family that just came from Jordan. Next door to them is like [a] third owner, divorced many times but, she's Korean and has a—I think—seven or eight or more young Asians are there and then go away and then they come back . . . . Next door to them is the American Samoan. Next door to them— they're from the Netherlands, but she was born in Beirut. Next door to them is Indiana. And that's just down that side [of the street]. My side is a gal and her mother . . . . : Greece; born here but I think mother might have been from Greece. Then a Jewish family and then next door to me has been a rental . . . . An Israeli family has been there the last ten years or more. And next door to me is Asian, both sets of parents came from Taiwan. Next door to them is Japanese . . . You see how it goes?

Respondents in East Palo Alto and Berryessa went through a similar exercise during the interview. East Palo Alto respondents generally pointed out who was Mexican, and their length of residence, while Berryessa respondents rattled off descriptions of neighbors with Vietnamese, Chinese, Indian, and Mexican origins. When respondents and their newcomer neighbors had lived in the neighborhood for a long time, respondents knew their neighbors' specific origins rather than only surface descriptors, like their race. The more detailed nature of these descriptions speak to respondents' familiarity with long-standing neighbors, an important factor in perceptions of social insiders and outsiders (more on this in chapter 4).

These informal demographic renderings of the cities and neighborhoods amount to on-the-ground depictions of a trend unfolding across U.S. metropolitan areas. The rapid increase of Latino and Asian immigrant populations has given rise to "global neighborhoods" where whites, blacks, Latinos, and Asians are all well represented (Logan and Zhang 2011). What is notable about these trends in residential integration is not the degree to which minorities have, over time, moved "up and out" of immigrant enclaves. Rather, it is the extent of integration experienced by both whites and blacks that stands out. According to sociologists John Logan and Charles Zhang's (2011) analysis of 2010 U.S. Census data from the twenty most multiethnic metro regions in the country, the share of blacks living in global neighborhoods grew from one in five in 1980 to nearly two in five in 2010; for whites, the share grew from one in five to more than two in five.[1] While these figures do not indicate residents' generation-since-immigration status, it is safe to assume that whites and blacks living in these global neighborhoods are predominantly established individuals because the overwhelming majority of U.S. blacks and whites were born in the United States to U.S.-born parents. Whites are still the dominant population in most metropolitan regions, even in neighborhoods where there is a large share of nonwhites, while whites are a minority in Silicon Valley and in the three cities that we studied. Silicon Valley thus stands as an amplified version of the global regions and neighborhoods found elsewhere. Still, there can be little doubt that the growing diversity in Silicon Valley, like that in other metropolitan areas, is defined both by immigration and by ethnic and racial difference.

The fact that these trends are more prominent across large metro areas like Silicon Valley was not lost on the people we interviewed. They often drew on time spent in other parts of the country to emphasize the degree to which immigration-driven diversity is part of Silicon Valley's identity. Standing out prominently in their stories of visits to the South, Midwest, or Pacific Northwest was how few immigrants there were in these other places and the lack of diversity that resulted.[2] Attending college, visiting family, or spending the early part of life living outside of the region threw the degree of diversity in Silicon Valley into vivid relief. Margarita Bartis, a white, forty-four-year-old dental hygienist whose son was dating a second-generation Asian American woman, compared living in Berryessa to the time she spent in Kansas:

> And it's funny because my dad lives in Kansas now. So when I go visit my dad everybody's white . . . . On my eye, it's very strange because I'm so used to the diversity here. And to go somewhere where everyone's white, it's very weird. Indians, we have here. We have a mix of people here. And it's very strange on the eye when you go somewhere and everybody's the same. It's very strange . . . . And there's not as many Caucasians anymore. It's no big deal, but just visually, you notice the difference with your eye. . . . I wouldn't move out of the area or go move to Kansas to be around white people. So I guess if I didn't like Asians, it would be bad. (laughs) But my son's girlfriend's Asian, so someday I may have little Asian grandchildren. (laughs)

Similarly, Melanie Davis, a black, unemployed twenty-nine-year-old in East Palo Alto, articulated the region's ethnic and racial mélange in relation to her experience visiting family in Jackson, Mississippi, where most of the individuals she encountered were black:

> Yeah, I like to see white people and Mexicans and Polynesians. I like to see that. I like to go to McDonald's and see that mixture. In Jackson, everybody is black. Everything is black. I seen a couple white people but that was about it. It's majority black. And I love black and I am black, but to see that many black people take me off guard because I've never been to the South like that; never go into an all-black college. Nothing like that. So to go in the McDonald's, and everybody working is black. Go to the grocery store, everybody there and everywhere you go, to where I, to me, that was just . . . I don't know—culture shock . . . . That was just crazy, mind blowing . . . . I mean here, it's all Hispanic, everywhere that you go. Every worker is Hispanic. But there, it was like, "Where is a Hispanic person? Let me see one!" It was Indian. Instead of the Hispanics it was the Indians, that's what took the place up. My mom was like, "Girl, you don't see them down here!" What?! But that's how it is out there. So I told her I'll visit but I think the Bay Area in California, and it's different to me. I think I'm just more Bay oriented. I never really left. So I've just stuck here. This is my big hole.

While African American respondents were not alone in expressing a preference for racially mixed areas, survey research suggests that they are more likely than whites to prefer living among people of different backgrounds (Charles 2006). Still, respondents from across the three cities we studied conveyed more than a hint of pride about living a place as diverse as Silicon Valley. In some ways, they portrayed the entire region as a "cosmopolitan canopy," the term that sociologist Elijah Anderson (2011) used to describe urban spaces where people from a range of racial backgrounds interact with one another with a high degree of civility. That regional character came to light when respondents like Melanie and others in all three study locales noted that less diverse regions of the country seemed "weird," "strange," or "boring," precisely because Silicon Valley's multiethnic scene had shaped their perception of the norm (see Voyer 2011).

That norm is not necessarily unique to Silicon Valley. In metropolitan areas across the country, the heavy settlement of immigrants means that established individuals and newcomers alike navigate contexts defined by diversity (Hannah 2011; Logan and Zhang 2011; Frey 2014). And like respondents in Silicon Valley that we interviewed, established individuals in other metro regions consider diversity a central feature of their particular region, defining what it means to be an Angeleno (Waldinger and Lichter 1996), a New Yorker (Kasinitz et al. 2008), a Houstonian, or a Nashvillian (Winders 2013). But as that diversity comes to characterize more regions of the United States, it will become harder for anyone to claim diversity as a truly distinguishing feature of their home region, for that diversity will be a defining feature of the United States as a whole.

"[IT] HAS ALWAYS BEEN A PART OF LIFE THAT I GREW UP IN": YOUNG RESPONDENTS AND THE UNQUESTIONED NORMALCY OF DIVERSITY

For older respondents, the current state of affairs in Silicon Valley represented a notable change from the past—a new normal. But for younger respondents, the influence of immigrants on the region's demographic and cultural character was an ever-present and thus unremarkable part of life. Respondents from the middle (age 35–54) and oldest (age 55+) cohorts were especially likely to compare the immigration-driven diversity that surrounded them to their experiences in the past or in other regions of the country. These respondents recalled growing up in much more segregated and homogeneous places, whether in Silicon Valley or in another locale. In contrast, younger respondents (ages 15–34) had spent their entire lives in a context where immigration was creating a majority-minority population (Silicon Valley crossed over that threshold in 2000). Immigration-driven diversity was thus normal for them, so much so that the terms "diversity" and "multiculturalism" did not register for them in the same way they did for the older cohorts. Whether they refer to "a demographic fact, a particular set of philosophical ideas, or a specific orientation by government or institutions toward a diverse population" (Bloemraad 2011), the terms "diversity" and "multiculturalism" connote the deliberate recognition and articulation of ethnic difference. For the young people we interviewed, diversity and multiculturalism were facts of everyday life that required no explicit articulation. Toya Rivas, a twenty-six-year-old, Mexican American rental-car company clerk in Berryessa summed up the sentiments of other young respondents when she said "[Being around immigrants] has always been a part of life that I grew up in, so I just take it for what it is."

Unlike the older cohort of respondents, young respondents were often slow to offer the ethnic and racial backgrounds of the people in their neighborhoods, workplaces, interpersonal networks, and schools—they did not flag diversity as noteworthy because it had been the norm for as long as they could remember. Because of their age and inexperience, many young respondents existed in a narrower frame of reference, and the degree of diversity found in their communities only became apparent to them when they went away to college or left the area to visit another part of the country. Though attitudes about race among young whites were not altogether different than the attitudes of older whites, their frame of reference may signal the emergence of a new racial order defined by blurred and crossed ethnic and racial boundaries (Hochschild, Weaver, and Burch 2012)

If young people were slow to articulate immigration-driven diversity and even slower to marvel at the diversity that defined their lives, the younger set's nonchalant acceptance of that diversity was one of the first things that older respondents noticed about them. The differences between the experiences of today's youth and those of their parents and grandparents were perhaps most apparent to older respondents in East Palo Alto, who came of age in the midst of an epic struggle for minority civil rights (Skrentny 2002). Though they still lived in an area of minority segregation, their lives and those of their children and grandchildren were no longer defined entirely by complete spatial isolation. Because there is no public high school in East Palo Alto itself, many young people from the city attend high school in adjacent affluent cities such as Palo Alto, Menlo Park, Atherton, Redwood City, and San Carlos.[3] They thus have ample interactions not only with the Latino and Pacific Islander newcomer individuals in East Palo Alto, but also with affluent whites and Asians in their schools. To be sure, poor and minority students tend to be tracked into more remedial classes, away from their more affluent white and Asian schoolmates. Also, rigid ethnic and class social cliques form within schools.[4] Nonetheless, parents in East Palo Alto marveled at the high degree of contact that their children had with racial others as compared to their own experiences in childhood. Michael Thomas, a black, forty-nine-year-old food-service worker, put it like this:

> My kids, they grew up around everybody because, even my older daughter and my youngest . . . OK the oldest [has been around] the Mexicans, Pacific Islanders, blacks. So they know everybody, all nationalities—white people, because they went to [Menlo-Atherton High School]. That kind of stuff. So it was just normal for them to be around all these different nationalities. Same with my youngest daughter. She goes to [Palo Alto High School], so you got white, you got, what, blacks—you do have there, the few. And they have Latinos. They don't have too many Pacific Islanders, at least not to Nixon [Grammar School]. And she has two of her best friends are white kids. She has play dates with them. So it's never been an issue of nationality or whatever. None of that stuff withstanding, the culture and that stuff, they hung with who they hung with. It didn't make a difference. It was never like, "We need to be around them"—that kind of stuff. And I never came from a household like that. Like [in my childhood]: "What you doing with that white boy? What you doing with that white girl?" That kind of stuff.

Parents in Cupertino and Berryessa similarly noted the difference between their own childhoods and those of their children. Daniel Gildish, a white, forty-eight-year-old corporate executive who grew up in Cupertino, echoed Michael's assessment of his children's experiences, though in terms that revealed the far greater social latitude that Daniel and his family experienced as a result of their racial identity. We sat poolside in Daniel's manicured backyard while he offered the following observation:

> Of course, now there's also people from all over. People from South America, Mexico City, Israel, everywhere—the Netherlands. There are people from all over the place now that have company schools. We didn't get that. We were very homogenous group of people here, I think, back then. And so I don't think we had the worldview as much. I don't think we understood other cultures. I don't think we had to deal with other cultures in our own daily life. So that's why I say it's completely different. So my kids know what Pakistani people are like. They know what Indians are like. They know what some Chinese people do and Koreans. They have friends whose parents are from Israel. So they know a lot about different people from all over the world. I think they're used to that. It's a normal thing for them. Whereas [in my childhood] it would be pretty abnormal to have somebody from . . . or a significant group of people from outside that had parents or were from outside the country, going to school with them. Back then for us, that was a big deal if maybe somebody came in from somewhere else. Even from out of the state was kind of . . . it wasn't abnormal, but I would say it wasn't usual. I don't think there were that many people that were born here and grew up here, that kind of thing.

Throughout the interviews, the significant contact between newcomer and established youth had an air of inevitability. Children could not avoid it, even when their parents intervened. Some parents, mostly from Cupertino, had placed their children in what they described as more "demographically balanced" schools in which their children were not part of a small minority (I discuss these dynamics more in chapter 3), and found that their children nonetheless ended up forming friendships across ethnic, racial, and immigrant-generational lines. Consider how things played out for Bob Russo's children. Bob, a white, fifty-one-year-old corporate manager, grew up in a virtually all-white part of the country. His wife was an immigrant from Mexico. Fearing that his son would suffer from being one of only a few non-Asian students in their zoned school, he placed his son in a school in another district. Bob explained the decision and the result like this:

I didn't want [our son] to be the only non-Indian/Asian child in the classroom. Because a friend of mine who lives in another part of Cupertino, where it's predominantly India . . . my friend is a Caucasian, his son is Caucasian. And there are three Caucasian kids in the kindergarten and they split them out. So his son was the only Caucasian out of twenty or twenty-five students. And I thought I try not to make that matter, but I think it does matter.

Q: How do you think it matters?

A: Well, I think he would have difficulty making friends because, from what I've seen, the Asian/Indian communities tend to be much more close knit. And I think it's hard for a Caucasian or a non-Indian, non-Asian to breach that community. And we wanted to make sure that he had friends as he was progressing through school.

Q: How has the decision to send him to the school in Los Altos worked in terms of that?

A: (chuckling) Ironically, his two best friends are Chinese and Indian! So good for him!

Richard Alba and Victor Nee (2003) explained that immigrant assimilation often happens as a byproduct of individuals pursuing their economic aspirations. As immigrants and their descendants look for better neighborhoods, better schools, and better jobs, they often find themselves coming into contact with people of other ethnic origins, which leads to other, more social forms of assimilation. As Alba and Nee put it, assimilation "is something that frequently enough happens to people while they are making other plans" (2003: 282). The same can be said of the established population. As the case of Bob Russo illustrates, significant contact with members of other ethnic racial groups and immigrant generations happened among the people I interviewed even when there were attempts to create some distance.

The reflections offered by respondents like Bob Russo also show that respondents were far from colorblind. They recognized ethnic and racial difference, and in fact respondents saw a less beneficial side to this diversity (as later chapters will show). For many, it made their own ethnic and racial identities uncomfortable parts of their social identity. Respondents also saw ethnic and racial difference as a strain on social cohesion. But as the quotes above show, these differences were thoroughly baked into the context that respondents navigated, making diversity not only familiar, but the norm.

NOT SO STRANGE, NOT SO MARGINAL: CONTACT WITH NEWCOMER INDIVIDUALS

Respondents' characterizations of the settings they navigated were more than general assessments of East Palo Alto, Cupertino, Berryessa, or Silicon Valley: they indicated the high degree of firsthand contact that interviewees had with immigrants and the second-generation children of immigrants in virtually every aspect of life. This contact was central to their experience of relational assimilation.

Silicon Valley offers abundant opportunity for such contact. Recall that first- and second-generation immigrants together make up roughly 56 percent of Silicon Valley's population. In East Palo Alto, Cupertino, and Berryessa, where newcomers make up almost half of the population, significant contact between the established population and newcomer individuals was nearly inevitable, whether in the neighborhood, at work, at school, or even in the family. These contacts were stratified by race and class, with respondents primarily having contact with newcomer individuals whose class status was similar to their own. But contact was universal: racial and class differences merely indicated *which* newcomer individuals they would have contact with, not whether they would have contact at all. And in its ubiquity and inevitability, this contact with newcomer individuals brought the immigrant experience into the daily lives of established respondents in both casual and more intimate ways. The most consequential contacts took place primarily in three kinds of contexts: the neighborhood, school and work, and romantic partnerships. Respondents also reported more casual contact in their everyday lives and through their participation in organizational and civic life.

Contact in Global Neighborhoods

The neighborhood was an especially prominent context for this contact. Sociologists who study immigrant assimilation place great importance on neighborhood composition as an indicator of assimilation. According to the "spatial assimilation" perspective (Massey 1985), assimilation takes place when, over time and across generations, individuals live in neighborhoods with fewer individuals who share their ethnic origin. The theory rests on the idea that immigrant assimilation involves moving away from urban centers where immigrants historically concentrate and to the city's edge (i.e., the suburbs), where there are not only fewer co-ethnics, but also easier access to the kinds of amenities that make for a nice residential life (Park, Burgess, and McKenzie 1925). A parallel line of research on racial segregation focuses primarily on the residential concentration of African Americans and is concerned with the implications of residential isolation for intergroup contact. It finds that when individuals live in integrated neighborhoods, they are more likely to come into contact with individuals of other ethnic and racial backgrounds (Iceland 2009).

These perspectives were conceived with an urban/suburban dichotomy in mind, framing urban centers as poor and largely minority-occupied, and suburban areas as containing a region's white as well as upper- and middle-class residents.[5] But the suburbs are no longer bastions of the white middle class. Today's suburbs are defined by heavy immigrant settlement (Alba et al. 1999; Lai 2011). Indeed, a majority of immigrants in metropolitan areas now live in suburbs (Singer, Hardwick, and Brettell 2008) or ethnoburbs (Li 2009) like those now established in Silicon Valley. The diversity that characterized urban areas in the early and middle parts of the twentieth century has migrated to the suburbs in the twenty-first (Logan and Zhang 2011).

Just as these theories of residential integration predicted, the large number of newcomer individuals in the areas that we studied meant that virtually all contexts lent themselves to contact with newcomer individuals. Respondents were quick to note as much. Chapter 4 discusses how respondents described the quality of interactions among neighbors. Suffice it to say here that respondents in all three locales believed that their neighborhoods and cities were less cohesive because of the large immigrant presence, but they were far from isolated from their newcomer neighbors. Respondents noted that they were most likely to interact with neighbors who spoke English fluently and who had lived in the neighborhood for long periods of time. While the quality of contact varied, virtually all respondents reported having some interaction with foreign-born neighbors and their children. The interactions ranged from mere cordial salutations to deep friendships. And because respondents lived in class-segregated communities, their contact with immigrants tended to be with immigrants who shared the same class status as themselves. In East Palo Alto, respondents reported significant contact with Latinos but also some with Pacific Islanders. Describing the nature of contact at the more intimate end of this spectrum was LaVaughn Agathe, a black, thirty-five-year-old grocery store clerk in East Palo Alto. LaVaughn was particularly gregarious, and it thus might be no surprise that he maintained cordial relationships with his neighbors. As he explained:

> I've noticed in other cities where you see little Saigon, little Koreatown, and stuff like that. It just don't happen here. Everybody kind of invite each other. We're all just such neighbors and we keep it almost a family atmosphere to where you don't really see the separate but equals and this is mine and that is yours type stuff—nah.

In Cupertino and Berryessa, most respondents' contact was with upper-middle- and middle-class individuals. These contacts did not necessarily approach the connectedness that LaVaughn portrayed. But interactions with newcomer individuals were nonetheless a prominent part of the neighborhood context that respondents described.

For respondents in all three cities, having children connected parents to immigrant neighbors who also had children. Though respondents in Cupertino and Berryessa often described second-generation children as overscheduled with activities meant to maximize an academic bottom line, when established and newcomer second-generation children living on the same street formed friendships, it had the ability to bring parents into the fold. My exchange with Lori Brewer, a white forty-year-old banker from Cupertino, highlighted the way that children connect their established population parents to newcomer individuals:

Q: What is it about [your Indian-immigrant neighbors] that you guys have been able to become friends with them and perhaps not some of the others?
R: Probably because the kids are best friends.
Q: If it weren't for the kids how do you think things would be with them?
R: Same as they are with the other people. Friendly, civil, but not connected.

Neighborhoods are not just places where people live. They are contexts that provide an opportunity for people to interact. And when established and newcomer families live side by side, the opportunities to interact increase (Blau 1977). Of course, simply being neighbors does not necessarily mean that people will interact with each other: the characteristics of the neighborhood must be conducive to interaction (Sampson, Morenoff, and Earls 1999). The presence of children in these neighborhoods made them quite a bit more conducive to interactions among parents, established and newcomer alike. Whether that interaction happened through monitoring the children, scheduling play dates, or observing norms of neighborliness, like inviting people in the neighborhood to a birthday party or family celebration, it resulted in instances of parents getting to know each other well and even forming friendships. In this respect, the findings from Silicon Valley reveal what can only be inferred from the spatial assimilation hypothesis, which focuses on residential location alone as an indicator of newcomer assimilation (Brown 2007; Park, Burgess, and McKenzie 1925). As newcomers move directly into the suburbs alongside established households, the contact that results drives a relational form of assimilation for both newcomers and established individuals.

Assembly Lines, Cubicles, and Schools: Contact Away from the Neighborhood

On top of the neighborhood diversity, the workplace presented ample opportunity for contact. Research in other metro areas suggests that the workplace may be far less segregated than the neighborhood (Ellis, Wright, and Parks 2004). For established respondents, work and school offered significant contact with newcomer individuals—often more than they found in their neighborhoods. This work contact usually was with immigrants of a similar class standing to their own—not surprising given that many people's class position is partly defined by their jobs (Katznelson 1981). Working together on a cooperative basis made the contact more sustained, and even more intimate. Whether they worked in professional technology jobs, blue-collar manufacturing, or service-sector occupations, respondents often had coworkers who were born in another country. Just as when they described their neighborhoods, interviewees readily pointed out that their coworkers were born abroad, and this was to them an important feature of their work environment.

The description that Derek Jackson, a fifty-six-year-old black assembly-line worker, provided of his workplace offered both a sense of the diversity that other respondents depicted and the nature of interactions among coworkers:

> There's a Vietnamese guy, [Ronnie]. There's a Filipino guy, [Mickey]. There's a Cambodian guy—two of them, well you got two Cambodians, [Bobby] and [Chann]. . . . But they talk about fishing a lot. They like to go out. They like the outdoors, and we talk about that a lot. Rocky's from the Philippines. And he told me about the culture at his house, how he grew up. Johnny's from Vietnam. He told me when he came over here when he was six, and he's been here ever since, so he speaks fluent English now, which is really good. But he still has his home native tongue with . . . which is good. (laughing) Sometime he be cracking us up by talking the Vietnamese stuff. But we don't pay him no mind. It's all funny, to me.

Professionals from Cupertino and Berryessa similarly described having a large contingent of newcomer coworkers. While the term "immigrant work" often conjures images of foreign-born workers shunted into low-wage, backbreaking work, Silicon Valley's entire labor force, from assembly lines to cubicles, is immigrant in character (Pellow and Park 2002; Saxenian 2006; Wadhwa, Saxenian, and Siciliano 2012). Bob Harmon, a white forty-nine-year-old engineer and manager at a major technology firm, provided a description of his workplace that was typical of those offered by other professional respondents:

> Today, I spoke to Olga, who is Israeli-Russian; Luc from Taiwan; Manjaya from India, Hassan—Pakistani; Ed is second-generation Taiwan. We had a guy from Nigeria. It's a diverse, diverse group. We go, (chuckling) "Yeah. Us poor white guys—we're in the minority here, too." It adds. The guys give me crap. We were supposed to go out to Indian food today. "Sorry. I went out with Mike from Canada." He's a Canadian. "We went and had sushi, instead. Next week, Manjaya." It's just a melting pot [at work].

Respondents from the youngest cohort described spending the bulk of their days in schools that were even more newcomer in character than their neighborhoods. High schoolers formed friendships with first- and second-generation immigrants, even if these friendships were less common than those with other established-population individuals. Young respondents described having especially significant contact with new-comer individuals in the classroom and through extracurricular activities such as sports, drama, and other school-sponsored clubs and organizations. Tyler Takahashi, a twenty-year-old college student from Berryessa of Japanese descent, had frequent contact with Asian newcomer individuals at school and with Latino newcomer individuals while playing soccer, coloring his sense of Berryessa's demographics. He noted:

> Well, I've been playing soccer for my whole life and I've been playing in the Berryessa area for most of my life. And most of the kids on my team . . . I'm usually the only Asian kid on the team. There's a few white kids, but it's mostly Hispanic. I don't know. My parents don't agree with me but I think there's a large Hispanic, a large percentage of the population of Berryessa I would consider to be Hispanic. But my parents think it's mostly predominantly Asian. But I think it's mostly . . . Well, it's probably just based on the people I know, but it's mostly Caucasian or Hispanic people I know around here.

Marquez Litt, a black, seventeen-year-old East Palo Alto resident, was a star high school football player and top student. As East Palo Alto had no public high school within the city limits, East Palo Alto high school students who stayed within the public school system attended school in one of the wealthier neighboring cities. Marquez went to a high school that was a mix of wealthy whites, wealthy Asians, poor Polynesians, poor Latinos, and a few poor blacks. As I observed firsthand, there was heavy segregation at the school. Moving from "the green," a grassy area where wealthy whites and Asians hung out during lunch, to "the courtyard," where Latinos, blacks, and Polynesians congregated, was like moving between two entirely different schools, even though the two areas were divided only by a bank of classrooms. Participating in athletics tended to break down these barriers for students who took part. Like Tyler, Marquez reported having the sort of intergroup contact with teammates that seemed to belie what I witnessed during lunchtime:

> We're just like a big family! We have like practices before football really starts. So our coach makes sure that he wants that bond. No matter what race you are, he wants that bond. So he brings us to lift weights, run on the track. We just do everything together. Go to each other's house and eat. We have big

festivals like that so we can be one basically and get along, so we can win some games. So that's one thing . . . .

Q: What about the racial or ethnic background of the kids who play football?

A: All that really doesn't matter. Like they just have that bond and basically focus on football and becoming as one basically. So that's one of the good things about it . . . . Never comes up. Never comes up. That's the weird thing about it.

Q: Why do you think that's weird?

A: Because we have all these problems outside of that. But when we come to something that we all love, I guess we want to win so we just do whatever it takes and we just get to know each other. But that's a good thing also because then outside of football, like when we do see each other, we got that relationship now where we can just chill, talk to each other and so on. So that subtracts the more negativity and more problems with each other.

Young people who participated in sports were especially likely to report significant and meaningful interactions across ethnic and racial lines because those activities created the conditions under which ethnic and racial boundaries could become porous (Allport 1954), even if those barriers were clearer in the rest of the school.

Dating and Marriage: Contact and Contact by Proxy

The contact that respondents described in their neighborhoods, schools, and workplaces could also be found much closer to home, in their own families. For some of the established people we interviewed, the immigrant lines of the family tree were not just relegated to distant branches. Marriage to immigrants or to second-generation children of immigrants could introduce (or reintroduce) a sustained and intimate contact with newcomers. Recall that Silicon Valley is something of an extreme case when it comes to the size and composition of its immigrant population. It is also an extreme case in terms of the scale of intermarriage in the region. According to analyses of 2007–8 American Community Survey data by sociologists Jennifer Lee and Frank Bean (2010: table 4.4), the intermarriage rate in the metropolitan area that includes a large swath of Silicon Valley was the highest in the country. More than 21 percent of marriages in the county involved interracial couples, more than three times the national rate.[6] Intermarriage rates are high among all of the major groups in the region: Lee and Bean's analysis show that 50 percent of marriages among blacks, 54 percent of marriages among Latinos, and 60 percent of marriages among Asians/Pacific Islanders were interracial. Although assimilation research tends to focus on intermarriage rates for minorities as a key indicator of assimilation (Waters and Jiménez 2005), intermarriage among whites, viewed through the lens of relational assimilation, is equally important. According to Lee and Bean's analysis, 24 percent of marriages among whites in Silicon Valley involved a nonwhite partner. The high rate of intermarriage in the area likely has to do with the composition of racial groups. Asians and Latinos together comprise a majority of Silicon Valley residents; these are also two groups that have extremely high intermarriage rates regionally and nationally (Wang 2012).

Intermarriage rates in the Valley are to some extent driven by residents' limited opportunities to meet partners of the same racial background (see Blau 1977). The small number of African Americans in the region makes it harder for African American partners to find each other, and thus makes intermarriage more common. The same can be said of the region's relatively small percentage of white residents compared to other locales. A smaller pool of same-race partners increases the likelihood that individuals of these groups will find partners of different racial backgrounds, raising their rates of intermarriage compared to national figures.

This does not necessarily mean that intermarriages involve *established* and *newcomer* individuals. Indeed, when intermarriage occurs, it is most likely among people who are more generationally distant from the immigrant generation—between established individuals of different racial groups (Lichter, Carmalt, and Qian 2011). Still, we found that intermarriage between newcomer and established individuals occurred to a large enough extent that it constituted an important form of contact between established and newcomer individuals, usually across ethnic and racial lines. Our respondents' most sustained and intimate forms of contact with newcomers emerged in their descriptions of family members, including spouses, who came from an immigrant household. These relationships were significant because they brought the established spouse into contact with an entire web of foreign-born in-law family members. In Cupertino, Bob Russo's wife was born in Mexico and had a large locally based family that served as the primary hosts of holiday and other family events, bringing both Bob and the children into regular and close contact with his wife's immigrant family. I interviewed Bob near Easter, prompting him to use the holiday as a reference point to explain his relationship to his wife's family:

> We do a lot of events with her family, birthdays, weddings, holidays. For example, on Sunday we'll go to a park for an Easter celebration. Everyone will bring something and it will be primarily Mexican food. And I'm the white guy they bring. I joke with them all the time and they joke with me about it. It's interesting because most of the events that we have with our [children] are around [my wife's] extended family.

Some young and unmarried respondents reported dating second-generation children of immigrants. Such pairings often crossed racial and ethnic lines. In East Palo Alto, heterosexual dating trends mirrored larger gendered patterns of intergroup romance, with black men more likely to date Latinas while black women tended to be in relationships with, or limit their partner searches to, black men. In Cupertino, white young men and women both dated newcomer Asians, contrary to the gender asymmetries found in larger interethnic dating patterns, where Asian women are more likely than Asian men to date outside their ethnic group. In Berryessa, white young men dated newcomer Asian women, while both white young men and women dated Latinos (Wang 2012).[7]

Even when individuals did not themselves seek romantic relationships outside their own group, other family members often introduced newcomer individuals to families through marriage. A Pew Research Center study reports that 35 percent of U.S. residents say that a member of their immediate family or a close relative is married to someone of a different racial group, a figure almost surely propelled by immigration-driven diversity (Wang 2012). Reflecting these broader trends, our interviews abounded with accounts of siblings, cousins, aunts, uncles, and even remarried parents who partnered with newcomers.

Contact with newcomer relatives was hardly relegated to the youngest or middle cohort of respondents. Those from the oldest cohort also described close contact with their diverse sons- and daughters-in-law. Changes in rates of and attitudes about intermarriage are partly a function of "cohort replacement," in which older individuals are replaced by younger cohorts who have greater opportunities for intergroup contact and hold laxer attitudes about intermarriage. The result is an increase in intermarriage over time (Wang 2012). The idea of cohort replacement would seem to suggest that age cohorts live in isolation: that the marriage patterns of younger cohorts have little or no bearing on older ones. The interviews suggest a different story, however. Take, for example, the case of Anna English, a white, seventy-year-old retired teacher of Portuguese descent in Cupertino. Anna explained that she had had regular contact with both whites and Mexican Americans when she grew up in the area, but that her parents' deep prejudices made the latter romantically off-limits. Yet her daughters, having grown up in a context of tremendous immigration-driven diversity, chose marriage partners whom her own parents would have rejected. As Anna explained:

> Now I have a daughter that's married to a Brazilian. She lived in Brazil for three years and speaks fluent Portuguese, plus she lived in Ecuador for a while with a family and speaks fluent Spanish. So she's trilingual. And so I'm the sandwich in between, where my parents told secrets so that we wouldn't know what they were saying. And then I hear her and her husband speaking Portuguese. And then my other daughter married a Mexican from the Yucatan. He is a brilliant guy and she's learned Spanish, not as fluently as [my other daughter], but she does.

Though Anna comes from a cohort whose intermarriage rates were low, suggesting much less interethnic contact among individuals of that cohort, marriage patterns among individuals in the subsequent cohort introduced diversity to the family networks of the older generation.

The effect could be even more profound for older African Americans, virtually all of whom told of the virtual impossibility of interracial relationships when they were growing up. They marveled at the relative regularity with which such relationships form now among their adult children and grandchildren. Black intermarriage rates are lower than for other nonwhite groups, indicating that the social boundaries between blacks and nonblacks are still relatively rigid (Lee and Bean 2010). Still, when older respondents in East Palo Alto discussed intergroup romance, the contemporary situation seemed to them a far cry from the Jim Crow segregation that defined their younger years. Many of their children and grandchildren had partnered across ethnic and racial lines and had mixed-race children of their own. Ronald Johnson, a black, fifty-eight-year-old retired plumber in East Palo Alto, had two sons and a daughter, all of whom had children with nonblacks, including one with a second-generation Mexican American. Ronald explained the rather ethnically complicated family tree that resulted:

> My [grand]daughter is black and white. And my son that's the plumber, he have a black kid, I have a white kid and a Mexican kid [from him for grand-children]. And my other son that's a legal secretary, he have a white kid and a Mexican kid. Well, my other son, he's with the mother of the Mexican child. But he's not with the first child's mother, which is Portuguese.
>
> Q: Do you ever get together with the families of your grandchildren's mothers?
>
> A: Oh yeah!
>
> Q: Tell me about what those gatherings are like.
>
> A: We just had one of them, my birthday in the park, [March] 23. And that son's wife['s] mother and father come to all, every event we have. And he's a Mexican guy, he's in construction. And his son's in construction. And he had two kids to get killed in Mexico. [T]hey praise me on how I raised me on my kids and I praise them on the way they raised theirs. And you know the father, he didn't do a good job with his two sons that got killed down in Mexico. And I told him, from the little bit I know of him, that I thought he did a wonderful job .... Father speaks it real good but his mother, she ain't never really worked, but she works as a housekeeper, cleaning people's houses and stuff.

As Ronald's experience illustrates, one family member's choice to be involved with someone of a different ethnic background and immigrant origin made the composition of the extended family more mixed and brought family members into close contact with members of other groups. The network ties that formed as a result sometimes made for particularly strong bonds across ethnic and immigrant-generation lines. Marquez Litt, the black student athlete from East Palo Alto quoted earlier, described what it was like to be around his second-generation Mexican American ex-girlfriend by referencing the diversity in his own family:

> I mean, it was slightly different because I know her Hispanic background was different than mine, different foods and stuff. So when I went over there, I ate the food that Hispanics eat. But it wasn't really a culture shock

because I have my second cousin, he's half Mexican, half black. And I'm really close to his Mexican part of the family, so it wasn't really a culture shock. It was just like regular . . . . My uncle on my mom's side, my mom's brother basically, married a Hispanic lady and had [my cousin]. And then, as he was growing up, me and him just connected. I was always with him, every day, every day. I call him my big brother because that's how we're just cool like that. That's my big brother instead of my cousin because we got that relationship. And he's somebody I look up to as well.

This contact did not wash away the group boundaries that respondents articulated, but it did make those boundaries much more porous. These partnerships across ethnic and national-origin lines had a profound effect on the composition of family trees—an effect that extended both up and down the tree to previous and future generations. This effect had important implications, especially considering that younger cohorts across the United States have more relaxed attitudes about interethnic partnering and are more likely to make relationship choices that reflect those more relaxed attitudes (Hochschild, Weaver, and Burch 2012; Wang 2012). As the experiences of our established respondents show, the choices that any individual makes in regard to romantic partnering reverberate throughout the family network (also see Vasquez-Tokos 2017).

Casual Contact in Daily Life

If neighborhoods, work, schools, and romantic partnerships provided established individuals with regular and significant interactions with newcomers, more casual contact offered equally regular, but less meaningful contact.

Respondents' descriptions of their participation in clubs, organizations, and leisure activities showed this casual contact in action. For many established individuals, these contexts had a smaller immigrant presence than they encountered in neighborhoods, workplaces, schools, and a less meaningful presence than they found through romantic or familial connections. Some newcomers were present in these contexts, but that presence did not necessarily lead to significant contact with established respondents.

Among these various activities, children's extracurricular pursuits created the most opportunities for casual connection. Involvement in recreation like sports and performing arts meant that young respondents made direct connections to their newcomer peers who also took part in these activities. Parents who were frequent attendees at their children's games or performances often became friendly with newcomer parents who were also present. Daniel Gildish's daughter was on a jazz dance team that had an active group of parents. Daniel explained the relationship between parents, some of whom were from China and India, like this:

> So it tends to be the parents participate and bring food to the competitions and work together and get really close to making it a positive experience for each participant. And like talking about each other's daughters and how they're doing in school and what's happening in each other's families and things like that . . . so you get to know them pretty well.

Daniel's experience, as well as that of other parents with children who participated in sports or performing arts, illustrates the way that organizations facilitate particular kinds of network ties. Using the example of day care centers in New York City, sociologist Mario Small (2009) noted that people are more likely to form ties when they have opportunities to interact frequently and when those interactions center on a cooperative activity. Daniel's experience illustrates a similar phenomenon in Silicon Valley. When children are involved in performing arts or athletic teams that require parental involvement, and when the group of parents involved represent a spectrum of nativity, racial, and ethnic backgrounds, ties that span these different backgrounds almost inevitably form.

While children's activities fostered some contact, there were several significant social contexts where established individuals reported little important contact with newcomers. Consider churches and temples, which are places where newcomers and established individuals alike might be expected to find close community (Foner and Alba 2008). While the churches and temples that established respondents attended provided some contact with newcomers, respondents described newcomers' involvement as largely confined to religious services: the newcomers would attend services and then go home, seldom staying to socialize with other members of the congregation. When there was a large newcomer presence, the immigrant newcomers were often part of a "parallel congregation," attending services at another time and in another language, or participating in aspects of the church where the primary language was not English (López-Sanders 2012).[8]

Respondents who took part in other kinds of clubs and organizations, whether political or civic in nature, likewise did not register their participation as facilitating meaningful contact with immigrants, perhaps because immigrants are less likely to participate in such activities alongside the established population.

Yet even though this more casual contact was less consequential than contact in the neighborhood, school, work, and romantic partnerships, it was nonetheless significant. The people we interviewed found it hard to imagine doing anything outside of their homes that did not include some contact with newcomers. A trip to the grocery store, a leisure walk, depositing money in the bank, a night out with the family, or mailing something at the post office almost inevitably included some contact with people born outside the United States. Combined with more intimate contact, these encounters saturated the everyday life of established individuals with an up-close and personal view of the newcomer experience.

More than a half century ago, the psychologist Gordon Allport (1954) asserted that this kind of contact between members of different racial groups, under certain conditions—equal status, shared common goals, institutional support—would produce more positive intergroup attitudes. The interviews we conducted do not offer a clear picture of whether the frequent and meaningful contacts in multiple aspects of life improved established individuals' attitudes toward newcomers. What the interviews do depict, however, is the extent to which the immigrant experience was infused into established individuals' daily lives, and resulted in their familiarity with that experience.

THE IMMIGRANT EXPERIENCE SHARED

Relational assimilation is not simply a matter of established individuals regularly bumping into newcomers in multiple realms of life. For the people we interviewed, this contact profoundly shaped the degree to which they saw newcomers as strange. Regular contact with newcomers gave established individuals a more nuanced picture of immigration and immigrant adjustment than that provided by the prototypical immigrant narrative—which is often comprised of harrowing stories of migration, struggles to learn English, poverty, and mobility (Agius Vallejo 2012). Most respondents' interactions with newcomer friends, acquaintances, coworkers, neighbors, family members, and strangers were void of overt references to what it is like to be an immigrant. But they described how the topic inevitably came up in casual conversation, manifesting as migration narratives or discussions of family dynamics, and sometimes extending to their becoming personally involved in the travails of being unauthorized. The overall effect was a newcomer experience that was hardly strange. Indeed, it was thoroughly familiar to established individuals.

Migration Retold

When the immigrant experience did come up as a topic of conversation with newcomer individuals, established individuals reported that such conversations centrally included accounts of the migration process. Respondents found these accounts especially memorable when they included harrowing details. Interviewees who lived in Berryessa and East Palo Alto were likely to live and work alongside Southeast Asian immigrants, who relayed traumatic stories of their home countries and their migration and settlement. Interviewees recalled these stories occasionally coming up in casual conversations during lunch breaks or across front lawns. Mike Cervantes, a fifty-eight-year-old, later-generation Mexican American electronics technician, lived in Berryessa and worked for a Mountain View-based company, mainly with East and Southeast Asian immigrants. Mike and his coworkers frequently swapped childhood stories over lunch. For his immigrant coworkers, these stories revolved around descriptions of the harsh conditions that led them to leave their homelands, the process of migration, and the struggles associated with settlement in the United States. Mike had a keen familiarity with the struggles of one of his coworkers as a result of these interactions:

> The guy I work with the most . . . . he's from Cambodia . . . . He was telling me that when he came over here [to the United States], only thought that Oakland, that's the way life was. No hope, no dream, drugs, fighting. Worked at McDonalds. He moved his way up as a manager . . . . He's told me some stories about the communist era over there in Cambodia. I don't see how he survived. He was toting an M-16 at ten years old—forced to. Seeing his daughter killed; father shot right in front of him, for nothing. Him and his brother trying to survive. . . . he's toting these rice bags at eleven, twelve. Can't eat till seven o'clock at night. Man. It's amazing how he made it— tracer bullets at night going over the bamboo. He doesn't know how he survived because he's seen the pits with bodies in them.

Mike's own father emigrated from Mexico during the early part of the twentieth century (his mother was born in Los Angeles). But Mike had only a fuzzy knowledge of the conditions under which his forebears lived prior to migrating. Working alongside immigrants, even if they did not come from his father's homeland, brought part of the migration narrative to life for him. These tales of the immigrant experience—of evading border security, trekking across deserts, long layovers in refugee camps, and life in the homeland—were not passed only from earlier generations to their children and grandchildren. They were also imparted to established individuals by their newcomer coworkers, friends, neighbors, classmates, and significant others. Paul Clark, a white, fifty-one-year-old computer engineer from Cupertino, described learning of the conditions under which his coworkers grew up:

> I don't hang out with anyone from work like in nonworking hours. But again, in my business there's a lot of pressure to deliver on deadlines. So the teams tend to get fairly close-knit because you're all working towards a common goal. When we need a break, we'll hang out, have lunch, talk, relax, talk about anything but work to get away from it a little bit. And then that's what we discuss, what it was like growing up when you were a kid, what it was like growing up for me as a kid. Just an exchange of experiences . . . . Maybe for some of my coworkers who grew up in India that came up from lower socioeconomic situations—their description of life there with rolling power outages and rolling water allocations, it's a little surprising. It's more from the standpoint of, "Wow. Are you serious? You would go two days without water?" And they talk about they remember as kids having to fill up their bathtub. When they had water they would fill up everything that would hold water because they might not have water for two or three days. Those types of experiences. It's interesting. And it's also a little shocking.

Even when interpersonal contact with newcomer individuals was limited to the workplace, these interactions imparted a level of familiarity with the immigrant experience that can only come from regular and sustained contact.

Similarly, the struggles that immigrants endured after migration gained significance and immediacy because of respondents' intimate connections to the newcomers who faced them. Assimilation theories conceive of the host society as part of the "context of reception" (Portes and Rumbaut 2006) that helps determine the ease with which assimilation unfolds for immigrants. But interviews with established respondents revealed that they were more than just part of a context of reception, judging newcomers' fitness to belong (Portes and Rumbaut 2006). They often shared in these struggles. Respondents were usually most intimately aware of the immigration struggles of people who shared their class background. The people we interviewed from East Palo Alto articulated a familiarity with the experience of being a poor, and even unauthorized, Latino immigrant. Cupertino respondents displayed a deep knowledge of the high-skilled immigrant experience, and established Berryessa respondents reported an awareness of multiple immigrant experiences, including high-skilled, unauthorized, and refugee. This familiarity often came about as result of involvement in schools and with children. Chloe Campbell, a white, fifty-eight-year-old retired social worker in Berryessa, recounted the travails of her son's friend, a refugee from Vietnam. In the course of extolling his remarkable work ethic, she recounted her knowledge of his experience:

> I watched this young man go through elementary, through middle school, he became a friend of my son's. And he would come here—his name is [Van]—and I would say, "Hi, how you doing?" I remember I had a candle on and he said, "[Chloe,] what that?" And I said, "Okay, that's a candle." [He said,] "Candle." He was learning. Still, but that kid got straight As. He's a dentist, now. He worked in somebody's business tailoring, making clothes. He made his own clothes in high school and he's a dentist now. So he really persevered. And when I worked at the middle school I saw the kids that would persevere were the Asian kids. They would . . . . The Caucasian kids were, "Eh." They were like, "Eh. I don't want to do that right now." They didn't persevere as the other ones did. So I did see that.

Q: Why do you think they persevered?

A: I asked one of them 'cause it always bugged me. It was like, "Why are they doing so well? Is it just something in their makeup?" So I asked one or two of them when I was working there, "When you guys go home, is it super strict? 'Cause you get such good grades and everything." And they said, "No." They said, "When we go home we have to do homework. We can't receive phone calls. If a friend calls us on the phone, everybody gets to listen to it. We don't want phone calls. We go to bed early. And we get whipped. We get whipped if we are not doing these things. We get hurt badly." So that was their incentive. Not to get hurt. They don't have a lot of socialization because they're not allowed to.

As respondents like Chloe told it, it did not take much to encourage immigrants to talk about what it was like to migrate and adjust to life in the United States. In the process, their stories made the experience far less abstract and more familiar to established individuals whose immigrant roots, if they had them at all, were many generations in the past.

Sharing in the Immigrant Struggle: Illegality and Parent-Child Conflict

The immigrant experience became even more immediate when respondents shared directly in the struggles that immigrants and their children confronted. Interviewees described familiarity with, and even direct participation in, two kinds of struggles intimately connected with today's immigrant experience: dealing with unauthorized status and the conflict that arises between immigrant parents and their second-generation children.

No factor is more acute in the immigrant struggle to belong than legal status. There is now strong evidence that being unauthorized or having parents who are unauthorized imposes significant hardship that may take generations to overcome, if it is overcome at all (Bachmeier and Bean 2011; Gonzales 2015; Menjívar and Abrego 2012). Silicon Valley has one of the highest rates of unauthorized residents in California. According to the Migration Policy Institute, about 8 percent of all Santa Clara County residents are unauthorized (Migration Policy Institute 2015). Some established individuals in East Palo Alto and, to a lesser degree, Berryessa had deep familiarity with what being unauthorized entails because they had significant and meaningful interaction with immigrants who lacked legal documentation. Though unauthorized immigrants and even their U.S.-born children generally do not announce their legal status, when established individuals developed close personal ties to them, the topic became relevant. In East Palo Alto, where the majority of immigrants are from Mexico and Central America (the largest sources of unauthorized migration), the tribulations associated with being unauthorized manifested as a collective issue that shaped the shared sense of community among residents. Carry Plimpton, a white, forty-seven-year-old head of a nonprofit in East Palo Alto, described the troubling effect of unauthorized status in the community:

> Usually the situation is we got a high school student whose parents may or may not be legal citizens, and the high school student themselves may or may not be legal citizens. In this community we're now seeing a lot of kids turn eighteen who were brought here illegally as kids. And they're asking us, asking around, "How do I survive in this country without being able to legally work? And I don't want to go back to Mexico. I hear about all the crime going on there. I don't have a relationship with people over there." So that comes up.

Young respondents in Berryessa also described confronting the issue in communal ways. When a schoolmate or friend revealed their unauthorized status, it was relevant to entire communities. Take, for example, the story that Elaine Hayes, a black, sixteen-year-old high school student who lives in Berryessa, relayed about a schoolwide discussion on the topic prompted by the impending deportation of one of her schoolmates:

> Well sometimes [immigration comes up] I guess, but last year we talked about it a lot in class and stuff like that. And my teacher, he made a good comparison because in our school we're going to have a lot more incoming freshmen than ever before. So he asked us how we felt about it and a lot of people said that they weren't that happy with it because they would get less attention and the school wouldn't be as . . . it's like a small community so everybody knows everybody and the teachers can help the students out and stuff like that. And so he compared that to immigrants, because that's how people feel about immigrants, you know. We also talked about the good facts of it too . . . . Well I don't think anybody in my class is [illegal], but I know

that there were some seniors last year that were. Oh, there's a senior that graduated two years ago, he went to [Columbia University] and he was being deported and so, yeah, we had to sign a petition to help him out and stuff like that.

Today's young unauthorized immigrants face a set of potentially permanent detours in their efforts to chart a path to adulthood (Gonzales 2015). Significant publicity of their plight made them more open to "coming out" about their status in recent years, though that coming out can be tamped down by any crackdown on unauthorized immigrants. When they do come out, it reduces the stigma of being unauthorized, and it also forces those who live and work around unauthorized immigrants to confront the issue (Abrego 2008). As Carry and Elaine's comments illustrate, established individuals could be motivated to collectively address the challenges of unauthorized immigration when they were connected to unauthorized individuals through schools and other institutional ties.

Lack of legal documentation entered into the lives of established individuals more directly when they had personal links to unauthorized immigrants or to the children of those immigrants. Young respondents in East Palo Alto and Berryessa told of friends whose lives were complicated by the unsettling way in which unauthorized status was entwined in every aspect of their experience. Young respondents in East Palo Alto, where Mexican immigrants predominated, were especially likely to articulate their familiarity with the plight of people who were "illegal." Roxy Taylor, a black, fifteen-year-old high school student in East Palo Alto, was a case in point. The electronic ankle monitor she displayed with more than a hint of rebellious pride was an apparent indicator of a checkered past. During one of Roxy's stints in juvenile hall, she had become friends with an unauthorized Mexican-immigrant youth through whom she became intimately familiar with how lacking papers and getting entangled with the law made for a toxic set of circumstances. As Roxy reported:

I be feeling bad because I had a friend, she was in juvenile hall with me and she didn't have papers. But she was [raised] down here and her family lives down here. And they all have papers and stuff for her. And they made her go back to Mexico and I was feeling bad because it's like, dang, she don't have no family in Mexico. Everybody came down here and they have papers. And it just makes me feel bad. And when they come and get them, people start running. And that makes me feel bad . . . . My friend doesn't have no family to go to. She don't have no papers and now she can't get papers until she's twenty-one. She's only fourteen. She's going to have to be on her own. And she said that they mistreat her in Mexico.

The lives of unauthorized immigrants have always been complicated by fear of authority and deportation (Ngai 2004). Recent efforts to more stringently enforce immigration laws in the U.S. interior have only exacerbated fears among immigrants (Menjívar and Abrego 2012). As the interviews highlighted, these fears struck a chord with established individuals when they had close ties to unauthorized immigrants or their children.

The precariousness of legal status was all too familiar to respondents with unauthorized family members. Interviewees who were married to formerly unauthorized immigrants, or to newcomer individuals who had family members in a state of legal limbo, sometimes found themselves ensnared in the difficulty of the situation. Consider the case of Fred Nugent, a white, forty-one-year-old software engineer in Berryessa. His sister-in-law, a U.S. citizen, married a Mexican national and gave birth in Mexico to Fred's now-teenage niece. Because of a variety of complicated circumstances, the couple failed to register his niece for U.S. citizenship, and she had been living in the United States without authorization since early childhood. After the girl's mother returned to Mexico with her husband, Fred and his wife took over their niece's care. Fred explained his involvement in the situation like this:

Our niece was born in Mexico. And we're still trying to get her papers straightened out. It's because her mother didn't do the right thing at one point, so it's been messy. She started living with us about a year ago. Since then, we're still trying. She has two brothers, but they were born in San Diego, so they're okay . . . . It seems like it's just the bureaucracy. But part of it is, from what we understand, only certain people can do the process, which in this case is her mother. And her mother hasn't been so forthcoming. Her mother lives in Tijuana with her husband who is—what's the word?—he was forced to leave the U.S. . . . . deported, because of some jail issues or felony . . . . But we started the process [of working out my niece's papers]. My wife went down there. They went to the U.S. Embassy in Mexico. We started the paperwork. They went in and found out, "Oh, we didn't have everything," so we gotta go back. Then we hesitate. I think the last thing was to get a birth certificate from Mexico. My niece's mother said that the niece had to be there. And we fear if the niece goes down there to Mexico she won't be able to get back . . . . So it's still been a challenge, even though her mother's American by birth.

Q: What's this process been like for your niece?

A: Somewhat depressing. Sometimes she'll say she doesn't feel like anybody, she's a nobody. Without the papers, can't get a Social Security number. Can't get a job.

Scholars have pointed out the way in which an individual's unauthorized status can reverberate throughout an entire family, even when other family members are in the United States legally or are citizens (Bean, Brown, and Bachmeier 2015; Gleeson and Gonzales 2012; Gonzales 2015). Fred's experience shows that these reverberations can be felt by an extended family made up largely of established individuals. These experiences also suggest that a more aggressive enforcement of immigration laws that includes mass deportations is injurious not just to deportees, their immediate families, and perhaps those who depend on the labor that unauthorized immigrants provide. As the experiences of the established individuals we interviewed illustrate, the lives of newcomers and established individuals can be so deeply entwined that fear of deportation and deportation itself is a stress that extends well beyond the prototypical "immigrant community."

It is important to note here that legal status was not as pressing an issue for immigrants in the upper-middle-class city of Cupertino and the middle-class area of Berryessa. Many of these immigrants had come on H-1B work visas, had green cards, or had already earned their citizenship. Though the high-skilled can be found among the ranks of the unauthorized, respondents from these locales (especially from Cupertino) were more likely to interact with newcomers who came from an elevated class position and were thus less likely to be unauthorized.

Legal status was not the only struggle characterizing the newcomer experience with which established respondents had intimate familiarity or direct engagement. Established respondents were familiar with conflict between immigrant parents and their second-generation children. They also often found themselves in the middle of that conflict. Scholars have documented the way in which immigrants and their children negotiate between the immigrant household they live in and an outside world where "homeland" ways bump up against ways of life viewed as more distinctly "American." The distinctive differences between the life experiences of immigrants and their children can be the source of parent-child conflict over everything from views about dating and sex, to corporal punishment and work ethic (Portes and Rumbaut 2001; Portes and Fernández-Kelly 2008; Waters 1999). Respondents who had close ties to immigrants had more than a front-row seat to this conflict. Interviewees in Cupertino and Berryessa showed considerable understanding of the conflicts that can arise from immigrant parents' expectations for their children's academic and professional success. Like other young respondents with many second-generation friends, Jennifer Schwarz, a nineteen-year-old college student of white and Japanese descent who lived in Cupertino, regularly witnessed the complicated relationship between immigrant parents and second-generation children:

> I've seen a lot of conflict between my friends and their parents because their parents are [foreign] nationals and my friends are American in terms of . . . in every way they may be Chinese or Indian, but they're as American as I am, and we're all at the same spot. There's conflict between them when their parents want them to do really well in school and like, "Oh, you had an opportunity I never had," like, "Do well." The kids are like, "I am doing well. What are you talking about? Just chill out." That's always something that I constantly saw . . . . Sometimes, in middle school and high school, some of my friends wouldn't be able to go out because their parents [were] like, "No. You have to stay home and study." Or, "You have Chinese school." Or, "You have to do well in such and such sport," not understanding that there needs to be a little more balance, and time for other things socially, as well. Sometimes, my friends with parents from other countries, there's more disconnect, not as much communication, or understanding between parent and child.

Established respondents sometimes became enmeshed in the sort of conflict that Jennifer described when their friends and romantic partners were second-generation immigrants. Brian McKenna, a white, eighteen-year-old college student who lived in Berryessa, was dating a second-generation Chinese woman. In the course of laying out his view of Chinese immigrants, he expressed tacit frustration over what he saw as strict parenting strategies that his girlfriend's parents imposed because it cut into the time that he could spend with her:

> [Chinese families] have really early curfews. My girlfriend's curfew is sometimes nine o'clock. She's seventeen and a half. And that's not even on a school night—on the weekends. It's just like the principle—they don't want them out. And a lot of them couldn't sleep over for a long time, they had to study. They make them read books. If you go to the library and walk around, it's 99 percent Chinese people in there and they have shopping bags with like twenty books. And then the kids start doing it because the parents do it and just naturally become really involved in education; it's just part of their life.

Other young respondents echoed Jennifer and Brian's characterization of Asian-immigrant households, noting how certain parenting strategies impeded their children's ability to socialize with friends or romantic partners outside of the school setting.

The Without a doubt, the struggles facing immigrants fall most squarely on the shoulders of immigrants and their children. But the regular contact between the established population and immigrants meant that these struggles rippled into the lives of respondents, often quite directly.

CONCLUSION

Part of what it means to be an immigrant is to get to know the way of life in the place of settlement. In the case of Silicon Valley (and likely in other prominent immigrant-receiving destinations as well), however, the way of life in the place of settlement is itself partly defined by newcomers. As these findings show, the give-and-take of adjustment—that is, relational assimilation—occurs through regular contact between established and newcomer individuals and the sense of mutual familiarity that it produces.

Although newcomers have been portrayed by scholars as strangers in a new land (Higham 1955), they were not so strange to the people we interviewed. Respondents saw the region, cities, and neighborhoods in which they lived as centrally defined by immigration-driven diversity. For respondents, especially the younger ones, this diversity was almost taken for granted. Their significant contact with immigrant and second-generation individuals—in their neighborhoods, at school, at work, and even within their own families—gave them meaningful access to the immigrant experience through tales of migration and settlement, direct involvement in the challenges that come with unauthorized status, and close experience of conflicts between immigrant parents and second-generation children. From the perspective of respondents, the stories and experiences that newcomers carried with them were not strange possessions of strange people. Rather, they were defining features of daily life for all who lived in Silicon Valley, regardless of how long their families had resided in the United States. It is important to note that, for all the contact established individuals had with newcomers, not every dimension of life facilitated that contact. In churches and temples, for example, established respondents described some newcomer presence, but they seldom had significant interaction with newcomer members of their church or temple. Indeed, the religious institutions were not significant facilitators of contact.

It is also important to note here what will become abundantly clear in chapters 3 and 4: this familiarity between respondents and the newcomers with whom they interacted was marked by considerable ambivalence. Along with their knowledge of the immigrant experience, their consumption of ethnic culture, and their praise for immigration-driven diversity, established respondents saw immigration as a destabilizing force in their experience of ethnic and racial identity and their sense of community. These more negative views coexisted, often uncomfortably, with the positive ones: in the end the positive views prevailed in large measure because of respondents' familiarity with the immigrant experience and the people who embody it.

How does ongoing contact and familiarity with the immigrant experience shape other dimensions of relational assimilation for the established population? The subsequent chapters take up that question, beginning with culture.

2 Salsa and Ketchup—Cultural Exposure and Adoption

The cultural imprint of immigrants across Silicon Valley is hard to miss. The signage in public schools is often displayed in three or four languages; strip malls prominently feature Indian, Mexican, and Korean markets; non-English languages can be heard in most public places; weekend festivals across the region center on ethnic traditions; and ethnically themed churches and organizations can be found in just about every city (De Graauw, Gleeson, and Bloemraad 2013). These signs represent the fuller flowering of a symbolic shift that took place in the early 1990s, when salsa overtook ketchup as the best-selling condiment in the United States (O'Neil 1992). But salsa is just the top of the chip bowl, as it were. For some observers, immigration's stamp on American culture is all too heavy. Immigration, in their estimate, is leading to the demise of what they conceive to be American culture (Buchanan 2006; Coulter 2015; Huntington 2004). For others, immigration's cultural influence is a celebrated triumph of diversity over forced assimilation (Kymlicka 1998). Whether they imagine an American society defined by a white core (Gordon 1964), or segmented by race and class (Portes and Zhou 1993), scholars have treated change in ethnic culture—defined as symbols and practices associated with an ethnic origin—as a zero-sum struggle between "foreigners" and "natives" over the survival of a distinctly ethnic way of life. Only recently have social scientists begun to rethink this struggle. Richard Alba and Victor Nee (2003) suggested that immigrant groups leave their imprint on the mainstream as they become part of it through assimilation, a process that unfolds over multiple generations. For instance, German and Italian traditions and cuisine once strongly associated with an ethnic origin now stand firmly as "American" aspects of life. Today, there is good reason to believe that the influence of ethnic culture is more far-reaching and that it moves more rapidly into multiple aspects of culture than in the past. The abundant cultural vibrancy brought by the contemporary wave of immigration and the opportunities that postindustrial societies offer for greater individual expression, including expressions of ethnic identity, have translated into widely held beliefs about the importance of maintaining and even celebrating ethnic culture (Alba and Nee 2003; Schildkraut 2010; Bean, Brown, and Bachmeier 2015).

Given this demographic and ideological state of affairs, how do the established individuals we interviewed make sense of the cultural vibrancy that surrounds them?

The large number of immigrants in Silicon Valley means respondents not only had lots of contact with newcomers, as I reported in the previous chapter. The interviews also show that the contact provided established individuals with regular exposure to and opportunities to participate in the cultures invoked by the newcomers around them. Their exposure came from being connected to institutions, like schools, workplaces, and cities, that value and celebrate ethnic difference. It also came from their everyday contact with newcomers. But this exposure did not lead to deep adoption: the ethnic cultures that respondents encountered almost never became part of a cultural repertoire they invoked on their own. Still, this cultural dabbling was influential nevertheless, shaping respondents' ethnic identities in complex ways. Their responses varied along racial lines. Among whites, the exposure produced feelings of ethnic blandness and a resulting desire to have a more robust connection to their own ethnic ancestries. Blacks in East Palo Alto did not feel "bland"—they expressed a strong sense of individual black identity—but the visibility of Latino ethnic cultures contributed to a view that black culture ought to be a more prominent part of East Palo Alto's civic identity, just as it had been in the past. Latino and

Asian established respondents reported an externally imposed expectation that they display a cultural know-how more likely to be found among co-ethnics who were closer to the immigrant generation.

The way respondents described their engagement with ethnic culture suggests that the cultural dimension of relational assimilation is characterized by exposure to ethnic culture rather than deep adoption of it. They described a local mainstream characterized not primarily by the specific ethnic symbols and practices contributed by various newcomers but instead by a norm of having strong connections to an ethnic culture. As established population interviewees explained, this was a norm that was often difficult for them to embody.

Before proceeding, it is important to clarify what I mean by culture. The concept is the subject of great debate in social science (see Small, Harding, and Lamont 2010). I use a "lean" version of culture here, focusing on symbols and practices regarded as ethnic in nature: for example language, music, art, food, style of dress, and observance of holidays. Certainly, some elements of culture lose their ethnic association over time. Alba and Nee (2003) have noted, for example, that the Christmas tree, leisure Sundays, and frankfurters are aspects of culture that were once associated with German ethnicity but that now no longer have an ethnic association and exist in the mainstream. In this chapter, I explore how established individuals engaged with aspects of culture that had not yet made such a leap: aspects that they categorized as ethnic.

ETHNIC CULTURE AS EVERYDAY CULTURE

There can be little doubt that the newcomers in Silicon Valley have contributed to a visceral sense of "super-diversity" (Vertovec 2007). But the debates about the proper place of ethnic culture in the public sphere that have been at center stage during the culture wars of the post-civil rights period (see Alexander 2006) were beside the point for the individuals we interviewed. Their exposure to a cultural mélange was not driven by a self-conscious desire to be cosmopolitan (Appiah 1997) or a proclaimed endorsement of multiculturalism (Bloemraad, Korteweg, and Yurdakul 2008; Kymlicka 1998). They simply lived in a region where immigration-driven diversity was a fact of life. Interactions in their neighborhoods, at their workplace, when socializing with their friends, and even in their romantic and familial relationships exposed them to a variety of ethnic cultures, symbols, and practices that were not necessarily connected to their own ancestry.

The ethnic cultural cornucopia in these contexts does not just affect the identities of the second generation, who often draw upon multiple ethnic cultures to develop what sociologist Natasha Warikoo (2004; also see 2011) called "cosmopolitan ethnicity." It also shapes how established individuals make sense of their own ethnic identity. Though our established respondents did not report significant adoption of the ethnic symbols and practices that were so abundant in Silicon Valley, their exposure to those practices informed a conception of the cultural mainstream that was ethnically multifaceted. For the people we interviewed, the local notion of the mainstream was composed of recognizably ethnic symbols and practices that were widely familiar and available to local residents regardless of ancestry.

Public Displays of Ethnic Culture

In contrast to early twentieth century views, which held that ethnic culture was properly deployed only in private life, ethnic symbols and practices are prominent in contemporary public life (Alexander 2006). In places with large immigrant populations, the symbols and practices that once hid inside private homes now make appearances on any given weekend in public festivals, schools, neighborhoods, and even casual encounters.

Ethnically themed public celebrations are a prominent part of public life in Silicon Valley and were reported in all three study locales. These celebrations exposed established individuals to immigrants' ethnic cultures. Though the majority of patrons were individuals whose own ancestry was reflected in the celebration, the events were ostensibly open to all. Even if established individuals did not attend, they displayed a keen awareness of the events' existence and purpose. In East Palo Alto, respondents were quick to identify Cinco de Mayo and Mexican Independence Day when asked about public celebrations in the area. Likewise, Cupertino respondents pointed out the Obon festival, Chinese New Year, and Diwali as events that dot the public calendar. Berryessa, as a subsection of a larger city, does not play host to its own ethnically oriented public events, but the city of San Jose boasts the largest Cinco de Mayo celebration in the country, a large Chinese New Year parade, and a Tet (Vietnamese New Year) festival. Most respondents reported having attended some of these celebrations. Though they were generally not regular attendees, they spoke about the festivals as part of the regular array of public events in their city and region. The awareness of such events displayed by Cliff Butler, a seventy-year-old, African American retired engineer in Berryessa, was typical of the sort of characterization that other respondents offered:

> The Chinese just celebrated a Moon Festival. The Japanese have what they call an Obon Festival. That's not living the life, but it certainly helps keep your culture alive. You have Cinco de Mayo. You see them just expressing the culture. And they're accepted in America, now. And not only are they accepted, but they themselves have become part of American culture. Think about it: we all eat Chinese food. We all eat all the different . . . . There's so many Mexican foods that it's unreal. Some of these things that we think of as Italian actually started in America. But we eat pizza. We have . . . you name it and we eat it. Every ethnicity you talk about. That's all part of the melting pot, too. That hasn't changed. They brought that here and they keep it here so it becomes American, also.

Cliff offered an updated version of the melting pot, where recognition and display of ethnic culture were core parts of local and, indeed, larger American national mainstreams.

If respondents from the oldest and middle cohorts of respondents had grown accustomed to ethnic celebrations in their respective cities and in the region more generally, interviewees from the youngest cohort took these celebrations, and particularly those that happened in their schools, entirely for granted part as of the cultural landscape. Virtually every high school in Silicon Valley has a day—often called "International Day," "Diversity Day," or some variant thereof—during which students display the artistic and culinary features of their respective ethnic cultures (Shankar 2008). The accommodations that schools make for these celebrations reflect larger institutional changes over the last four decades that have elevated diversity into a value that permeates institutions, including schools. That value translates into school-sanctioned recognition of students' various ethnic identities, particularly those students whose families arrived most recently from abroad. The primary audience for these public displays of ethnic culture is not just the individuals who connect their ancestry to the culture on display but also includes those whose ethnic ancestries are not connected. LaSunda Jackson, a seventeen-year-old black high school student in East Palo Alto, reported that she had been a frequent attendee at Cinco de Mayo celebrations at the local Boys and Girls Club as well as at her high school. As LaSunda reported:

> In EPA, we have a Cinco de Mayo thing. It's at the school, Cesar Chavez [Elementary School]. And then for Black History Month you'll see a lot of African Americans. Here, at the [after school club], we'll do something for Black History Month. Or for that, we'll sit in the front of the bus and stuff like that. And then, at my school, we have a whole cultural week where we'll celebrate every different culture. And people who will come today, if they're Mexican, they'll have their Mexican flag on, and we'll have something [for food,] tacos, whatever. And then for black people, chicken or whatever. And the Asian, Chinese, they'll have their day to celebrate what race they are . . . . I have went. It's a whole lot of fun, even though you can't really understand it because they're speaking Spanish. But if they can kind of like they're celebrating their independence. They're really thankful for being here and stuff like that. And it's kind of like a little parade and people eat, play sports and stuff like that, play games and stuff like that.

Having come of age in a time when public displays of ethnic culture were far less common and accepted, parents of the youngest respondents often spent more time discussing how normal these displays were in the eyes of their children than they did discussing their own exposure. Sarah Norton, a white, forty-seven-year-old homemaker in Cupertino, was very involved her daughter's school. She described the celebrations at her youngest daughter's school like this:

> We'll celebrate or educate the kids on all of the big holidays. So while they're learning about Christmas, they're learning about Hanukkah, someone comes in about that. Someone comes in and talks about [the Indian festivals of] Diwali and the festival of the lights. And Chinese New Year. And we have the celebrations that happen at the classroom level, and then we do this big international festival thing that just went on, on Friday. And that's for all the kids across the whole campus . . . . kids walk around with little passports and visit the different tables for different countries and learn things, and have to

answer questions so we know that they're learning about them. So we do celebrate. There's so many! I think that's interesting. So the sensitivity is that—and this is different actually. I would say probably ten or twelve years ago when my [older] girls were going to school, if you look at the calendar of the school it probably said things like, "Christmas party." Now you don't see that. Now it's very much like this is the "Winter season party," or something. So it's more generic now, so that we're really not excluding people from it, for those people who don't celebrate Christmas for example, or those people who don't celebrate Hanukkah . . . . Because the classrooms are made up of kids from all over the world.

The global classroom that Sarah portrayed is an apt description of classrooms across the region, including Berryessa. The reflections of Natalie Hayes, a thirty-three-year-old black homemaker in Berryessa, echoed Sarah's observation:

I go to people's homes and I see their culture, I see how they interact with their families. These are things that people can learn, but they don't take it away, take it home. When you say, "What did you try today?" I mean, at the preschool they even try to have a culture festival and whatnot. And I keep going, "Well, if I bring something, nobody is going to eat it." If it's not mainstream to what they think is black food, if it's not ribs, people won't eat it. They're not going to eat the greens or the ham hocks, things that people eat that are considered black. Those kids are not going to eat it because they've never seen it before. But because a lot of these kids have seen *pancit*, which is the Filipino noodles, they'll eat it. They're like, "I know this. I've seen it." So it's taken a lot of stuff out of, it's not just spaghetti any more. Different types of noodles, different types of treats that have changed the culture of the kids. So it's opened up everybody's eyes.

The exposure certainly opened everybody's eyes, as Natalie put it, but respondents generally did not "take it away, take it home": exposure to culture rarely led to outright adoption of that culture. These public celebrations are sporadic and respondents seldom described participating in any meaningful sense. Still, their exposure to an array of public ethnic displays had the overall effect of making the public deployment of ethnic culture a normal part of life.

To be sure, several respondents complained that the celebration of particular ethnic identities came at the expense of more collective celebrations that honor their more monotonic conceptions of a mainstream "American" history. In East Palo Alto, for instance, several respondents noted that ethnic festivities, particularly those that honor Mexican heritage, drown out African American celebrations such as Juneteenth and the Collard Green Festival. Respondents from Cupertino sometimes expressed frustration over the number and frequency of ethnically themed events at the city's largest public park at the expense of "American" displays. In chapter 4, I discuss interviewees' views on these matters more fully. Suffice it to say here that there was a great deal of ambivalence across the sample and even within individuals about the effects of these cultural events. Nonetheless, they were an important means through which respondents came to see, even if reluctantly, the multicultural reality of the places they lived, worked, and attended school.

Ethnic Culture and Interpersonal Contact

As discussed in the previous chapter, interpersonal contact was a primary way that respondents came to understand the immigrant experience and even to engage directly with it. Such interpersonal contact also granted respondents access to symbols and practices that came from ethnic ancestries other than their own. Across the three study sites, interviewees mentioned that their interpersonal contact with newcomers had resulted in frequent and significant exposure to ethnic culture, mostly in the form of celebrations, holidays, and artistic expressions. Virtually every respondent could recall having attended at least one wedding, birthday celebration, or religious ceremony at which some element of non-white, non-African American ethnic culture was prominent.

Interviewees from the middle and oldest cohorts reported contact with newcomers in their neighborhoods and at work who offered significant exposure to ethnic culture. In the neighborhood context, older interviewees occasionally characterized their relationships with their neighbors as distant because of linguistic and cultural barriers. But they also described having close relationships with immigrant-origin neighbors who had lived in the area for a long time. These immigrant-origin neighbors regularly invited respondents to events—like birthday parties, weddings, and religious observances—that prominently featured ethnic culture. Noel Keats, a white, forty-seven-year-old administrative assistant from Cupertino, spoke in general terms about how living in the same neighborhood with so many newcomers had affected her exposure to different ethnic cultures:

> I think a diverse population adds a lot of different cultural events, different foods because you have the restaurants. It just adds exposure to a lot of things that you might not have if there weren't such a diverse population.

Q: What's that been like for you?

R: It's been awesome! In just my immediate block here we have people from South America, Italy, Vietnam, India, China, Russia, Mexico and I'm sure a handful of other places too, but that's just my one block that has people from all those different places in the world who are first generation here, not born and raised here with parents who came from out of the country. So that really allows us to learn a lot about different people and different cultures and it's just really awesome . . . . I just think different customs, different ways of doing things that maybe I didn't know of before. We have a little bit of language issues sometimes. That hasn't presented a big problem, just an extra challenge in communication with people. But we've learned of different holidays that people celebrate and just cultural awareness.

While few respondents were as effusive as Noel in explaining their exposure to ethnic culture, they described similarly limited levels of engagement. Donna Williams, a forty-year-old white homemaker in Cupertino, depicted how her family dabbled in public and private observances of Chinese New Year and public celebrations of Diwali. When asked whether she participated in private events that reflected an ethnic ancestry, she replied:

> No. I don't, meaning not consistently. We've been invited to various Chinese New Year events with our friends. Not that our neighbors aren't friends, but kind of our peers and stuff. So we do that. But [in the neighborhood,] yeah, we do. Thinking of . . . have we gone to anyone's home for Diwali? We've gone to Diwali events, other things around town but not . . . And then friends that have had special . . . what is it called? The ginger egg, the special thanks for the kids that are born, special celebrations that families do—the dim sum restaurants and all those kind of things. We've done a lot of those special things. But more with our Chinese friends. I'm trying to think about anything East Indian . . . not really.

Q: Can you tell me a little bit about the Chinese New Year celebrations that you went to with friends?

R: Just for the kids, lucky money, red envelopes and special foods. Really just
    kind of dinner parties and dragons and being silly and running around and
    just little tchotchkes and kid toys.

As Donna's comments indicate, contact with newcomers can create tremendous awareness of a range of ethnic cultures. But it was very rare for
the people we interviewed to describe deep engagement with these cultures, much less any sort of adoption of new cultural elements into their
own lives.

Much as in the other two research locations, respondents in East Palo
Alto were often invited to family celebrations that expressed the ethnic origins of their neighbors, especially when those neighbors had lived in the
area for a long time. In these neighborhoods, mariachi and *banda* music
emanating from backyards was a soundtrack to weekend afternoons, as
immigrant-origin Mexican residents celebrated weddings, birthdays, and
anniversaries at parties that often included ethnic outsider attendees.
LaVaughn Agathe, the black, thirty-five-year-old grocery clerk from East
Palo Alto quoted in the previous chapter, told me that he is a frequent guest
at these parties because his Mexican-born neighbors are sure to invite him.
LaVaughn described a set of community dynamics that were located on the
more positive end of the spectrum of intergroup relations that respondents
offered. He explained how these invitations worked:

> If there's a barbecue going on, the back gate is open. If anything, bring some
> more beer. And if there's a *quinceañera* [a Latina debutante] or a little
> wedding party or whatever—side gate is open, the band is playing. Pick
> a table and someone will bring you some food. I've got [a] neighbor that
> literally stays right around the corner from me and when the party goes on,
> he'll either send one of the kids or my other neighbor—who is black, right
> across the street from him—[he will] will send him to me and be like, "Tell
> him to get his ass over here . . . ." I mean it could be *quinceañera*, maybe
> birthdays, which in the daytime will always be the baby parties and in
> the nighttime is the grownups party. If I'm around and it's going down, I'll
> stop [by].

As often as East Palo Alto residents might attend these celebrations, they
described their role at the events as more observer than participant.
Similarly, the black teens we interviewed reported having attended, in

some cases, multiple *quinceañeras*. But it seemed that no matter how many they had attended, their exposure never translated into a sense of full comfort at these events.

The workplace was another central context that broadened respondents' notion of the cultural norm. Professional and working-class respondents alike spoke of the way that lunch breaks offered an opportunity to get to know immigrant-origin coworkers in a social setting and sample the cuisines of these coworkers' ethnic origins. The cafeterias at many companies, and especially at technology firms, reflect the tastes of a workforce that is heavily immigrant-origin. Menus feature Indian and East Asian cuisine that is primarily enjoyed by tech workers from India and China, but also by established population individuals. Cupertino and Berryessa respondents, who largely worked in professional positions, described their exposure to the culinary aspect of their coworkers' ethnic cultures during lunches and after-work events. Andy Zulfan, a white, fifty-four-year-old engineer from Berryessa, worked for one of Silicon Valley's technology giants, which employed a substantial number of South and East Asian engineers. Andy was one of the few non-Asians in his division, which was dominated by Indians. Andy's close working relationship with these engineers provided him with a glimpse into Indian culture. As Andy explained:

> I eat with these [Indian] guys every day and so a lot of the guys joke that I'm part Indian or something like that. There's an Indian dress that a guy wears when he gets married or goes to a formal occasion, and I was given one of those things by one of my Indian friends. And things like that. So no doubt I've learned a lot about it by talking with these people . . . . I have gone to a wedding, which . . . . was an Indian guy and a white woman. I've gone to Indian festival events, Indian day and that kind of stuff . . . . It's really just an appreciation of another culture. I was friendly with another Indian family outside of work because my kids swam together. And she taught Indian dance and so we went to see Indian dance and that kind of stuff. So I appreciate the culture, but it's not in that intimate kind of thing where I want to do it kind of thing.

Andy's experience shows how social interactions at work led to invitations to ethnically themed events after work hours. A similar story was related by Josie Whatley, a black, fifty-one-year-old social worker from East Palo Alto, who had frequent interactions with Asian newcomers because she worked in San Francisco's Chinatown. Her coworkers and clients were mostly Asian (Chinese in particular), and Josie was often a guest at their weddings, birthday parties, christenings, and other events where ethnic culture was prominently featured. Josie had thus become familiar with Chinese culture, but this familiarity had not made its way into her own cultural repertoire. When asked to provide an instance of the kinds of events she had attended, Josie relayed a recent example that underlined how established population respondents' tastes and traditions can gently bump up against those that newcomers observe:

> I work in Chinatown, so I was invited to the Buddhist temple last Saturday for a wedding. That was different (laughs) . . . . First of all, one of the things I've been working on for twenty-something, thirty years, is being open to try all different types of food. In terms of trying it and not having a reaction to it, do you know what I'm saying? (laughs) Because, I think it's rude when you're sitting with people and then they offer you something and you just say no. People say that's OK, but I don't think it's OK. I think you should try, you should try . . . . So, I brought fruit. I'm a Christian. I brought fruit for the Buddhas. They have these special things where they have fourteen Buddhas at the temple, and my coworker was also having her wedding ceremony, also that evening, the same day. So, when I brought the fruit, I thought I was just going to give it to the Buddhas. I give food to people, anyway. She wasn't around, so the people in the kitchen, and all these people there, she said, "Wash the fruit." And I'm like, "Well, if it's for Buddha, is there a certain way you're supposed to wash it?" (laughs) So, I'm kind of like, "OK." And then there's someone looks at me just standing there, and I'm like, "Well, how should I wash it?" They said, "Oh, just wash it." So, when I washed it, this particular lady said, "Bring it inside the temple." And I'm bringing the fruit. So she says, "Here lay it . . . " I had my basket and she had another basket. So she puts it down. So she's saying, "Bow, bow." So I said, "Oh, no. I can't." [They said,] "It's OK. It's OK." You know, I didn't want to be rude, because I don't want to worship false gods. I don't worship statues. So, she kind of looked at me . . . . That was really different, because I was kind of in an awkward position on dealing with my own spiritual beliefs and then trying to be respectful of others. And it was a lot of others! (laugh) I didn't want to get cursed!

Andy and Norma's comments echoed a central theme that emerged from respondents' discussions of their exposure to ethnic culture. Such exposure did not do away with the perceived strangeness of these cultural events, or the feeling of being a stranger when attending them. In fact, that exposure led them to reject elements of other cultures that were not compatible with their own tastes. But for Josie and others, the exposure did make what was strange about the events and the participants a more familiar part of their understanding of newcomers' ethnic culture.

Even if respondents did not describe significant participation in any given display of ethnic culture, many, and especially the younger respondents, felt that their exposure to and knowledge of multiple ethnic cultures gave them a particularly cosmopolitan outlook. These young respondents often eagerly discussed their knowledge of artistic dimensions of ethnic culture. In Cupertino, Indian music and dance were especially central to youth culture and were familiar to young people regardless of ethnic background. Even if they did not see Indian culture as part of their own ancestry, they could see it as part of a regional identity that they viewed as very much their own. Kristin Morrison, a white, twenty-four-year-old teacher who lived in Cupertino, explained how the knowledge of Indian bhangra dance and Bollywood that she gained while growing up in Cupertino was something of an anomaly when she attended college in the Midwest:

> I remember being in ⌈the Midwest for college⌉ and trying to explain bhangra to them and they didn't understand. And I was like, "We had that at junior prom and everybody got in a circle and there's this song and we have a bhangra club and they come and perform." And I was so excited about it. And they were like, "All right, that sounds a little weird. You mean Indian dancing?" I said, "It's not (just) Indian dancing. It's really cool." And they just couldn't get it. Now, a few years later, it's on, "So You Think You Can Dance" [a television reality show]. It's on TV and it's called Bollywood, which annoys me, but that's OK. I feel like I don't really have the right to be annoyed by it but I'm like, "I was here first and I knew about it and it was so cool. And nobody got it."

Like other respondents, Kristen did not claim ownership of the ethnic culture with which she was so familiar. Doing so, as her comments implied, would require some ancestral connection to the cultural symbol or practice being deployed. Yet the contrast she raises between her knowledge and her Midwestern classmates' incomprehension also suggests that some ethnic cultural literacy is part and parcel of growing up in Cupertino and Silicon Valley. She could claim some amount of authenticity and even a degree of hipness—as she put it, "I was here first"—in her mostly white,

Midwestern college because she had engaged with this aspect of Indian culture well before it hit mainstream popular culture. Likewise, Kiaya Butler, a black, twenty-year-old college student in Berryessa, described her exposure to an array of ethnic cultures because of her frequent contact with immigrant-origin peers:

> My mom always says, "You guys look like the United Nations," 'cause in our Facebook pictures—it's like one of every one of us. The people that I meet are all different. And since I meet different people just because of my personality . . . I don't do one thing. Some people are just, "I'm a guitarist." That's what they do. I have a little bit of everything . . . . I've taken a lot of Indian dance class. My friend, he plays the guitar and in the band. I've gone to Cuban cooking classes. My friend goes to Chinese school. I went to that one time. My other friend—or not friend, these are all people that I know . . . . They're from Africa. Their families are families who took people in as exchange students, not their real family, so I've experienced a little bit of the African culture, had dinner with them, gone places with them and learned things and . . . . My friend that moved away, he was into everything. So he tried to learn about every culture imaginable. I was with him. He would always take me 'cause he know that I was always interested. We would do things like Japanese drumming—Taiko drumming. And all that good stuff.

For Kiaya and other young respondents, this kind of easy exposure to different ethnic cultures was an expected part of everyday life. Indeed, to some degree, the cosmopolitan ethnicity identified largely with a second generation (Warikoo 2004; Warikoo 2011) appeared to belong to the established population as well.

Romantic and familial connections could deepen that sense of cosmopolitanism. Young interviewees were particularly apt to have familial and romantic network ties that reached across ethnic boundaries. In East Palo Alto, where it was not uncommon for African American men to date, and occasionally marry, Latinas, young respondents explained how their familiarity with Mexican ethnic culture was the result of their or their family members' romantic connections to Latinos. Aaron Mullin, a black, twenty-three-year-old delivery truck driver in East Palo Alto, was in a serious relationship with a second-generation Mexican American woman with whom he had a child. Aaron had Latinos in his extended family. As he explained, the symbols and practices that he and his girlfriend invoked involved more mixing than melting, a dynamic familiar to him because intermarriage had diversified other branches of his family tree:

> We have Hispanic people already in the family. So [being with my girl-friend] wasn't nothing new or out of the ordinary or extreme . . . . I guess it's a mix [in our house]. Seems like it's not really something you could define unless you're cooking food . . . . Not to put my girlfriend down, but I do most of the cooking. But she is a good cook herself but there have been some things that I have introduced her to that she didn't have an idea about . . . . Like gumbo. She loves gumbo now. She heard stories about it and she asked, so now she's fanatic. Or thick Texas chili, because that's where my father was from. That's pretty good. She introduced me to authentic Mexican, hand-made tortillas, enchiladas, everything made from scratch—so many things, I can't pronounce the names. I don't speak Spanish, so I don't want to try to pronounce it and massacre the word. But pretty much everything she has cooked so far I haven't had a problem with. And we alternate nights on cooking. So I might cook a dish and the following night she'll cook a dish. It's been a pretty good experience so far. No fussing. So we're pretty open-minded.

If an established individual we interviewed was not in an interethnic rela-tionship himself or herself, someone in the family—a sibling, aunt, uncle, cousin—often was. As a result, other ethnic cultures often made an appearance in the form of food, music, and religion at respondents' family gatherings. As sociologist Jessica Vasquez-Tokos (2017) points out, inter-marriage does not necessarily lead to diminishing recognition of ethnic and racial difference. Quite the opposite can be true: intermarriage can lead partners to greater awareness of the boundaries that define a signifi-cant other's experiences, as well as mutual adoption of the cultural prac-tices that come with each other's particular ethnic ancestry.

The exposure to ethnic culture that respondents reported as a result of their romantic partnering reached to the extended family. Take, for exam-ple, the experiences of Marquez Litt. As described in the previous chapter, Marquez's close cousin had Mexican and black ancestry, and Marquez had some connection to the immigrant experience through these family ties. That cousin's mother had passed away, but Marquez's uncle later married a woman from India, introducing even more diversity and a wider array of ethnic culture to the extended family. This contact led Marquez to see the cultures associated with these origins as normal part of the way his family does things:

> So [my uncle] remarried to an Indian lady some time back. It was a differ-
> ent culture, but I got used to it. When they had their kids, it was the same
> thing. Me and them just grew up together and so I got to know their culture
> instead of judging it. So I really got to know their culture. So, I just adapted
> to it.

Social scientists tend to conceive of the effects of romantic unions across ethnic boundaries as generationally forward-oriented, shaping the bound- aries and cultural repertoires of those involved in a particular union as well as those of their offspring (Lee and Bean 2010). In this conception, intermarriage redraws color lines, reducing the salience of any particular ethnic culture among future generations. As I outlined in the previous chapter, however, respondents described the effects of these unions as generationally backward-oriented too, affecting the cultural repertoires of previous as well as subsequent generations. Take the experience of Mona Danby, a multiethnic, sixty-three-year-old retiree from Berryessa. Mona and her husband each traced their ethnic lines to multiple, though mostly European, ancestries. Her son was in a serious relationship with a second- generation Mexican American woman, shaping not only Mona's knowl- edge of Mexican culture, but also the kinds of ethnic practices in which she partook:

> Well, I've picked up a lot more of the Mexican culture, because we only have
> a little bit of Mexican [in my family background], but I learned a lot more
> with my son's girlfriend, [with her] being Mexican. So the *quinceañera*, and
> what I found out in my family, because when I mentioned it they said, "Oh
> yeah, we used to do those way back when." And I go, "Oh! Well why did our
> family stop doing it?" "Oh they were just too expensive." Oh, OK. So once
> you start asking those questions, then you find out, "Oh we used to do that
> but it was just too expensive so our family quit doing it." OK, sounds good to
> me because I don't want to do it. So I've gone to two or three *quinceañeras*.

The reintroduction of Mexican traditions into her family as a result of her son's girlfriend is an instance of ethnic "replenishment" (Jiménez 2010a), in which new waves of immigrants make ethnic culture—and potentially ethnic boundaries—more significant in the lives of more firmly established generations. For other respondents from the oldest cohort, their children's romantic involvements with newcomers of Chinese, Mexican, Indian, Brazilian, Filipino, Japanese, and Iranian backgrounds expanded the range of family traditions that they observed. Respondents did not take the initiative to invoke these forms of ethnic culture themselves. Still, these displays of ethnic culture became part of the familial ethnic and cultural repertoire so long as newcomer family members maintained them.

The fact that the high level of exposure to ethnic culture that abounds in Silicon Valley did not produce a significant degree of adoption among the people we interviewed should not diminish its significance. It might be easy to dismiss descriptions of occasional enjoyment of food, festivals, holiday celebrations, and artistic expressions as "happy talk" about shallow forays into ethnic culture (Bell and Hartmann 2007). But the established individuals we interviewed saw this exposure as part of a cultural literacy that comes with—and perhaps is required for—living in the rich immigrant context that is Silicon Valley. Indeed, the effect of ethnic cultural exposure may be even more far-reaching. Experimental psychology research shows that contact with individuals of other ethnic groups sparks interest in that group's culture, and that freely participating in a task relevant to that culture reduces bias over the long term (Brannon and Walton 2013). Though the interviews did not offer a clear view of whether this was happening in respondents' lives, respondents' frequent contact with newcomers and their high exposure to the ethnic culture of these individuals suggests that such an effect may have been present. Since both contact (Allport 1954) and exposure to culture (Brannon and Walton 2013) predict a reduction in prejudice over time, it is more than likely that contact and culture serve as twin engines facilitating more harmonious intergroup relations in the contexts we studied.

SHAPING INDIVIDUALS' ETHNIC IDENTITY: PROMINENCE OF CULTURE VERSUS CULTURAL CONTENT

Even though established individuals seldom went so far as to adopt the cultures to which they were abundantly exposed, that exposure nonetheless had a significant effect on them. Respondents saw their exposure to

ethnic cultures as normal and viewed having strong ties to an ethnic culture as an identity norm required for anyone who wished to fit in in Silicon
Valley. The cultural vibrancy surrounding them spurred white, Latino-,
and Asian-descent respondents to ethnic introspection—an examination
of their own relationships to the cultures associated with their own ancestry. For African Americans in East Palo Alto, the immigrant presence was
an uncomfortable reminder of the diminished state of African American
cultural expression and prompted a desire for a more robust collective
expression of black culture.

Searching for a Way Out of Ethnic Blandness

Because respondents were several generations removed from their immigrant ancestors, most offered a rendering of their connection to their ethnic ancestral cultures as a kind of *symbolic ethnicity:* "a nostalgic allegiance to the culture of the immigrant generation, or that of the old
country; a love for and pride in a tradition that can be felt without having
to be incorporated in everyday behavior" (Gans 1979: 9). Established
whites can achieve the seemingly competing American desires for individuality and communal identity by asserting themselves as ethnically distinct for enjoyment but stowing their ethnic distinctiveness when it better
suits them to define themselves in other terms (Tocqueville [1840] 1994;
Waters 1990). According to scholars of ethnicity, symbolic ethnicity is an
advantage to whites as compared to nonwhites because ethnic distinctiveness is an option for the former, but an unshakable and possibly negative
aspect of identity for the latter (Waters 1990). In our interviews, white
respondents' descriptions of the roles that their ancestral cultures played
in their lives were entirely consistent with symbolic ethnicity. However,
they did not see this form of ethnic identity as an advantage. The shedding
of a strong ethnic identity, and its replacement with symbolic ethnicity in
a current context that celebrates a more vibrant ethnic identity left the
young whites we interviewed feeling ill-equipped to find a place for themselves in the ethnic mosaic around them.

White respondents often relied on comparisons with their immigrant-
origin peers to describe the role that ethnic culture played in their own
lives. In contrast to some of the early scholarship on white racial identity

that portrayed whiteness as the invisible racial background against which nonwhite identity stands out (see, for example, Frankenberg 1993), respondents' comparisons portrayed white identity as highly visible in the ethnically complex spaces they inhabited. Even more, many respondents described whiteness as culturally hollow, whereas other ethnic identities seemed fuller. Such comparisons were made almost exclusively by young respondents, whose core ethnic identity formation was still very much in play. Mike Peterson, a white, twenty-two-year-old recent college graduate from Cupertino, described the relatively weak significance that his Greek ancestry had for him by referencing the more robust significance that culture and ancestry had for his Indian friends. Ultimately, the comparison led Mike to lament that his Greek ancestry played such a minor role in his life:

> I more think of myself as just white American. Or if someone specifically asks me, I'll say yeah, I'm a quarter Greek. Because that's always the interesting question for me is, "Do you identify with something else?" And that's kind of the tough question. It's like, "Yeah, I'm a quarter Greek, but I don't speak Greek, I've never been to Greece." Whereas I know some of my friends speak Indian and they've been to India and they practice the different things from there and religion. And so it is like, yes, it's a kind of fallback thing, but I don't really think about [being Greek] a lot, it doesn't really shape my life . . . . I don't know. I think a lot of it just comes back to the ideals that I was raised in with democracy and respect for people. I think especially living around here you have to be very tolerant and very open to different things because you're just exposed to them all the time. You see them all the time. . . . Sometimes it's tough for me too because people that identify as like Latino or they identify as French, they have this specific culture that they can always fall back on. Or Native American, they have that culture, whereas if you identify as an American you kind of have a culture, but it's not really specific and it's not something I would say I could put my hands around and hold like that.

For young respondents, such comparisons inspired an expressed desire for their ethnic culture to play a larger role in their life. Andrew Hawkins, a white, seventeen-year-old high school student in Cupertino, described himself as "white," which he implied signifies a connection to multiple, though perhaps unknown, ethnic threads. Yet being at a school with so many newcomers inspired Andrew to make the threads he was aware of a brighter part of his identity tapestry:

I consider myself white pretty much. I think I'm one quarter Spanish, one quarter Polish and all kinds of different things. There's nothing that I consider myself one specific race. There's a bunch of different things. There's no culture that we really participate in from the European background at all.

Q: Does the topic ever come up in your family?

R: I always ask my parents what I am exactly because they have a hard time telling me. My dad's trying to trace back our family tree and my grandma just came over and we don't have that much paperwork or knowledge about my grandfather's family, his past ancestry. So it's kind of an unknown to me as far as the major amount of kinds of blood I have.

Q: What prompts you to ask your parents?

R: I'm just curious about it. I feel like I should know what I am. Pretty much just curiosity.

Q: Was there something in particular that made you want to know?

R: I guess having so much different diversity at our school. It just kind of made me want to know what I am.

Q: Is there something in particular that stands out as kind of making you want to know?

R: I'd say just a bunch of little things, not anything in particular . . . . Just at our school, just being around all kinds of different people.

Similarly, Michelle Yates, a white, twenty-one-year-old college student in Cupertino, reflected on the choices that multiethnic individuals in Cupertino made about their identity. Her reflection revealed her desire to have an ethnic cultural vibrancy that she felt her life lacked. According to Michelle:

I think if I had any ethnic ties, I would definitely go more towards that because white is not very ethnic unless you come from another country, like if you're German or Swedish. If you come from there, it's just kind of fun to have a culture and to surround yourself with a culture . . . . [I'm a] mutt! (laughing) I've traced my ethnicity back and it's a combination of ten different places that I come from. And so I'm sure I could pick and choose which ones I want to identify with, but I just don't feel connected to that . . . . But yeah, I always told myself growing up, "Oh I'm going to marry someone who is very ethnic, and then my kids can have that to identify with." For me, there's a lot of cool things that happen in other cultures that I'm a little bit jealous of . . . . I guess one of the cool things, I've never been to India or anything but their wedding is so much different than our culture as just an example. It's intriguing to me. Their wedding is so much different and they have this huge ceremony and they do the paintings on the hands and it means something. It's not just for decoration, it means something. And they wear their sari that's super pretty and everything means something. It's very meaningful for them to do this ceremony. Because I went to [an Indian] wedding yesterday and I was thinking to myself, "Why is this such a big thing? People just pay all this money to basically throw a big party." But in other cultures it's very meaningful.

Young white respondents' sense of ethnic blandness, and their corresponding desire for a more vibrant ethnic identity, had built over their lifetimes as they accumulated more exposure to the medley of ethnic culture around them. Kristin Morrison, a white, twenty-four-year-old teacher in Cupertino, attended a birthday party in third grade that turned out to be a formative experience in how she evaluated ethnic culture's actual role in her life, versus her ideal. As a teacher, Kristin celebrated Indian and Chinese culture in her classroom in ways that seemed to affirm the lesson that she took away from that childhood birthday party:

I remember going to the birthday at [my friend's house], and she lives right there . . . third grade and thinking that her mom was the coolest ever because she . . . like we did Indian dancing at a birthday party and I don't remember what it was but she told us stories. And it was all about that culture and I still remember that being the coolest birthday ever. We went to Chuck E. Cheese first, but then we went back to her house for a sleepover and did all kinds of cool things. That was pretty much it. I think just being around it helped, but I didn't . . . that was kind of on the first layer. Never went deeper into celebrating other cultures or learning more about them than seeing them. And I think I was lucky to have seen them but I really didn't get to go any deeper. And now, teaching them, I get to do holidays around the world in my classroom and everybody gets really excited for Diwali and really excited for all of the other holidays. And I don't remember doing as much with them. We did like Chinese New Year necklaces out of macaroni. That's pretty much it . . . . I think growing up, I felt left out because we went to these culture fairs and there were booths with such interesting and rich things. And my mom did the America booth and I was like, "Well this is boring!" They had an American flag and some hot dogs and sometimes I went to the Germany booth and I was like, "Well, we're really not that German so it doesn't really count." And I remember being so jealous of the rich culture that they had and how connected they were to that. And I still think that it's so cool to be both, and they could identify with the American culture and they could identify with this other culture, so they got double. It's kind of like being Jewish and Christian and getting two holidays. And I was like, "What? Why don't we get both?" So I think that I admired how connected they were to a culture that was so interesting. And I think I admired how much they knew about it. They knew about their holidays more. They knew the traditions and what went on. And if you asked me things about Germany, it's a long time ago and it's my grandpa's culture. And I still know a little bit but it's not right there with me and it's not something that I live in my everyday life. And that's what I admired.

These young respondents saw little advantage in their merely symbolic attachment to an ethnic identity and the weak role that ethnic culture played in their lives as a result. Their cultural longing may have stemmed in part from the fact that the purveyors of the ethnic culture to which they had exposure were from high-status groups. If, for example, the relevant comparison were African Americans or Arab Muslims perhaps the longing for a vibrant ethnic identity would not have been so strong. Still, what the young whites we interviewed responded to was largely the salience of identity around them—the fact that a strong connection to an ethnic identity was a cultural norm in their community. Indeed, they saw whiteness as visible precisely because it stood out against a backdrop of ethnic vibrancy. While they could choose from among several ethnic options (as described by Mary Waters [1990]), the choices appeared too slim and insignificant to be on equal cultural footing with those embraced by their immigrant-origin peers.

For other young white respondents, the large newcomer population and the recognition of immigrant ethnic heritages by institutions like schools intensified their frustrations over a search for a strong sense of ethnic identity. One small group of young white respondents had engaged in a mostly dead-end search to claim a piece of this recognition in form, if not substance, by attempting to form their own, racially based organizations. However, attempts to form "white" or "Caucasian" groups on campus did not go over well with school administrators. Take, for example, the experience with such efforts reported by Ashton Howard, a white, nineteen-year-old college student in Berryessa. Ashton was one of the few white students in a high school that was majority Asian but that also had a substantial Latino population. From his perspective, the school's Asian and Latino students took a great deal of pride in their ethnic backgrounds partly because of their closeness to the immigrant generation. Seeking to develop a similar sense of pride, Ashton attempted to form a "white" organization at his high school, an effort that school officials blunted. Ashton described that effort in the context of explaining his search for an ethnic identity:

> I've tried looking for [my ancestors] myself, like in my family tree—who I derive from and all those years before, but I could never really do it. And I really want to know where in Ireland or where in Scotland my ancestors came from. I feel it would give me a little bit more cultural pride and stuff like that if I found out. But I don't really know how I can . . . . And I'm not allowed to have white pride because . . . that's why I see myself as white. I'm not allowed to have white pride because I get in trouble if I do . . . . But apparently we're not accepted into being a club . . . . Yeah. It's not completely unusual but definitely a lot of the races usually always hung out with their own races. Like I said, sometimes I'd get jokes like, "Whoa! Where are all your white friends? Why don't you hang out with your real friends?" And I'm like, "They're not my real friends." So I was always known as being the one white guy in the group, always the one white guy with the group of Asians. So I guess it was pretty unusual. I think [I'm more willing to hang out with Asians because] the whole fact that I don't really have cultural pride. Like I said before, I don't really know where my ancestors are from and I barely really know any of many of my family. I'm not really that prideful of my race or cultural stuff. So I'm white but I don't really even call myself white, I call myself Asian half the time because I can relate more to Asian people. So that's why I feel like I don't really care.

Clearly whiteness did not show up as invisible in his daily life. Like other young white respondents, Ashton saw himself as an ethnic canvas bearing only blurry cultural imprints that could be interpreted and reinterpreted on the fly. An explicitly articulated pride in the bluntest interpretation of his identity—being "white"—was met with opposition from school officials, likely because expressions of white pride are associated with supremacist groups. And so Ashton searched high and low for some sense of ethnic identity, including affiliating himself with other ethnic origins (Jiménez 2010b), rhetorically at least, as seen in his identification of himself as "Asian" in part of because of his Asian friends. (One of the four members of his close group of friends was second-generation Filipino and Salvadoran, and another was second-generation Vietnamese.) Indeed, Ashton's whiteness, and that of other respondents, was visible precisely because it was an amorphous identity relative to the more defined notions of ethnic identity that so many of his peers displayed.

Why did a similar longing not emerge among older white established respondents? It could very well be the case that growing up in an earlier era, when multiculturalism was far less influential, made having a strong connection to an ethnic identity less fundamental to their sense of their overall social identity. It could also be that the young respondents were still working out a social identity that would become more settled as they moved into adulthood. As others have shown, individuals in their late teens and early twenties try on different identities that they shed later in life. For example, some of the 1.5- and second-generation Mexican Americans in New York that sociologist Robert Smith (2014) studied identified themselves as "black Mexicans," an identity that they thought improved their chances of academic success. However, Smith found that black Mexicans largely shed any sense of black identity by their late twenties, when their overall social identity had largely solidified. Whatever the future held for the young white respondents we interviewed, their formative years were defined by an ethnic vibrancy to which they aspired to conform.

Of course, white identity may be regionally inflected—it may not be as bland everywhere else. Ethnic distinctions among whites on the West Coast, both in terms of socioeconomic position and ethnic identity, may be much flatter than those in other parts of the country. Analyses of the Los Angeles region in the 1990s, for example, showed a tendency for different strands of white ethnicity to be woven indistinctively together into a larger white or "Anglo" identity and socioeconomic trajectory (Waldinger and Lichter 1996).[1] Western states' legacy of colonization and the historical racial milieu that pitted white settlers against Native Americans as well as Spanish, Mexican, and, later, Chinese and Japanese immigrants created a system of relations that distinguished whites, broadly speaking, from everyone else (Almaguer 1994). Moreover, differences between East and West Coast labor market opportunities for early arriving immigrant groups, like Italians, yielded a weaker sense of ethnic attachment and looser ethnic institutions in the West (DiLeonardo 1984). These dynamics may account for more visible expressions of white ethnic identity on the East Coast compared to the West Coast. Still, it is important to keep in mind that studies establishing the distinctiveness of different strands of white ethnic identity are mostly a generation old or more. The distinctiveness that showed up then may have washed away since, though it is difficult to know for certain given a notable lack of contemporary research in this area (Gans 2015).

BRINGING BACK BLACK

While young whites in Cupertino and Berryessa attempted to bring the blurry elements of their multiple ancestral ethnic strands into clearer focus, blacks of all ages in East Palo Alto expressed a desire to regain the black cultural prominence that once defined their city. Much as Asian newcomers were a point of reference for whites in Cupertino and Berryessa, Latinos were the relevant comparison group for blacks in East Palo Alto. Blacks can hardly be said to experience a symbolic ethnic identity in the same way that whites can (see Lacy 2007 for argument to the contrary). While whites can don and doff ethnic identities with relative freedom, blacks' skin color and its position in a racialized system of white dominance make it virtually impossible to ever opt out of blackness (Bonilla-Silva 1997).[2] But they nonetheless shared in common with their young white, middle- and upper-middle-class counterparts a desire for a more vibrant ethnic identity. However, this was not a desire for a greater sense of individual ethnic black identity; rather, they called for stronger collective identity. These respondents made two interrelated comparisons. The first was between the prominence of black culture in East Palo Alto today as compared to an earlier time, when the city's civic identity was built on blackness, and even self-conscious Afrocentrism (Hoover 1992). The second comparison was between the relative prominence of black culture versus Latino culture in the city today. Both comparisons, often articulated together, led to the conclusion that blacks needed to do more to recognize their heritage. Respondents' articulation of this desire centered on their perceptions of collective observances—like the Collard Green Festival and

Juneteenth, in comparison to Latino-themed events like Cinco de Mayo—rather than individual expressions of ethnic identity. According to black respondents in East Palo Alto, the prominence of the Latino-themed events brought the diminished state of African American events into vivid, and even disappointing, relief. Kareem Johnson, a black, eighteen-year-old college student, said that it was a daunting but necessary task for African Americans to maintain a strong sense of identity amid the cultural shifts. Like other young respondents in East Palo Alto and beyond, Kareem explained he enjoyed and was even accustomed to sampling the symbols and practices that came from other groups. For example, he was an avid member of a local Japanese anime and film club, and one of its only African American members. But he nonetheless emphasized the need to stay culturally connected to a sense of black culture precisely because of the brightness of other cultures:

> It's just one thing is because it's an overpopulation of one race, that your community can start to turn into that, can start to get that theme. Like if it's a lot of Mexicans, it's going to become that type of neighborhood. I'm not worried about it, I'm just saying that I'm a real culture junkie. So you can start to lose your own culture within someone else's culture. So I don't really have a problem with it, you just have to stay centered within your culture and you shouldn't have a problem. It's not like I hate or despise anybody, but you just have to stay clinging to your culture.

As Kareem's comments imply, the overshadowing of black cultural displays by Latino ones contributed to a perceived inversion of the foreigner/native dynamic, in which blacks felt themselves to be cultural foreigners in a city that was once defined by its black residents and accompanying black cultural displays. Edgar Culliver, a black, forty-four-year-old social worker in East Palo Alto, made a similar observation, folding in the declining importance of black-themed events with the violence that had racked the community, declining respect for elders, and a preference among youth for general diversity over particularistic black pride:

> When I grew up, here, it was predominantly a black neighborhood; at least 75 percent black. Not only that, we had a sense of family . . . . And back then, when I did go to the Juneteenth festival, you'd see a host of black families. The tradition of cooking those sweet potato pies, the yams, the black-eyed

peas, the collard greens, the corn bread, fried chicken, fried fish. You had neck bone. You probably even have some pig feet over there. You would see all that and knew you belonged here. That sense of . . . where by now, I think we lost that through pretty much violence, greed of money. Not knowing we had this sense of family and religion with God. We've lost that through greed and trying to get material things. I push for education and believe in it, as well, but I don't believe in it to where education should rob you of your spiritual foundation or take you way out of your ethnic culture background, where you no longer desire to be here with us but you want to go move in the suburbs. And so you forget about being a positive role model here and instead you vacate it. So the difference is, now, with my children growing up, the sense of respect for adults is not there. I've had to really instill that, because mine grew up in church, they knew it. Since the family is not really here, but mine know it because of our church, I bring it up. Diversity is pretty much the norm for my children. So much so that my children don't desire to be in a crowd of black people. They don't . . . none of them desire that. They like to be in a crowd of mixed. Not just black. It's funny. They'll be like, "Uh-uh: too many of them together." They just start acting, what they call the term, "ghetto," or what not.

Part of what sociologist Orlando Patterson (1998) calls the "ordeal of integration" includes a paradox related to integration: as relations between blacks and nonblacks ease, black solidarity breaks down. That paradox was all too real for older black respondents in East Palo Alto. While none of the East Palo Alto respondents we interviewed expressed a preference for the days when Jim Crow reigned, they recalled the vibrant black culture that came with a concentration of African Americans and lamented its loss. The importance of cultural events to a sense of black collective identity had added importance when considered in the larger Silicon Valley context. Because the African American population is so small in the region (less than 3 percent), opportunities to celebrate black heritage are few and far between, especially relative to the myriad chances to observe Latino- and Asian-origin ancestries. Thus, the declining significance of events like the Collard Green and Juneteenth festivals in East Palo Alto represented the near disappearance of African American events as they were dwarfed by Latino- and Asian-themed ones.

The sense that African American collective identity was too understated in East Palo Alto was compounded by the American cultural norm that people have a connection to an immigrant-origin identity (Schildkraut

2010). The slave trade long ago severed any hopes for contemporary African Americans to have a precise sense of a homeland or collective identity centered outside the United States. While collective experience of successive waves of European migrants built the idea of a "nation of immigrants" (Kennedy 1964), knowledge of their history before blacks came to U.S. shores rang hollow for African American respondents. That hollowness was especially apparent when black respondents considered their ethnic identity relative to those of the large immigrant populations around them. Rosa Johnson, an eighty-year-old retired city clerk, gave me the following in explaining her beliefs about the importance of retaining ethnic traditions:

> But I think everybody should be able to hang onto their traditions if they wanted to. That doesn't have anything to do with their citizenship. It means that you are together and you got certain things you'd like to honor. Because I wish now, you know, I think the biggest thing that's missing in [African Americans'] path, we don't have the identity. And everybody gets all . . . Africa is big. You never know what part of it you're from or whatever. And then you get over here and they got a block that comes in. Then you wind up, after they sold you, you went to whoever. Then you took their name and then you get in a family name and something happen they gonna sell you again, so you sold over and over and over again. You don't have any way to . . . I'd kind of like to know where we came from. I really would; pin it down other than just this particular area. That's one thing that we don't have. So I don't know, maybe we can get it as science keeps making progress, I think we might be able to get down to the point where you can get close to where you know.

The advent of mass genetic testing that Rosa alludes to offers clues to a putative sense of ethnic ancestry (Duster 2005; Morning 2014; Horowitz 2016). Yet it is still a crude tool with which to reconstruct details of an ancestral past that predates U.S. history. That historical severing has long been recognized as elemental to the tragedy of slavery. The heavy presence of immigrants, with their vibrant cultural expressions and strong ties to a sending country (Smith 2005), highlights blacks' inability to readily identify with a non-U.S. homeland. This comparison with immigrants, combined with the comparison to the way things once were in East Palo Alto, added to respondents' deep desire for a celebratory sense of African American ethnic identity.

Immigrant Replenishment and the Ups and
Downs of Cultural Vibrancy

While whites and blacks reported that the growing prevalence of Latino and Asian ethnic cultures spurred a desire to reclaim a stronger sense of their own heritage, established Latinos and Asians found that the cultures connected to their ethnic ancestries were so abundant that they not only wanted to be more familiar with those cultures, they felt uncomfortably *required* to do so. For Latino and Asian respondents, the heavy influx of immigrants from the same ethnic origin represented the replenishment of an ethnic culture that had been lost as group composition shifted from foreign-born to native-born (Jiménez 2010a). The way that established Asian American and Latino respondents described the effects of abundant ethnic culture affirmed what other social scientists have shown among nonwhite, established individuals in other contexts: they enjoy ready access to the culture associated with their ethnic ancestry, but they also experience pressure to know about and readily display that culture in order to prove that they are "authentic" ethnic group members (Jiménez 2010a; Tuan 1998; Vasquez 2011).

By far the most important way of authenticating culture was language. In spite of the United States' immigrant history, most newcomer families stop speaking their home country language within a generation or two, even in regions with large immigrant populations (Rumbaut, Massey, and Bean 2006). However, the presence of large numbers of non-English speaking immigrants reinforces the tie between language and ancestry, and makes language a marker of authentic group identity. Latino- and Asian-descent individuals whose immigrant ancestors arrived generations ago were especially apt to feel as though they needed to speak the language of their immigrant ancestors to substantiate their claims to group membership. Take, for example, the case of Sandra Gallegos, a twenty-six-year-old dental assistant of African American and Mexican ancestry in East Palo Alto. In spite of having grown up around a large Mexican-origin population, Sandra felt distant from Mexican-descent individuals because she did not speak Spanish. This feeling of distance motivated her to make sure that her daughter, whose father was African American, learned Spanish. Sandra explained:

I think that's really my purpose of [my daughter] being in the Spanish immersion program. So she can learn Spanish and know the culture. Because I wish that I would have known Spanish. Not just because that it's a lot of people are looking for bilingual people; just because that's part of my culture. And I feel like, if I knew Spanish, I think I could relate to them more. I feel like I'm kind of, I guess distant or whatever because I don't know Spanish. And I think that's a big part of the Hispanic culture is knowing the language. I think if I knew Spanish, I think I would be more accepted from the Hispanic people, and they would know that I am Mexican . . . . I feel like I could relate to them more. Because I somewhat know the culture as far as like food and . . . . But I feel like just knowing the language, I think that would make a big difference . . . . I think I would feel more comfortable—more comfortable with me, and I think I would be more comfortable with them. 'Cause now, if they don't speak English, we have that barrier. And then, sometimes I feel that I don't speak Spanish, and I have the last name of [Gallegos]. It just . . . it's hard. 'Cause, it's like, I want to be a part of both cultures, not just feel like I'm very distant from my Hispanic side.

For Mexican-origin respondents, this expectation played out in daily life as they interacted with Mexican immigrants. Rebecca Salas, a fifty-four-year-old county court clerk from Berryessa, had both Mexican and Portuguese ancestries. Despite having grown up in San Jose's East Side, a long-standing Mexican *barrio* (Pitti 2003), she did not grow up speaking Spanish, and Spanish monolinguals often asked her to interpret in vain. As Rebecca reported:

I think because I look Mexican people assume not only am I Mexican, but that I came from Mexico, that my parents came from Mexico, and that I should be speaking Spanish. I get that all the time. People just start talking Spanish to me cause they just take for granted that I . . . I think just because of my looks they take for granted that that's . . . . And my age . . . . A lot of time people expect older Mexicans to speak Spanish whereas I don't think for my kids it's . . . people don't think twice, "Oh, you don't . . . Yeah, 'cause you were born here. So that's why you don't . . . " Whereas for me, because I'm older, they take for granted that I should have the language . . . . Because I work at the [courthouse] there's a lot of people who come in and they just come in and they'll start talking to me because they need information or something. They'll start speaking. I'll have to tell them, "Sorry. I don't." Or even a lot of my coworkers used to bring people and say, "Oh, [Rebecca], can you talk to these [Spanish speakers] . . . " And I'm like, "Sorry."

Interactions between established respondents and immigrant co-ethnics revealed intra-group fissures largely defined by language as well as by knowledge and deployment of other cultural elements. While social scientists have focused on these fissures among groups whose immigrant populations are nationally prominent, like Mexican Americans (Jiménez 2008; Jiménez 2010a; Ochoa 2004; Vasquez 2011) and Chinese Americans (Horton 1995; Tuan 1998), some immigrant replenishment is more regionalized, as with the ethnic Polish population in Chicago (see Erdmans 1998). Likewise, Portuguese immigrants have been coming to Silicon Valley for over one hundred years, producing a mix of Portuguese Americans of different generation-since-immigration statuses. As with other ethnic groups whose immigrant populations have seen a great deal of replenishment, established Portuguese Americans face strict criteria for positioning themselves as "authentic" people of Portuguese descent. Anna English, a seventy-year-old retired teacher in Cupertino, frequented the various Portuguese-themed festivals that take place throughout the region. While she found these events mostly enjoyable, she was less pleased when Portuguese immigrants greeted her display of Portuguese national costume with challenges to her nationality and her ability to speak the language:

> I've got the Portuguese dress and everything, and I go [to the Portuguese events] and they'll start talking to me. I'll say, "Oh, I don't speak it." [They say,] "What?!" And I remember having fights with them. They would tell me, "Well, you're not Portuguese!" I said, "I am! I have my ancestry. I've got it stacked with baptisms, weddings, and everything for four hundred years. I'm 100 percent Portuguese descent." [They say,] "But you're not Portuguese." And I said, "How could you say that?" [They say,] "Well for one thing you can't be deported if you commit a crime." Because I was born here. Right? If you're not naturalized then you could get deported for a crime. I said, "Well I'm not going to commit a crime so I'm not really worried about it. But that doesn't make me any less Portuguese." [They say,] "Well, you don't speak the language." "Yeah, I can agree with that. So? What else? I'm still . . . Nope." And we would have fights. And the Chinese feel the same way about the ones that have been here, like [our friend] who is second, third, fourth, I don't know what his generation is. And [another Chinese American friend] that I've talked to says he's lived here twenty years and even the Chinese coming over go, "You're Americanized. You're not . . . " So you've got the ones that just come off the boat, same with Portuguese as Chinese. And then you've got the ones that have been here twenty years. And they go back . . . like I

know a Portuguese guy who went back to the Azores and they said, "You're American now. You're not Portuguese." Even though he speaks Portuguese and everything.

As Anna pointed out, later-generation individuals from many groups experience similarly strong expectations about ethnic authenticity as a result of immigrant replenishment.

While all of these respondents experienced a set of expectations about language as a result of their assertion of a particular ethnic identity, the replenishment that Asian respondents experienced was more rooted in a shared appearance with contemporary Asian immigrants, regardless of ancestry. Japanese American and Chinese American respondents from Berryessa and Cupertino reported that it was not at all uncommon for Chinese immigrants to initiate conversation in Mandarin simply because the respondent appeared Asian, even if their specific Asian origin was not Chinese. Echoing the comments of other Asian American respondents from Cupertino and Berryessa, Sarah Schwarz, a fifty-three-year-old homemaker of Japanese descent in Cupertino (who was married to a German Jewish man), reported:

> I run into a lot of people that think I'm Chinese and will try to speak Chinese to me. But . . . . there aren't a lot of Japanese Americans here. Most of the Japanese are Japanese from Japan, they're Japanese nationals. So nobody is really looking to me to speak Japanese. I think most of them can't tell that I'm Japanese. They think I'm Chinese and try to speak Chinese to me. Well, whenever I go to the markets, if you go to the Asian markets here in Cupertino, they always try to speak. So that's on a more regular . . . like last month or something I was in one of those markets. And I was asking for extra rice or something like that and they responded in Chinese. I'm like, "No, no, no, English." Because those stores are so heavily populated by mostly Chinese. So I think they just assumed I was Chinese.

Similar to the established Americans of Chinese and Japanese ancestry interviewed by other scholars (Tuan 1998; Tsuda 2016), the generationally established Asian Americans we talked to felt lumped together with the immigrant-origin Asians who represent a majority of the Asian-origin population. For these respondents, the replenishing effect brought by newer co-ethnics challenged a sense of ethnic authenticity that had emerged over their generations in the United States. Other respondents, who navigated a context that was heavily defined by immigrants but who lacked a connection to their homeland, reported no such experiences at all. Instead, they described having the option to invoke an ethnic identity without it being challenged (Gans 1979; Waters 1990), even if this thinner identity left them feeling less than ethnically fulfilled.

CONCLUSION

The role of ethnic culture in individual and collective identity is an important part of immigrant assimilation. It is also a central part of the relational form of assimilation in which established individuals are engaged. If the relational assimilation is a back-and-forth adjustment and readjustment, the cultural adjustments for established individuals in Silicon Valley had a lot more to do with the salience of ethnic culture than the specific content.

The ethnically themed public celebrations that abound in these three locales, and in the Silicon Valley region more generally, offered respondents plenty of opportunities for exposure to culture unconnected to their own ethnic ancestries. A regular version of this exposure came from interpersonal contact with immigrant-origin neighbors, coworkers, schoolmates, and neighbors. The ubiquity of ethnic culture, far more than its content, shaped local norms that ethnic culture *ought* to play a role in individual and collective identity. White respondents from the youngest cohort said that being around so many peers for whom ethnic culture was an important part of life made the lack of cultural salience tied to their own ancestry all too apparent. Growing up in a time of heightened immigration, when multiculturalism and the value of diversity are institutionalized, made white youth in particular feel as though the weak and symbolic ways they invoked ethnic culture did not advantage them socially. Indeed, none of their ethnic strands seemed like good "ethnic options" (Waters 1990) because they all appeared so fuzzy relative to their peers' much more pronounced deployments of ethnic culture.

The vivacity of immigrant-origin ethnic culture had a similar effect on African Americans in East Palo Alto, except that they described a desire for black culture to be a more prominent part of their community's collective identity. The city's historical status as Silicon Valley's most important black community, combined with the rising prominence of Latino (and especially Mexican) ethnic culture, led East Palo Alto's black residents of all ages to long for a return to the time when blackness was more visible in the city's cultural scene.

For established individuals with ties to ethnic groups prominently represented in Silicon Valley's immigrant population—mostly Latino and Asian, but also Portuguese—the effects of a vibrant immigrant-origin ethnic culture were visible in both the prominence and content of the culture. The pressure to exhibit a cultural know-how—especially in the form of language—that was more likely to be found among the immigrant and second generations imposed expectations about the role that ethnic culture should play in these respondents' lives. Being multiple generations removed from an immigrant origin, these respondents felt unable to fully participate in displays of ethnic culture that newcomers defined.

Would respondents in the three study locales have felt differently without the presence of a large newcomer population? Perhaps. Historian Marcus Lee Hansen (1952), observing shifts in ethnic identity among the children and grandchildren of European immigrants, noted that, while the second generation tried to appear less ethnic in order to distance themselves from their parents' "old-world" ways, the third generation looked upon these same old-world ways with a sense of nostalgia, and even tried to rekindle their essence in their own lives. In the 1970s and beyond, efforts to revive a stronger ethnic identity among the descendants of European immigrants were aided by a wave of multiculturalism that followed on the heels of the civil rights movement. They often celebrated an immigrant heritage in an attempt to claim their place in an emerging version of American identity that rejoiced in the country's diverse ethnic components (Jacobson 2006). The desire of later-generation descendants of early immigrants to maintain a strong sense of ethnic identity was driven partly by this new multicultural thinking (Glazer 1997). But later research ultimately showed that any such efforts by the third generation added up to a merely symbolic form of ethnic identity (Alba 1990; Waters 1990). The interviews with established blacks, whites, Latinos, and Asians in Silicon Valley offer hints that their desire to be more strongly connected to an ethnic identity sprang out of their multicultural way of thinking. But they felt their ethnic identities fell short compared to the vibrancy of the newcomers surrounding them. That was clearly the case for some whites, who could at best muster only a symbolic form of ethnic identity. But even nonwhites, who might be expected to have maintained a stronger connection to an ethnic identity, struggled with the thinness of their ethnic identities compared to the more robust ethnic identity shown by the newcomers around them. Given that respondents of all ethnicity, race, and class categories expressed similar desires to be "more ethnic," and articulated that desire by pointing to newcomers, it would appear that their desire for a strong ethnic identity stemmed from the combination of the clear salience of ethnic identity among newcomers and their own multicultural view of the world.

At the same time, these findings could also be describing the other side of the relational assimilation coin, in that they parallel the processes the research literature portrays taking place among newcomers. For all the differences in the salience of ethnic identity for newcomers and established individuals, the way established individuals experienced and made sense of ethnic culture comported in many ways with accounts of how more recent immigrants did so in other regions with large immigrant populations. Research on the second generations in New York (Kasinitz et al. 2008; Warikoo 2004) and Los Angeles (Lee and Zhou 2015) showed that the second generation adjusts to local contexts where, often, no one ethnic group predominates. As a result, the second generation has a kaleidoscopic view of the cultural norm, much like the one that I found among established individuals in Silicon Valley. Alba and Nee (2003) argued that, over the long term, the mainstream is a composite of ethnic cultural elements that have lost their association with an ethnic origin. That vision of a mainstream—one that includes cultural elements contributed by post-1965 immigrants—may very well emerge in the future. However, the findings I present here, along with those on the second generation in other locales, suggest that in the short term, the heavy immigrant presence makes ethnic vitality itself into a norm. In twenty-first century immigrant destinations, fitting in may entail displays of ethnic cultural vibrancy more than blandness.

3 Spotlight on White, Fade to Black

Respondents' familiarity with the immigrant experience and their exposure to ethnic culture makes it easy to assume that their experience of relational assimilation was relatively smooth.[1] But it was not. Sociologist Herbert Gans's (1992a) portrayal of assimilation as "bumpy" is an apt descriptor of relational assimilation for established individuals. Traditionally, scholarship has held that the bumps in immigrant assimilation are, in part, a matter of immigrants adjusting to a new racial landscape (Waters 1999). But mass immigrant settlement in places like Silicon Valley shifts the racial terrain underfoot even as immigrants attempt to adjust to it. The result is that established individuals' experience of relational assimilation often entails a bumpy adjustment to new forms of racial identity that emerge as the immigrants who live among them strategize how to make their way in American society. Immigrants, regardless of national origin or class status, bring an amped-up motivation that they apply to conventional avenues of advancement in the United States: work and school. Immigrants also attempt to create a sense of cultural comfort by establishing linguistic, culinary, religious, and artistic contexts that resemble, as best as possible, those that exist in their homeland.

Newcomers' economic striving and cultural adaptation—and the success that results—can have implications for the racial identity of the established population. This chapter examines those implications for respondents who identified with America's two most prominent racial categories—black and white—in aspects of their lives where those implications appear most prominent: education (for whites) and civic belonging (for blacks). According to both black and white respondents, immigrants were outgunning everyone when it came to educational and economic achievement. But the effects registered differently depending on locale. In Cupertino, and to a lesser degree in Berryessa, whiteness was a highly visible—indeed a "marked"— racial identity as far as educational achievement was concerned. In these two locales, Asianness represented the pinnacle of intelligence and academic achievement, perhaps no surprise given the prevalence of beliefs about Asian racial identity (Fiske et al. 2002; Kim 1999). But in Cupertino this racial inflection of educational achievement marked whiteness as representing academic mediocrity and laziness. Though whites were doing well by most standards, Asian immigration introduced a new, racially encoded set of standards that placed whites in a subordinate position where academic achievement was concerned. Berryessa respondents reported a similar dynamic, but also reported that Latinos and blacks were buffering whiteness's fall to the bottom of the achievement hierarchy. Still, high-achieving whites in Berryessa described whiteness as a deficit in a place where the honors track was dominated by immigrant-origin Asians. Like whites in Cupertino and Berryessa, blacks in East Palo Alto found themselves displaced down a status ladder by newcomers. But in East Palo Alto this displacement rendered blackness *less* visible, rather than more visible as happened with whiteness in Cupertino and (to some degree) Berryessa. For black respondents, the large presence of Latino immigrants in East Palo Alto, combined with the declining black population, was eclipsing blackness in both symbolic and material ways, from public recognition of black identity to jobs and services for blacks.

In some respects, these shifts in the meaning of racial identity reflected respondents' local experience of relational assimilation. But at the same time, white and black respondents' reactions to being out-achieved by newcomers also reflected deeply embedded, historically rooted notions of privilege and disadvantage. Whites often described the immigrant work ethnic exhibited by Asians as strange, never suggesting that Asian immigrants represented a model that they themselves should emulate. Black respondents, in contrast, held up Latinos and other immigrant groups as examples of a successful collectivist approach to advancement that they believed blacks would do well to adopt. In short, established individuals' reactions to immigrant success reflected existing systems of privilege. White respondents did not display any sense of responsibility for their lower achievement relative to Asians: they maintained an internalized position of privilege. Black respondents, on the other hand, internalized responsibility for blacks' perceived lack of advancement relative to Latinos, replicating their position of disadvantage.

Rather than offering a full accounting of how race operates in every aspect of life, this chapter lays out how the meaning and status of racial categories are challenged, when they are challenged, by newcomers. By showing these challenges, the findings illustrate how a relational view of assimilation reveals a fuller picture of the dynamics of immigration and racial identity. Respondents' accounts and interpretations of their experiences with race show that, rather than simply fitting into established racial categories as they assimilate, immigrants can serve as a foil against which the meaning and status of some racial categories are recast, while those of others become more entrenched.

AN UNWELCOME SPOTLIGHT ON WHITENESS IN CUPERTINO

In the United States, whites have historically been the dominant norm against which all other groups are evaluated. For much of that history, white racial identity has been invisible, a blank wall against which nonwhites stand out, until and unless there was a threat against it. Whites have been able to summarily put down such threats by crafting policies that grant access to valuable resources—citizenship, homeownership, voting, jobs, unions, etc.—to whites only (Fox 2012; Haney-López 1996; Katznelson 2005; Omi and Winant 2014).

There is no doubt that white privilege still reigns. But there may be cracks in that privilege. For example, while survey research customarily gauges how minorities fare by comparing the socioeconomic outcomes of minorities to native-born whites, data on socioeconomic attainment shows that this is a questionable standard. The highest earning and most educated racial group is not whites. That spot belongs to Asians. According to data compiled from the American Community Survey by the Pew Research Center, the median household income for Asians in 2010 was 22 percent higher than for whites (sixty-six thousand dollars versus fifty-four thousand dollars). Differences in educational attainment were even greater: 49 percent of the adult Asian population had a college degree compared to 31 percent of whites (Pew Research Center 2013).[2] To be sure, there is variation in each of these larger racial categories. Southeast Asians tend to be poorer, and many, like the Hmong, are faring far worse than other Asian subgroups (Pew Research Center 2013; Keister, Agius Vallejo, and Aronson 2016). But the difference between whites and Asians should still be regarded as significant.

That significance registered powerfully among respondents in Cupertino, who did not describe whiteness as an unquestioned norm against which minorities were evaluated. Instead, their achievement norms were defined by the Asian-origin population, a shift that flipped the meaning and status of whiteness on its head. By most standards, Cupertino breeds success. This is an upper-middle-class area with highly engaged parents and some of the best schools in California.[3] In fact, the quality of the public schools is Cupertino's primary attraction for high-skilled immigrants who are what Jennifer Lee and Min Zhou (2015) call "hyper-selected"—their level of formal education far outpaces both the average in their home country and the average in the United States. And so success in Cupertino does not follow the standard pattern. According to interviewees, the influx of high-skilled Asian immigrants significantly lifted achievement standards, an observation shared by virtually all of the people we interviewed. Summarizing this view, a teacher at one of the area high schools, who was also an alumnus, noted:

Football was very strong here until about the early nineties.

Q: What changed?

R: Oh, the demographics changed. The size of the kids changed. The interests of kids changed. This has always been known as an academic school since it was founded, but the academics have gotten stronger and stronger and stronger.

The impact of high-skilled Asian immigration dominated almost every respondent's characterization of the city, especially their descriptions of the area's schools. For example, Sarah Schwarz, a fifty-three-year-old homemaker of white and Japanese ancestry, offered:

> I would say it's a great community; it's a great place to raise kids. I think anybody coming in, at least potentially looking at it as a place to live, would need to know that it's highly Asian—lots of Chinese families, East Indian families, and there is a mix. But I think, because of the heavy influence of the Asian population, it's a very competitive academic atmosphere for kids. . . . . It's just a phenomenal school system. But it's very competitive. So if that's a worry for you, if you don't think your children can handle a very multicultural, multiracial, multiethnic community, maybe it's not the place for you. If you're looking for some place with [an] excellent school system that's going to provide your kids with a really good background and start for college, it's an excellent place to be.

Young people, parents, teachers, and school officials alike portrayed Cupertino's schools as extremely competitive, even to an unhealthy degree. They nonetheless noted that the norms of academic excellence and the accompanying pressure prevailed. These informal observations made by respondents in Cupertino square with what more systematic observations suggest. Take the 2012 elementary school district data from the California Department of Education, which assesses schools according to their Academic Performance Index (API) score, a measure of performance on state-issued student assessments. On a scale that runs from 200 to 1,000, the district-wide score for all students was 888. The API score for Asian students was well above that average, at 953; and at roughly the district average—887—for non-Hispanic white students. The California average for all elementary schools was well below either of these scores, at 753. As these scores make clear, students in Cupertino, Asian and white alike, are doing much better than their peers in the rest of the state.

These disparities reflected the class origins of Cupertino families and the associated strategies that parents there employed to help their kids get ahead. Norms that prevailed in Cupertino might characterize any upper-middle-class community, where parents work every angle and invest an enormous amount of time, money, and energy in their children's success (Lareau 2003; Weis, Cipollone, and Jenkins 2014). In Cupertino, however, these norms carried a heavy racial connotation. The explanation of Asian academic success outlined by Lee and Zhou (2015) is on full display in Cupertino: hyper-selected immigrants from South and East Asia use the resources that come with their upper-class status to support institutions (tutoring centers, afterschool programs, college preparation programs, cram schools, etc.) and a guiding frame of success that pushes children to achieve. In the U.S. context, the class origins of this success appear ethnic, supporting strong stereotypes about Asians that associate the group with academic competence, intelligence, and hard work (Fiske et al. 2002; Lee and Zhou 2015). But in Cupertino these stereotypes of Asians also entailed a rather atypical stereotyping of whites. Where whiteness is often associated with intelligence and academic success in mixed settings (Ferguson, Ludwig, and Rich 2001; Fryer Jr. and Torelli 2010; Tyson, Darity, and Castellino 2005), in Cupertino it stood for the very opposite: low achievement, laziness, and academic mediocrity. Marcus Peterson, a white, twenty-two-year-old, recent college graduate, characterized whiteness in just that way:

> I would almost say [Asian immigration] kind of brought about the stereotype, at least [in high school]. The Asian kids and the Indian kids were really smart and they were really good at math and they were always going to do really well in the AP [Advanced Placement] classes, whereas the white kids were less academically oriented. And they did okay, but they didn't put in as much effort. Some of that in some cases was true but it almost did become a stereotype kind of thing.

Respondents were aware that Cupertino was atypical in its racial definition of academic success. This knowledge only made the racial encoding of achievement in Cupertino more apparent. Mark Estes, a white fifty-six-year-old chemist, moved to Cupertino from a small, mostly Latino city in California's Central Valley in the 1990s. His description of the difference in his daughter's experience between the two locales highlighted the very particular meaning of whiteness in Cupertino:

> I mean, the [Central Valley], where we came from, was probably about 60 percent Hispanic. So you had that culture which was a lot different than our culture in a lot of ways, and it's different than the Asian culture here.... First of all, the Hispanic community has just the reverse opinion [from Asians in

their approach to school] (chuckling). They put more emphasis on family, so there is more time to play, there is more time to just grow and kick around like kids. And education is, "Yeah, well, that's nice but you don't need it." Where the Asian community is just totally the opposite. I mean that's the whole driving thing. . . . . And it was hard for our daughter because she went from the Hispanic community, where the white kids were the smart ones, because we do think highly of education. But so she was considered an overachiever—got As and Bs in everything down there. When we moved here, then she became the dumb kid, and it was just a really inverse situation for her.

This inflection of whiteness was part and parcel of daily life in Cupertino, reflected in colloquialisms students used to describe academic success and failure. According to the young respondents and the teachers we interviewed, an "Asian fail" meant receiving a B, or even a B+ on a school assignment, while a "white fail" meant receiving an F grade. Students casually used such racial categories as shorthand for academic commitment. For instance, one teacher recounted hearing the following exchange between two students: "Somebody will ask them, 'Well, are you taking AP?' [and the student responds] 'Oh no, I'm white.'" Though the student's comment was likely sarcastic, the clear implication was that a racial label alone allows others to infer a student's approach to school.

The link between high academic achievement and Asianness, and, conversely, low achievement and whiteness, was even clearer when respondents explained the nuances of the stereotypes and their accompanying terminology. Students racially recoded individuals who were phenotypically white if they displayed a commitment to academic pursuits that was more typically associated with Asianness. Likewise, Asians who broke from stereotypes by taking a more "easygoing" approach to life—for example by participating in nonacademic activities outside school, going to parties, drinking alcohol, or using recreational drugs—were often recoded as "white." Angelica Mills, a seventeen-year-old high school student who was white with some Asian ancestry (her paternal grandmother was Japanese), explained:

If you're really studious and you're white, you're called "Asian at heart" . . . . Just like there's the white people who act Asian, there's the Asians who act white. They're the Asians who party. It's definitely a smaller percentage. I'd say there's only 20 percent of the school who actively goes to party or drinking and smoking and stuff. There's people who socialize and they do community service on the weekends and have sleepovers with friends. There's not as big of a population, but you can find it.

Flexibility in the use of these terms also reflected the relevance of nativity. Respondents pointed out that the Asian students who were most likely to "act white" were those whose families had been in the United States for several generations—in other words, people who were part of the established population. Respondents asserted that established individuals of Asian ancestry were "whitewashed," a term that described not just the low importance of ethnic culture in their lives, but also their more casual approach to academic pursuits. The perceived distinction between established Asian Americans and immigrant-origin Asians was apparent in the comments of the established Asian American respondents. Melanie Chang was a seventeen-year-old high school student of Chinese and Japanese descent who was heavily involved in extracurricular activities and who maintained a strong GPA. While she had several friends who were growing up in immigrant households, she reported sharing more in common with white households precisely because of similarities in the way these households were run, including the approach to academic pursuits:

> I feel like white households are more open. I guess I base it off my brother's friends because they are so open to have my brother over, have any other friends over, they can just walk into the house. That's what I think . . . . I think it's the families that their kids are the first generation . . . definitely more secluded. They have to plan stuff, plan to have friends over. But then, people that have been around here more, for longer, they're more open to have people walk into their house, like it's fine, it's nothing . . . . I keep going back to the academic thing. I don't think [white families] focus as much on academics. I think they focus more on how their kids are and that they want them to have fun. I think they're more open to having friends over because of the kids and the wellbeing of the kids . . . . We want to have fun. But when it does come down to academics, we can do our work but still have fun at the same time. And sometimes the academics get put on the back burner and the fun takes control first. My household's definitely not focused on studying at all.

Indeed, in the Cupertino vernacular, "whiteness" was associated with a more casual approach to school and work that could be embodied by anyone, not just those with white skin.

And yet the first impressions of students, parents, and even teachers were nonetheless shaped by racial phenotype—the racial encoding of achievement was inescapable. The teachers in Cupertino we interviewed, none of whom had Asian ancestry, subscribed to it, despite their best efforts to the contrary. According to one teacher,

> Oh, it's just a reversal of roles! I mean whites usually kind of get to sit at the top of the heap for whatever reason, whether they mean to or desire to or meant to. And it's just kind of interesting to see. You look at someone who is white and you kind of assume that they're probably not the best student, and then . . . okay, a group of students have just walked in and, as the teacher, I try not to stereotype of course, but after a while, I guess I just assume . . . even I am beginning to assume right now that when kids walk into the classroom, the white kids probably aren't going to be my very, very best students. They may do great work, but they won't turn it all in or something. If I were to go back and look at the grades I've given . . . I'm sure that the GPA for the white kids I've had would be lower than the GPA for the Asian kids I've had. I'm sure of it.

Another high school teacher related that colleagues openly rejoiced with each other (but not in the presence of students) if there was a white student in an AP class because it was such a rare occurrence. Teachers' view of students was not lost on the students themselves. Kara Chang, a seventeen-year-old high school student of Chinese and Japanese ancestry, noted:

> I feel like [teachers] had a little bit more leeway for the non-Asian kids because . . . maybe because they need to pass the class or something, I don't know. But what I feel is the general consensus is that we just maybe assume—which is negative and that's bad—but like that [white students] may not be as smart as the Asian kids.

Kara's view of the way teachers treated Asian American students resonates in other contexts. Sociologists Amy Hsin and Yu Xie (2014) used survey data to show that teachers rate the effort and academic performance of Asian students well above white students. These subjective perceptions may have psychological implications. In their research in the Los Angeles area, sociologists Jennifer Lee and Minh Zhou (2015) showed that teachers assume that Asian American students are intelligent, precipitating "stereotype promise," wherein even low-achieving Asian Americans, over time, live up to stereotypes that Asians will be successful. Both white and Asian American respondents in Cupertino saw a similar dynamic at play in their schools.

Given that academic achievement was highly valued among all parties in Cupertino, this particular racial encoding of academic achievement not only frustrated established respondents, it also shaped their interactions and perhaps even their academic performance. The young people we interviewed were explicit about the ways in which it shaped their interactions with peers, especially when conversations turned to exam results. Angelica Mills, a top student quoted earlier, recounted an instance in which she believed her skin color (she had Asian ancestry, but appeared white by her own reckoning) led other students to perceive her differently:

> I've gotten a lot of feeling like I'm not taken seriously because I'm a preppy white girl. Or, I don't know what they would call me, but I know that after a chemistry test last year, we were all comparing answers that we got on the test afterwards and they were like, "Oh, what did you get for that one? What did you get for that one?" to each other. I said, "Oh. I know how to do that one." And they were like, "Oh, okay," (dismissive tone) and then asked their other friend anyway. It was two Indian guys, and I was like, "Do you not think that I know the answer?" And he's like, "Well, I just wanted to see what he had to say." And I was like, "Is it because I'm white that you don't think that I know?" And he's like, "Well, I don't know if you know or not." [I said,] "Could I just give it a shot?" I guess I constantly feel like I have to prove people wrong. I don't necessarily care if other people think that I'm really smart, but it's kind of nice when they see my tests when I get them back.

No one explicitly reported that notions of whites as a less-than category in the realm of achievement had a negative effect on their school performance. But research by experimental psychologists suggests that stereotypes about Asians as smart and academically successful, even when subtly invoked, can dampen the cognitive performance of whites and lead them to divest from a school-oriented identity (Aronson et al. 1999; Handron 2014). No definitive corroborating evidence emerged from the interviews, but the strategies respondents described for dealing with the particular racial encoding of achievement in Cupertino were consistent with these findings. When reflecting on their children's experiences in school, some parents recalled their children dialing back their efforts because they felt that they simply could not compete. Melanie Peterson, a white, fifty-one-year-old nutritionist in Cupertino, spoke sympathetically about her son's negative response to the pressure to excel that came from living among a large Asian newcomer population:

> The Asian population tends to value education very highly and I think that's fabulous. But they often push their kids to perform at levels that are maybe unreasonable. They go to Chinese school on Saturdays and they study extra math and they study extra this and study extra that. And I think for my kids sometimes it was hard to feel like they could ever keep up, or that they wanted to keep up with that level of academic pressure. There was a lot of pressure that came along with that . . . . I think that that was one of the hardest things for them because they never felt quite like they were good enough. And for one of [my children], because he couldn't be good enough, he just decided to check out and not do [schoolwork] at all.

The degree to which the settlement of high-skilled Asian immigrants shifted not just the standards of achievement, but also its racial encoding, led at least three white respondents in Cupertino to either move residences, transfer their children to other high schools in the district, or send their children to private schools. These exit strategies were a response to a context where whiteness no longer represented the achievement norm. Cupertino has a unique set of characteristics that make this particular encoding of racial achievement possible: the immigrant population is large, highly skilled, and almost entirely from Asian countries, and the racial makeup of the city is defined exclusively by Asians and whites. Comparing Cupertino to Berryessa provides insight into how variations in these factors might lead to different outcomes in other places.

MIDDLING IN BERRYESSA

Wandering the main high school in Berryessa might make one wonder if whiteness is even a relevant category. In the sea of slightly awkward teens strolling the halls on the way to their first period class there are few white faces. Asian and Latino students socialize with members of their respective groups, and there is an occasional black student. No one seems to take special note of the ethnically mixed cliques sprinkled in. Like the schools in Cupertino, Berryessa schools, including the main high school, have a large Asian population. At this main high school in 2010, 60 percent of students were Asian, 20 percent were Latino, 12 percent were white and 4 percent were African American. Reflecting the demographics of the Berryessa neighborhood, the overwhelming majority of Asian students were of Vietnamese origin and unlikely to share the class origins of the predominantly Chinese and Indian students in Cupertino. Still, as Lee and Zhou (2015) demonstrate, upper-class Vietnamese immigrants are highly selected when it comes to education and income, and they support a set of resources and institutions, as well as role models, that guide the academic success of the Vietnamese second generation. The stereotypes linking Asianness to intelligence and hard work applied in Berryessa, where respondents described Asianness and intelligence as intimately linked. As in Cupertino, whiteness in Berryessa was constructed as a less-than category when it came to achievement. However, the position of academic laggard did not fall as squarely on the whites in Berryessa. As respondents explained, lower-achieving Latinos and blacks occupied that status, leaving whites in a middle and almost invisible position. Still, in a heavily tracked school, where "smart" students wind up in AP classes, the kind of racial ranking of academic success found in Cupertino also showed up among the high achievers in Berryessa.

The description of Asian achievement voiced by Berryessa respondents was nearly interchangeable with what we heard in Cupertino. Asians, according to the people we interviewed in Berryessa, were supremely focused on school and came from households where academic achievement was so important that children who fell short faced dire consequences. It may be no surprise, then, that immigrants were drawn to Berryessa, where schools have long been considered to be good, especially relative to other schools on San Jose's East Side. As Berryessa's established respondents saw it, the presence of Asian immigrants burnished the reputation of area schools. When asked what her life would be like if there were not immigrants in the country, Margarita Bartis, a white, forty-four-year-old dental hygienist, zeroed in on the effect of Asian immigrants on Berryessa schools:

[S]o the scores [at the main high school] are really high because there are so many Asians there and they score high. So that school and [and another] are the two, number one schools in the district. So for me, bringing it down a notch to my community, if the school was not so much Asian as it was, I think academically it might not be as good of a school. . . . . If it was all Hispanic and white like it was before, who knows? It might have been more troublemakers at the school or not as educationally advanced as it is because there's more Vietnamese people who tend to be more studious and good students and such.

Even though Vietnamese, who tend to have a lower class standing than their East and South Asian counterparts in Cupertino, dominate Berryessa's Asian newcomers, Berryessa respondents in all cohorts asserted that Asian children were driven by an Asian style of parenting that focused heavily on school success, which they often compared to their own, laxer approach. As a result of having multiple close ties to Asians, young respondents in particular spoke with a degree of familiarity. Kyle Zell, a sixteen-year-old white (with Jewish ancestry) high school student in Berryessa, was an excellent student who was well on his way to a good college. His father was a successful computer engineer at one of Silicon Valley's tech giants, and his mother was a successful professional. His closest friends were second-generation Asian Americans. He referred to these friends in explaining the differences between white and Asian approaches to education:

My dad, he's all about not pushing me; let me accomplish my own goals. There's no need to work your ass off. He wants me to have fun this summer instead of going to some SAT class and just wasting my time, well, not wasting my time but just working my butt off to get a better SAT score. He thinks it's more fun to cherish my adolescent years and have fun rather than attend school and work hard for my future. And then have fun in the future. And that's also a difference between whites and Asians: Asians are definitely more pushy and they want their kids to accomplish as much as they can.

Kyle's comments might reflect the security that comes with being from an upper middle-class white family whose position is relatively stable. Asian immigrant families, on the other hand, have to fight to find a foothold for themselves and future generations (Lee and Zhou 2015). Be that as it may, there was near consensus among respondents in Berryessa and Cupertino that "Asian" was synonymous with intelligence and hard work, and that the large presence of Asian immigrants had enhanced the reputation of public schools.

But these conclusions about Asianness and achievement did not have nearly the same implications for what it meant to be white in Berryessa. While Cupertino respondents explained in no uncertain terms how whiteness stood in stark contrast to Asianness, Berryessa interviewees did not see the effect of Asianness as diminishing the meaning and status of whiteness, nor did they directly contrast the two. To be sure, they saw whiteness as less automatically associated with academic aptitude than Asianness was. While Asianness put whites in an unfamiliar, second-place position in achievement, second place was not last place, as was the case in Cupertino, where the only two categories in play were white and Asian. The people we interviewed in Berryessa laid out an achievement hierarchy that consisted of whites sandwiched between high-achieving Asians and lower-achieving Latinos and blacks. Isabella Adamsen, an eighteen-year-old recent high school graduate and waitress of Mexican and white descent, attended two different high schools in Berryessa. She offered this assessment of the hierarchy:

> Black people are always the dumb ones. Mexicans are the slackers. White people were up there, sometimes more ahead than Asian people, but usually not. There was always, yeah, Asian people were the smart ones.
>
> Q: What is your perception of things?
>
> A: In this community, I think maybe it's true just because their parents' focus—like I said, they don't keep up their houses. They're very more like, "Oh, get good grades. Go to college." That's their mindset. Mexican people—just the ones I've been around, like: "Have fun but try to stay in school." White people: "Yeah. Get good grades, but still have fun at the same time." But Asian people, it's always been like that's their goal. At my graduation, the valedictorians, all but one were Asian.

That rendering of the academic racial order shows up in in more quantitative forms too. The overall 2012 API score for Berryessa's high school district was 747; it was 859 for Asian students, 789 for white students, 673 for black students, and 652 for Latinos. Parents in Berryessa shared this reading of the academic racial order too. Larry Smith, a white fifty-eight-

year-old corporate executive, echoed Isabella's comments and those of
other parents when he noted:

> The Mexican and Asian and the Caucasian and white environment are the
> ones that stand out. The Asians: very pro-education, very good. The
> Mexicans: I think, their education is not as valuable. And then, as far as us,
> the white, probably a little bit of both. . . . I think actually the Asians value
> the education in total more than even the white population does . . . . I think
> they're probably a smarter group and I put Caucasians next, then the
> Mexican population below that—although you're not supposed to do that.
> (laughs)

This three-level achievement hierarchy meant that, in general, it was
Latino and black students who had to fight against negative stereotypes, not,
as in Cupertino, white students. Take, for example, Michael Romero, a fifteen-year-old high school student of Mexican descent in Berryessa. As a high
achiever enrolled in AP classes, Michael bucked stereotypes about Mexicans
that prevailed at the school. Exhibiting behavior at odds with these stereotypes made Michael the target of occasional ribbings from his peers.

> [Some people] told me, they're like, "Oh, well, you're pretty smart then, for
> a Mexican." And I'm like, "Okay. Thank you." I wasn't sure how to take it . . . .
> I would say, honestly, for me, I was expecting [my Asian friend] to be smart
> because of the same stereotype. I've heard that because you're Mexican
> you're not the smartest person in the world. But I was never expecting any-
> one to say, "Oh, well you're pretty smart for a Mexican . . . ." I guess in a way
> it does push me, too. It pushes me to do better, or wanting to do better, just
> to break the stereotype that Mexicans aren't very smart, or they're not sup-
> posed to be smart. It gives me motivation to want to do better.

Although Michael knew that these comments were often meant in jest, he
also knew that they reflected the prevailing achievement hierarchy, and
this knowledge motivated him to resist living out the stereotypes that
defined that hierarchy.

While lower-performing Latinos and blacks buffered whites from falling to the bottom of a racially inflected achievement order in Berryessa,
high-achieving white respondents saw a penalty for whiteness in the
encoding of Asianness as high-achieving. Their depictions of their classroom experience were a scaled-down version of dynamics that were in

fuller bloom in Cupertino. A teacher, who was also second-generation Asian American, offered the following portrayal of the honors classes:

> There's all these clubs [that] are very academic and they're really focused on college. In my honors classes . . . . there'll be maybe three or four white kids and then maybe one Hispanic kid, but everybody else is Asian. So then I think [whites] feel a little out of place because it's the opposite of what I experienced. There's no one else that looks like them in the classroom versus before, it was the other way around. It was just me and everybody else is white. So I think that's daunting in some ways.

Indeed, teachers in Berryessa remarked on the scant number of whites in honors courses, a trend that was partly a function of the relatively small number of whites in the schools, but also of the way that high achievement in Berryessa is racially encoded. A long-time high school teacher in Berryessa, who offered several honors English classes, discussed this encoding in her class in general, and how it affected her son's experience in particular. I entered her classroom as she finished teaching one of her honors courses, which by my count included only one white, and one Latino student; the remaining dozen or so students were all Asian. The interview took place during a prep period and was punctuated by the arrival of a notably more Latino and white group of students who were there for the teacher's non-honors section. It was against this backdrop that the teacher offered the following assessment:

> This is, again, where I get in this part where I'm uncomfortable, where I feel like I'm making racial stereotypes, but if I look at the . . . it's pretty rare if I have a Latino student who shines in honors, and pretty rare, and they're very memorable. But for the most part, I would say that the Mexican kids who come into my class ends up not going on. They end up being in over their head. Part of it is they don't have support, for this, where the Asian students will have [parents who say], "We will do everything for you to get your A. We will go to any length." And [Mexicans] just don't have that kind of history in their families . . . . I will say, [my son's] own experience . . . . [he] said, "Papers get passed back and the teacher says, 'One person got a perfect score.'" On a regular basis it would be [my son], both in writing—[he's] pretty extraordinary—and math. [He] says, "Mom. No one ever asks if it's me. They'll turn around and go, 'Was it you? Was it you? I bet it was this one. I bet it was that one.'" [He] says, "No one ever says, 'Was it you,

[Michael]?' No one." And it took [him] . . . by the time [he] was a junior, when teachers started saying, "[Michael] actually got the high score," or whatever. But [he] said that Asian students didn't want [him] to be [in] their groups because [he] would say—my students would tell me the same thing—Asian parents teach their kids: "Don't . . . You're not going to study with white kids. They don't have that work ethic. They're not going to work hard. They're going to bring you down."

High-performing white students affirmed these observations, noting that their whiteness pegged them as academic stragglers, a stereotype that became apparent when they were one of the few white students in an honors course. Take, for instance, the experience of Ryan Jordan, a white twenty-three-year-old recent college graduate who, like many people his age, moved back home after graduating (Newman 2012). As we sat in the kitchen of his parents' sprawling, cluttered home, he explained how his white skin and sharp intellect were an anomalous combination at his high school:

I guess there's the stereotype of Asians being very good in math and science and since I was up there [in academics], we had a lot of Asians in our class, but I was not always the top of the class, but I had the best intuitive sense of the subject even though I didn't study as much, as hard. And I always sat in front just because I liked being up front. But we didn't talk about it much but it seemed to be sort of, yes; we understood—not understood but thought of it as an oddity that the white guy's at the front of the class when . . . the other people at the top of the class were all Asian . . . . During graduation noticing how we had . . . I think they were all officially called valedictorians, but we had many of them because we had many of my friends who were up there who got As all four years . . . . I don't remember any white students up there, like myself. I wouldn't go so far as to say I was the best or brightest white student in my class, but that seemed to be a reputation I had.

The numeric minority status of white honors students like Ryan and Isabella meant that they experienced their whiteness as a highly salient and visible part of their identity. Whereas Cupertino was defined entirely by whites and Asians, in Berryessa Latinos and blacks prevented whites from falling to the bottom of the achievement hierarchy. But the honors track in the school was, for select students, similar in its dynamics to Cupertino. Where there were almost no blacks and Latinos in these classes, whites did, in fact, occupy the bottom rung of the subhierarchy.

FADE TO BLACK IN EAST PALO ALTO

As whites did in Cupertino and Berryessa, blacks in East Palo Alto saw immigrants as the cause of a hit to the status of blackness. But in East Palo Alto, the settlement of immigrants reinscribed blackness's traditional historical status, rather than upending it, as happened with whiteness in Cupertino. As the one-time heart of the black community, East Palo Alto was seen regionally as a place where blackness was highly marked and salient. Within the city's confines, blackness was once a majority status, and black identity defined life in the city. According to respondents, the settlement of Latino immigrants contributed to the fading of the city's black identity. As with whiteness in Cupertino and, to some degree, Berryessa, immigrant settlement imbued new meaning to blackness in East Palo Alto. But rather than turning blackness on its head, according to respondents, immigrant settlement reinforced the subordinate status of blacks. In East Palo Alto this was most apparent not with respect to education, but with respect to civic identity.

If scholars of racial identity have generally treated whiteness as the unstated norm against which visible and subordinate minority groups are measured, blackness has stood out as the most visible of these groups. This visibility is associated with residential segregation (Massey and Denton 1993), everyday encounters with racism (Feagin 1994), lower levels of education and earnings (Feagin 2010; Massey 2007), and entanglement with the criminal justice system (Western 2006). And during the time of the interviews, even as the sharp knife of inequality cut deeply into the African American population, public attention had turned away from American blacks.[4] Possibly informed by a "race-blind" view of inequality, which holds that any individual's station in life has nothing to do with race (Bobo 2011; Bobo and Smith 1998; Bonilla-Silva 2006), the plight of poor blacks was sidelined in the national social policy scene during the period when these interviews were conducted (Massey 2007).

Black respondents in East Palo Alto described their city as a microcosm of these larger, national dynamics. For all of the city's history of violence and drugs, longtime black residents expressed pride in East Palo Alto's forays into Afrocentrism and the struggle for civil rights that were central to the city's history. Yet black respondents also emphasized the diminished visibility of black identity in East Palo Alto—a decline resulting, in part, from the presence of a large and poor Latino population that had become the material and symbolic focal point of the city.

Material Invisibility

In a city whose institutions once focused on its black population, respondents said the rise of Latino immigration had rendered blackness nearly invisible in terms of material resources. For most respondents in East Palo Alto, the issue of educational achievement that loomed so large in Cupertino and Berryessa did not have the same resonance. It is not that blackness had no meaning in relation to achievement; quite the contrary. During the time of the interviews, East Palo Alto students attended several different high schools, all of which were outside the city limits, in wealthier neighboring cities like Palo Alto, Menlo Park, Redwood City, Woodside, and San Carlos. There are few African Americans at these schools partly because the number of blacks in East Palo Alto has declined, but also because East Palo Alto high schoolers are scattered across five different schools as a result of a court-mandated desegregation order.[5] While wealthy white and Asian students at these schools work on replicating their parents' upper-class position, blacks struggle to get by. This state of affairs was an unfortunately all too familiar to East Palo Alto residents. What was new was what they described as a virtual disregard of the plight of poor African Americans. As respondents from East Palo Alto saw it, the large presence of poor and often unauthorized Latinos had shifted attention away from needy blacks, deepening their invisibility. As Rachel Abernathy, a black 37-year-old executive assistant who was born and raised in East Palo Alto, put it, "This is a city that was built or known perhaps as an African American community. And now it's more of a city, to me, skewed toward the Hispanic community." A skewing of resources seemed particularly apparent to older respondents who had been residents of the city throughout the major immigration-driven demographic shift of the last two decades. They recalled a time when governmental and nongovernmental services were oriented toward African Americans. Now, they said,

Latinos and the complications associated with immigration—legal status, language, et cetera—were dominating the agenda of service agencies. Some respondents, like Elaine Middlefield, a black sixty-year-old freight service warehouse worker, recalled firsthand experiences when racial identity excluded African Americans from accessing resources:

> I find that being an African American sometimes it's hard to go to the community and get, like if you need financial help or Medi-Cal or AFDC or food stamps. I just find that [Hispanics] more ready to help their friend's race than they are to help African American race.

Q: Tell me more about that.

A: Well, I tried—when I was pregnant with my youngest daughter, the place where I worked closed down. My husband was working as a security guard and we were having difficulties trying to keep the family fed with just one paycheck. So I had gone up to the community center on Bay Road. And I wasn't asking for cash, all I was asking for was Medi-Cal and food stamps . . . . They didn't approve it. But yet, and still, the Hispanic immigrants come in and they get pregnant, they have babies born here, but they know how to work the system where everything they need they get. They get WIC, they get Medi-Cal, they get food stamps, they get cash aid. But yet, and still, I go to work every day, pay into these programs and when I need the help, I don't even qualify for it. That pisses me off. And when you put Hispanics in the upper positions to help other people, they make sure their race gets every little thing that they qualify for and they'll tell you, "Oh no, you don't qualify" . . . . And I was talking with my sister-in-law and she said, "We are a minority within EPA right now." It's like 65 percent Hispanic and the rest is made up of Orientals, whites, Pacific Islanders, and blacks. So yeah, I've seen the community go from one race to another and that's just the way it is.

Respondents from East Palo Alto accepted that focusing on Latinos was logical given the city's large Latino population. This view did little to take the edge off their lamentations that blacks seemed to be invisible to service agencies, partly as a result of Latino staff who "help their own." Arincha Robinson, a thirty-two-year-old multiracial full-time student, offered comments that echoed Elaine's:

> I think the equal opportunity shifts where they may feel the need to help their own versus being equal, and keeping things right, morally right and fair, by helping the next person who is in line. So if you had Michelle Johnson—I'm just making a name—who is in line next for the housing

certificate, and you had a Hispanic, and you see Silvia Fernandez, do you really have something in you to do what's right and not put Michelle Johnson's application up under Silvia Fernandez. That's the type of thing that might cross my mind or concern me, because I've seen it happen. Or, if the county is saying we need to put some percentages in place here. We know the majority's Hispanic, but we're going to make sure that we have a percentage that we give out housing certificates to Hispanic as well as to black as well as to Pacific Islander, Caucasian, according to the ratings or statistics of who lives in the county, relatively to the percentage of those who live there.

Black respondents in East Palo Alto expressed this assessment regardless of whether they had accessed services or needed them currently, though the people in current need spoke about the circumstances in much graver terms (for similar findings in other contexts, see Gay 2006; McDermott 2011). Respondents' sense that blacks had been disappeared from policy priorities had historical parallels. Social policies, like veterans' benefits (Katznelson 2005) and the New Deal (Fox 2012) that ostensibly applied to all were far less available to blacks than they were to whites and even Latinos. While I cannot say with certainty whether respondents were experiencing a modern incarnation of the racial favoritism that characterized past social policies, it is clear that African Americans in East Palo Alto felt like an afterthought in the provision of resources that go toward the community's needy.

Symbolic Invisibility

The feelings of black invisibility that East Palo Alto respondents expressed went beyond access to material resources, to the symbolic level. The decline of East Palo Alto's black population brought with it a diminished sense of collective black identity that was especially apparent to the city's older residents. These individuals carried with them a local history that included East Palo Alto's rise as a place that celebrated black identity in spite of the area's problems with drugs and violence. The people who had been at the center of this history were particularly apt to point out the decline of black identity. At a meeting of black leaders I attended, one participant offered the following general observation about the state of black identity in the city:

We don't feel we fit. We definitely are the minority. Definitely what he's saying, where people don't respect you because they don't see a presence of your
culture. And so not that it needs to be negative but just that we say, "We
belong too." And I don't sense that any more.

In a separate interview, another community leader lamented that the
decline of the black population was undermining the city's rich history of
activism as well as the general awareness of the role that activism had
played in the city's development:

And we see a lot of that where people come back into the community and
say, "Hey, the Walkers used to live there." Well, the Walkers don't live there
any more. There's the Martinez family. And what's really interesting is that
the Martinez family can't tell you a thing about the Walkers. Can't tell you a
thing . . . . Our storytellers are gone. . . . I was in [a meeting] and here's a
great image: we had Malcolm X's birthday, it was a holiday. Cesar Chavez's
birthday is a holiday. Dr. Martin Luther King as well. There were three very
significant days where we're about to give kids a free day off. So we had a
sixth grade class do a paper on who are these guys. What's the best way to
honor them? Oh my god! If you could have read some of the papers—
couldn't connect the dots. So I'm not harping on the eleven-year-old's inability to know who Cesar Chavez is or Malcolm X or Dr. King, but the storytellers in the homes are no longer there celebrating the life and the legacy of
these individuals as a part of their family traditions. And the kids are like,
"Man I don't care who he is! I get a day off from school. Man I like him, he's
cool . . . ." "I don't care who he is." So what does that mean when you talk
about EPA that says Mrs. Gertrude Wilks or a Barbara Mouton [early black
leaders in the city]; when you say that to a Latino family today the majority
of them don't know who they are?

Black leaders acknowledged the importance of Latinos to the struggle for
civil rights. But they also recognized that the Latino civil rights leadership
lionized today emerged well before the newcomer Latinos who reside in
East Palo Alto arrived in the United States. Because these immigrants had
arrived on the scene after the major struggles of the civil rights movement,
African Americans in East Palo Alto saw a disconnect of consciousness
among most of the city's Latinos: they did not seem to understand or
appreciate the history or the struggles that had shaped the city. In a similar vein, sociologist Mario Small (2002; 2004) noted how a dual historical
frame of reference helped account for the level of engagement among

older residents in a largely Puerto Rican housing project in Boston. Residents from younger cohorts, Small showed, lacked this historical frame of reference, and thus were not as invested in the welfare of a community that they had always known to be a nice place to live. Black East Palo Alto residents identified a similar dynamic, except that the cohort change was racial as well as generational. The city's young people not only lacked the same historical frame of reference, their more recent history of struggle was characterized by different challenges, those that come with immigration and assimilation. To be sure, the city's institutions and leaders had made efforts to integrate Latinoness into the city's identity, including observance of César Chávez Day and Cinco de Mayo. Yet the older African Americans we interviewed were concerned that what started as inclusiveness had turned into the symbolic drowning out of black identity.

For East Palo Alto residents who were less directly involved in the city's historical struggles, the invisibility of black identity resulting from immigration-driven change took on concrete forms. Several respondents, for example, noted that the renaming of one of the city's largest grammar schools to Cesar Chavez and Green Oaks Academy represented a visible and significant shift in the identity of a city that had once had a thriving Afrocentric school (Olewe 2015). Others cited the diminished state of once-vibrant public celebrations of black identity. East Palo Alto has a Collard Green Festival and a Juneteenth Celebration, which commemorates the emancipation of the United States' last remaining slaves. Black residents saw these once lively events as shells of their former selves. To emphasize the point, some compared these black celebrations to flourishing Latino-oriented ones, like Cinco de Mayo. The comments of Michael Thomas, a black forty-nine-year-old food service worker, captured these widely-held sentiments:

> Well it's supposed to be America, but it's almost like it's turning into not too far away from where the majority is gonna be Latino. So now everything has a multicultural bent to it. It's not like . . . even the Juneteenth is only a half day now and it's not even where it's reflecting what Juneteenth is supposed to be about. The fact that in Texas, they was the last one to find out that they're free and that's what Juneteenth was supposed to be about. Recognize that slavery was over. It's not really like that no more. We don't really have

anything else, festivals that acknowledge it. And being now, not even a truly black community any more because now we're the minority in this community . . . . Yeah, there tend to be some others. Even the Cinco de Mayo celebrations and stuff they have. It's like the naming of the schools and stuff in EPA. The elementary school I went to used be Cavanaugh. Now it's Cesar Chavez. And that one I can pretty much understand because Chavez didn't have jack shit but he organized the country. So I gotta give him his credit for that, because even though he organized all that shit, he still didn't have crap. He didn't even own his own home! So I give him that credit. But like I say, as a whole, they be down for each other a little bit more. Maybe that's also because this is not their country, even though more than half their country is over here! But they do celebrate their heritage as much as they can.

Michael's comments suggested that the disappearance of collective black identity under waves of Latino immigrant settlement represents an inversion of the usual immigrant-native dynamic, in which foreign-born guests are strangers in a land where the norms and culture are defined by the native-born hosts. Aaron Mullin, the twenty-three-year-old black delivery driver with a second-generation Mexican American girlfriend, introduced in the last chapter, described a similar inversion of the usual dynamic in his take on ethnic celebrations in the city:

I remember the annual Juneteenth Festival that EPA has. They had it every June, this celebration when the slaves got emancipated. I remember that used to be a big festival in EPA and it was cool. It was like predominantly black and had boutiques and stuff. You go down there with your family for the day and play games and eat food, listen to performances and stuff. And see your community leaders and stuff and learn about things going on in the community. Now we barely even have one. The last one we had, I don't know how they can call that a festival! It wasn't even a festival. It seemed like it was last minute. They had it on the school grounds. The sprinklers came on while the vendors were out there. They had one performer. It was like somebody just threw that at the last minute. Man this is what it's come to?! . . . Seems like they're more leaning towards the Latino community because that's the bigger population and that's probably where they're getting the most income, from that population. So I guess it all comes down to politics and business. It's just sad that some of the activities that the city used to pride itself on, they really let them go. And it's sad because sometimes that makes people feel foreign too, knowing that you can't even stay within your own city and have some type of festival.

As Michael's and Aaron's comments illustrate, respondents in East Palo Alto saw the shifting symbolic representation of Latinos as a natural outcome of the city's changing demographics. Still, their comments were tinged with the irony of finding it difficult to experience a collective sense of blackness in a city that has for so long stood as a black capital of the region.

If the decline of annual festivals is a large but infrequent reminder of the invisibility of black identity, the city's retail landscape is a regular prompt. Black barber shops and soul food restaurants, important and rare institutions in Silicon Valley, are now hard to find in East Palo Alto. Respondents explained that the Latino retail scene has become much more vibrant instead. The decline of black retail institutions is partly due to the razing of "Whiskey Gulch," the city's former semblance of a downtown, and its replacement by a Four Seasons hotel and a large office complex. Whiskey Gulch used to be home to several liquor stores and bars, but also to music stores, a wig shop, and soul food restaurants that served as black cultural anchors (Levin and Brink 1996). East Palo Alto residents cited the demise of these black institutions and the rise of Latino establishments as evidence of the city's changed character, but also as part of what made it difficult to experience a deep sense of blackness locally. Rachel Abernathy, the executive assistant, mourned the disappearance of black institutions. Throughout the interview she recalled growing up with several Mexican American people whom she regarded as similar to blacks in their struggles and general approach to life. But, she said, contemporary Mexicans in East Palo Alto seemed more distant, a perspective she supported by laying out the city's institutional landscape:

> Well, they had special, at least in my world of EPA, they had schools in particular that was geared for African American teachings. Like they had [Afrocentric school], which I went to but I was real young. I went there when I was like fourth grade. And then my son went there when he was in the eighth . . . . So they had schools available for that type of resources in general and when I was growing up, I don't know if they do it now with kids. But we had field trips where we used to go to this, I think it was the African American library up in San Jose somewhere. So they just had more things available or resources of teaching more of the foundation of being an African American . . . . Soul food for the most part. A lot of barbecue places. Like here on this main street

here, I think this is University [Avenue], mostly now you see most of the markets are Hispanic or just some of the restaurants are mostly to me Mexican restaurants. But where before it was a little nightclub and they had more barbecue restaurants and just more black-owned businesses.

The growing prevalence of Latino institutions and the declining number of black ones presented an assimilation challenge posed not by a putative white mainstream, but rather by a Latino population whose symbols and practices had grown visible in inverse proportion to black culture.

The invisibility experienced by blacks in East Palo Alto locally is not necessarily an indicator of the invisibility of blackness more generally. Indeed, there is ample evidence that blackness remains a highly "marked" category with largely negative consequences. However, the specific role that East Palo Alto once played as the black cultural hub of Silicon Valley was a key reference point for how respondents there evaluated its symbolic prowess today. The centrality of place comes into clearer focus when the views of East Palo Alto black respondents are compared with those of Berryessa's middle-class blacks. Whether in the neighborhood, workplace, or school, Berryessa's established blacks were perpetually navigating non-black spaces where their blackness was highly visible and not always welcomed. Respondents reported harassment by police, disrespect in everyday social interactions, and feelings of isolation in the workplace. The rare times when these middle-class blacks found themselves in largely black contexts stood in stark contrast to their usual lives. Consider Natalie Hayes, whom I introduced in the previous chapter. Natalie grew up in Berryessa, but attended high school in Sacramento, a city 120 miles away with a much larger black population. The visibility of her blackness in Berryessa was a sharp contrast to the sense of comfort she felt living in Sacramento:

> Really, when I got to be around black people is when I went to Sacramento. I had culture shock. I never knew that many black people existed. It was unbelievable for me. I was going, "Are you kidding me?" I had never seen anything like that in my life.... I actually loved it.... And so it was just like people who had families, who weren't just the one black person who married into the family.

The sort of comfort that Natalie described in being around a larger black community was still available to East Palo Alto respondents to some extent: the city's black population was large enough that respondents there could still get a taste of the cultural and psychological ease that came with being around other blacks. But the public spaces that respondents said had once made East Palo Alto a cultural home were now muted by a large Latino presence that rendered the symbolic representation of blacks virtually invisible. As the comparison with middle-class blacks shows, the invisibility that East Palo Alto respondents expressed is rooted in comparisons to a time when blackness was a much more prominent part of the city's character.

Myrisha Jackson, a black twenty-nine-year-old, unemployed woman from East Palo Alto, summarized the state of affairs when she offered these thoughts: "And blacks: we're so confused because our culture is dead. It died. We just lost." For Myrisha and other respondents in East Palo Alto, African American identity was being lost in the sea of Latino identity and institutions that now defined a place that once stood out for its blackness.

PRIVILEGE AND BLAME

In all three of the places we studied, relative group power shaped how respondents made sense of racial identity. At the same time, the accounts of racial identity cited thus far flip the typical assimilation equation, in which immigrants and their children are understood to form new racial identities in response to the established racial order. Seen through the eyes of Silicon Valley's established individuals, large immigrant groups have some power to reshape a community's racial structure in ways that force established-population individuals to adapt to new and often uncomfortable inflections of racial identity.

But these experiences do not exist in a local vacuum. Respondents made sense of the local inflection by drawing on notions of race that extended beyond their particular cities, schools, or the Silicon Valley region. Among both whites and blacks, accounts of the local meaning and status of whiteness and blackness reflected larger notions of race, privilege, and disadvantage. Whites tended to exert their privilege by deflecting responsibility for the diminished meaning of whiteness; blacks, however, tended to internalize responsibility for their invisibility vis-à-vis Latino immigrants.

Pointing the Finger of Blame Outward

Many of the usual manifestations of white privilege did not show up in the lives of white respondents in Silicon Valley. Whereas white privilege is typically associated with racial invisibility and a presumed superordinate position (Frankenberg 1993; McDermott and Samson 2005), Silicon Valley's large and concentrated high-skilled Asian immigrant population prevented whites from accessing that privilege in full. But the privileges associated with whiteness manifested in the subtle way white respondents assigned blame and responsibility for their position. They fully recognized that Asians set the standards for academic and even professional achievement. Yet they drew on larger notions of whiteness as the norm to cast Asian immigrants' approach to achievement as outside that norm—as "weird"—almost never pointing the finger of responsibility inward. Over and over again, we heard white parents and young people express frustration that Asian newcomers predominated in schools numerically and in terms of status. They chalked this positioning up to the immigrants' electric work ethic and commitment to academic excellence, yet they almost never suggested that established-population whites needed to elevate their performance to keep up. Instead, whites cast the "Asian" approach as odd. Indeed, Lori Brewer, a white banker from Cupertino, put things in those very terms in the process of critiquing of the Asian parenting approach. Her view mirrored the stance taken by other established parents. As mentioned in chapter 1, Lori and her husband were close friends with an immigrant South Asian Indian couple that lived on the same block. These close friends served as an example of what Lori saw as a strange approach to childrearing:

> [The kids are] either in daycare after school or they're in tutoring or music or everything, all of the above. So they overtax their kids, they really do. They come here with this huge work ethic, over the top. I think, as Americans, we tend to want to have a more balanced childhood for our kids and we're interested in academics but we also want to have them do swimming or music or whatever. But we want down time, too. And my husband's

always kind of . . . not fighting, but sort of play fighting with [our neighbors and friends from India] about homework because . . . . they're just on [their son] all the time about the homework. Yeah. And so [my husband] is like, "Lay off the kid! Come on! You're going to burn him out before he's even in junior high . . . " [Our neighbor was] like, "Yeah when we went to [Lake] Tahoe, my husband was making [our son] do the homework." [I said,] "It's vacation!" . . . But people come here and they want to make sure that they're a success. And [our neighbor] works until 10, 11 o'clock at night. They do not eat dinner until 9. He comes home, they eat dinner and then the kids are up until 10 or 11, too. It's really weird.

Parents and teens described a putatively immigrant-origin Asian approach to achievement—what is now popularly known as "tiger parenting"—as throwing "normal" childhood off kilter. Legal scholar Amy Chua (2011) offered a biographical account of what she called her Asian "tiger mother" approach to parenting, which emphasized academic achievement and family and employed authoritarian and dictatorial methods to achieve those ends. Chua's book had not yet come out when we did our interviews, and it was thus an unavailable frame for respondents to make sense of different parenting approaches. But even if they did not reference the parenting style by name, they recognized the pattern and rejected it in spirit, expressing a desire for a more "balanced" approach to school. Although the perceived Asian approach they criticized accounted for the diminished status of whiteness, they nonetheless offered their more relaxed approach—characterized by placing value on academic success, but also valuing freedom for children to chart their own course—as the right one. Michelle Yates, a twenty-one-year-old white college student from Cupertino, reflected on the difference between her approach to school and the one that her immigrant-origin Asian peers exhibited, hold-ing up the former as superior:

I remember people breaking down in class and bawling if they got a B, a high B. And I was like, "It's fine. It's fine. It's a good grade for me!" That was good. And they'd say, "No, it's not an A." So who wants to handle someone like that? When I was in high school all I was concerned about was having fun—drinking and having fun. That's all I was concerned about. These kids never . . . they go to SAT study groups on the weekends. It's too much! . . . Like I said before, I think there's a totally different work ethic in their culture, especially coming over here and trying to succeed. Maybe as a second-language speaker or whatever. I know a couple of people [from another country] whose parents had just paid for them to come over here and go to school here. And that must feel really like a lot of pressure, that they paid all this money for you to come over here and then if you don't succeed . . . . There must have been a reason why they were crying as well. I don't know if their parents beat them? I don't know!

Interestingly, respondents in Berryessa were less insistent about the righteousness of a "balanced" approach to achievement than those in Cupertino, where the inverted meaning and status of whiteness was most pronounced. The more noticeable change in the meaning and status of whiteness in Cupertino was thus accompanied by a proportionally forceful assertion that the balanced—i.e., white—approach to school and life was the more normal outlook and strategy. Some parents' perception of the outsized influence of immigrant-origin Asians on achievement standards led them to look for an escape hatch. Take, for example, Denise Miller, the white thirty-nine-year-old homemaker and former corporate manager. Denise and her husband had a tremendous track record of conventional success. Both had attended elite schools, and both had distinguished professional careers. But Denise expressed concern about how the school environment in Cupertino would affect her young children in the future:

And it's just, "Wait a second. What about our social growth, our emotional growth, this balance?" . . . So that's been frustrating for us. Looking again at a lot of this as a parent, even though I grew up here, we don't want our kids to go to the high school that we're zoned for . . . which is an excellent school. It produces amazing graduates. But, again, there's just a high level of competition, unfortunately a high level of cheating, a high level of negative parent pressure on teachers for, "Why doesn't my kid have an A?" All of this stuff over there that's again left out a whole piece of the development of the child. So we want our kids to go to [another high school], which is right over the bridge here. They don't have transfers to that so we're likely going to have to move within district. And my husband's business is here, and our family and everything is here. But to track our kids for the right schools that aren't so over the top with kind of just a real risky, negative approach to success—we don't want our kids to be in that.

Denise and her husband moved shortly after our interview to be in a school district that was *less* competitive.

Notable in the responses from whites in Cupertino and Berryessa is that they saw their approach to achievement as normal, and tacitly superior, but also that they never interpreted the shifting meaning and status of whiteness as a wake-up call to adopt the new norms pervading their neighborhoods and schools. Put bluntly, the privileges of whiteness appeared in the fact that whites never blamed themselves for their inability to keep up with the changing standard of achievement. Instead, they held fast to the belief that their way was the normal and thus right way while still recognizing that they were being outgunned academically.

Pointing the Finger of Blame Inward

This absence of any sense of self-blame for the current state of affairs among whites may not seem notable on its own. But it is remarkable compared to the reaction that African Americans had to a similar sense that newcomers were outpacing them. Whereas whites in the other two study locales virtually never cited the "Asian" approach to achievement as evidence that whites could do more to get ahead, blacks in East Palo Alto pointed to the supposed habits of immigrant groups as a basis for an approach to collective advancement that blacks ought to follow. Folk theories of racial inequality often cite the success of immigrants as evidence of the deficiencies of native-born minority groups that have been unable to lift themselves out of a collective depressed social and economic state (see Kim 1999).[6] African Americans in East Palo Alto seemed to have internalized this logic, calling for greater self-uplift on the part of the group. To be sure, respondents cited historical and present-day racism as powerful forces impinging on the fortunes of African Americans. But they were even more ardent in mentioning what they saw as blacks' own shortcomings in overcoming racism. Take, for example, the comments of Mike Bly, a thirty-four-year-old African American in East Palo Alto, who made a living in the underground economy:

> We've got strikes against us. We came out of the womb with a strike against us. It's just a real struggle. Everybody's in it at the same time. We're all crowded in a bucket. Everybody's always pulling the next person down. We don't know how to stick together as a race. It's just been like that. Maybe our grandparents, in that era, maybe they came up, reach one, teach one, and all that. But

in my age growing up, and I'm in my thirties, it's just every man for himself. Everybody's just straight cut-throat-ish. And that's what it is. Where, opposed to other races, everybody sticks together, struggles together, and comes up. There's just not that many African Americans that think like that.

Q: What other races think like that?

A: Hispanics. The Asians. All the other races. Maybe even the Hindus and Indians. I know for a fact, you see corners, taco spots everywhere around this place. They stick together. There's nothing wrong in that. There's nothing wrong with that at all. In a bad situation ten heads may be better than one. Them, the Asians, that's just what they do. But us—everybody's for themselves. Basically that's what it is.

Their characterization of Mexicans, and occasionally Asians, as having a collectivist approach to advancement echoes social-scientific theories about the benefits of the co-ethnic community. According to these theories, ethnic networks anchored by more established immigrants provide newly arrived immigrants with access to resources such as jobs and housing, softening what is often a rough landing for greenhorns (Portes and Bach 1985; Zhou 1992). Interviewees often cited the willingness of Mexicans and Asians to live together in large numbers (a response to the area's high housing costs) in order to get by. Blacks' perceived inability to do the same was, for these respondents, an ever-present example of blacks' lack of cohesion. Yvonne Winston, a forty-three-year-old black medical-billing examiner, articulated this oft-invoked comparison:

I admire the fact of other cultures how they can build and live together versus my own brothers and sisters. Because for some reason we have a selfish demeanor about ourselves, where we have to be forced to live together without someone getting hurt or some type of animosity builds or argument or fight. Just something will go wrong. I admire how the Asian community can live together, grandma and grandpa take care of the grandkids. And the husband and wife go out to work. And how they work together to run the household. Everybody has a role, everybody fulfills their role. Hispanic does the same thing. They do the same thing. Whoever is home, they do the cooking and the cleaning. If the baby is too small to go to school, baby stays home with them. But the expenses are minimum and the dads or the sons will go out and produce money to keep the roof and the heat and food flowing. I just wish that the African American could learn how to do and coexist like that with each other, in family. But they don't.

Rebecca Lawrence, a thirty-two-year-old black teacher who was born and raised in East Palo Alto, moved back to the city after receiving a bachelor's degree. When asked whether there was anything about other groups that she admired, she echoed Yvonne's assessment:

> I'm not going to try to be stereotypical. I do like how, for example, Asian culture—even though I know there's some parts of it that take it to the extreme—but how they emphasize, and also African [immigrants], the emphasis is on education. I think one thing that we as, African Americans, lack sometimes is the emphasis on education, like the de-emphasis on education and emphasis on the bling. (laughing) I see it always. The quick money, real fast. Forget the education thing. So I like that [about Asian culture]. I also like the same thing of Jewish people; what they went through with World War II and how they're able to . . . . And Native Americans, they went through a lot but they're still here. Not as strong numbers as they were before the Spanish came, but they're still here. With my students here I also like how . . . I can't name them by name but the different cultures kind of stick together as far as the community. Like the last time I could reference is the civil rights movement when African Americans really came together as a community and mobilized by helping each other . . . . So the emphasis on family in the Mexican culture for example, Filipino culture, even African culture. I don't think we focus on that enough. Quick money sometimes is where it is.

Although the question of whether respondents admired anything about other ethnic groups was not designed to prompt a comparison, African American respondents made just such a comparison. And when they did, they concluded that blacks would do well to emulate what they saw as immigrants' collectivist habits.

These immigration-inspired critiques of African Americans by African Americans echoed findings from other research. Jennifer Lee's (2002) study of relations between Korean and Jewish merchants and their mostly black clientele offered an assessment of black mobility that echoed what we heard in East Palo Alto: Lee's subjects too believed that immigrants offered a model of collectivist strategies for advancement. Mindiola, Niemann, and Rodriguez (2002) uncovered similar views among African Americans in their survey and interview data from Houston. Like the people we spoke to in East Palo Alto, their respondents lauded Latinos' collectivist approach to socioeconomic advancement. Similarly, political scientist Jennifer Hochschild's (1995) study of African Americans' view of the American Dream showed that poorer blacks, like those we interviewed in East Palo Alto, are more likely to believe in the attainability of the American Dream than their middle-class counterparts. Such a view among less-well-off blacks is consistent with the implications of the sort of self-critique interviewees offered, which is that blacks are in control of their own fate. Such self-critiques belie the widely held stereotype that blacks are quick to blame any bad circumstances on factors beyond their control, like systemic racism (Salter et al. 2015). The sentiments expressed by East Palo Alto's black respondents confirmed that they hardly put it all on "the system."

CONCLUSION

The relational form of assimilation that established individuals are undergoing has powerful implications for their racial identity. Immigrants make uncomfortable adjustments to the new racial context that they encounter in the receiving society. But they also shift the racial terrain in which they settle, requiring an adjustment on the part of the long-established residents of these contexts. In some respects, the changes that whites in Cupertino and Berryessa and blacks in East Palo Alto experienced as a result of the heavy immigrant presence were quite similar. In all three contexts respondents shared the view that immigrant groups were outdoing everyone, knocking blackness and whiteness down the status ladder in certain realms of life. Their interpretation of that impression, however, differed by race and class setting. In Cupertino and Berryessa, respondents saw Asian immigrants and their children as excelling over and above the established population in educational achievement. In East Palo Alto, respondents emphasized that immigrants had leapfrogged them in economic advancement and in garnering material and symbolic recognition. Counter to established academic views of racial identity, immigration has made whiteness *more* visible and blackness *less* visible in this region. In the upper-middle-class city of Cupertino, high-skilled Asian immigrants have introduced an amplified version of an already elevated academic achievement standard. This new standard has an explicit racial coding:

Asianness stands for high achievement and intelligence; whiteness, by contrast, stands out as lower achieving and less intelligent. Whiteness in Cupertino, then, is a visibly marked category that has been turned on its head relative to its conventional meaning. A somewhat similar relationship between race and achievement exists in Berryessa. While Latinos and blacks prevent whiteness from serving as the absolute bottom of the achievement hierarchy, whites in the high-achieving track of Berryessa schools reported experiences around racial identity that strongly resembled those described by whites in Cupertino. In East Palo Alto, by contrast, blackness—the dominant racial identity among established-population respondents there—has become *less* visible as a result of the large Latino immigrant presence. Black respondents reported that the material and symbolic salience of black identity in Silicon Valley's historically black city had been drowned out by Latino immigrants. Unlike whites in Cupertino and Berryessa, who tended to see the social norms upheld by immigrant-origin families as strange and not to be emulated, blacks in East Palo Alto viewed Latinos as exemplars of a collectivist strategy for advancement that blacks lacked.

The findings from this chapter offer a portrait of how notions of race shift as a result of a large newcomer presence. In so doing they add to existing evidence that immigration is changing the racial landscape (Frey 2014). But beyond documenting the existence of the shift, they are perhaps more valuable as insights into *how* that shift takes place. Scholars have largely focused on how the presence of newcomers reinforces the existing racial order: either the newcomers fit into existing racial categories (Ignatiev 1995; Roediger 2005; Waters 1999) or the order reacts to them in a way that reinforces the existing racial categories (Haney-López 1996).

The experiences of established population respondents in Silicon Valley suggest another possibility. The presence of immigrants can be a foil that recasts the meaning and status of a particular racial category. In Cupertino, and to a lesser degree in Berryessa, the large number of high-skilled Asian immigrants has contributed to making whiteness highly visible, inverting its meaning and status when it comes to achievement. In this case, Asian-origin immigrants shape whiteness not by becoming white, nor by serving as a contrast bolstering what it means to be white. Rather, their presence flips whiteness on its head relative to its typical meaning. But it is also the case that the settlement of immigrants in Silicon Valley reinforces the meaning and status of particular categories. Though blackness has become less visible in East Palo Alto, what it *means* to be black has been reified by the presence of the large Latino immigrant population.

These findings suggest that the presence of immigrants causes cracks in some dimensions of the racial structure, but that it makes other dimensions firmer. Respondents' different reactions to the changing status and meaning of racial categories in the three different research locations indicate that, even as white privilege comes under threat, there is a vast reservoir of rationalizations that white individuals and institutions can muster to reestablish the racial hierarchy (see Espenshade, Radford, and Chung 2009; Samson 2013). In some respects, the way respondents make sense of these changes reveals the ability of privilege to reinvent itself (Jackman 1994; Omi and Winant 2014). And yet some respondents' rhetorical attempts at reinvention swim against a local current that forces them into a subordinate position when it comes to achievement. Whites' rejection of the perceived Asian approach to achievement is an attempt to patch cracks in a racial structure that whites have dominated for all of American history.

Over time, however, Asian-white relations may not turn out to be a competition for resources at the top. Consider a historical parallel. When in the 1920s and 1930s the number of Eastern European Jews admitted to Ivy League schools, then dominated by white Protestants, grew, administrators attempted to cap that growth (Karabel 2005; Keller and Keller 2001). Those efforts ultimately failed because of pressure by alumni and civil rights groups. The result was not Protestant whites losing out to Jews in the competition for elite status. Instead, elite whites ultimately had to make space for a select group of Jews to *share* elite status at Ivy League schools and beyond. A similar process may be unfolding for Asians today. There can be little doubt that Asians often have to work much harder to gain admission to elite educational institutions (Espenshade, Radford, and Chung 2009).[7] Still, Asians are overrepresented at colleges and universities, and large numbers of Asians are entering jobs at the top of the occupational hierarchy alongside whites (Alba and Yrizar Barbosa 2015; Alba 2009). Moreover, the racial status of Asian men and women does not appear to adversely affect their chances of getting those jobs or dampen their wages relative to whites (Alba and Yrizar Barbosa 2015). It may very well be that white elites are presently being forced to make room at the educational and occupational top for elite Asians, much as the case was a century ago for Eastern European Jews. The situation in Cupertino may depict that process beginning to unfold.

East Palo Alto, in contrast, is a microcosm of processes that block blacks from finding a place in the American status hierarchy alongside whites. In East Palo Alto, African Americans, and particularly poor African Americans, expressed a sense of being overpowered by newcomers. They also internalized a critique regarding the need for group uplift, reinforcing the recurrent and intractable narrative of African American subordination (Bobo and Smith 1998). There is a troubling harmony between analyses of nationally representative data on occupational status and the views we uncovered among established blacks in East Palo Alto. Unlike Asians, who are reaching near-parity with whites, or Latinos, who are catching up, blacks appear to be gaining no ground in occupying jobs at the top of the occupational hierarchy (Alba and Yrizar Barbosa 2016; Alba 2009). Combined with grossly high incarceration rates (Western 2006), persistent segregation (Sharkey 2013), and lower levels of educational attainment, the general advancement of more recently arrived immigrant groups gives credence to the view of East Palo Alto's established population that blacks are being left behind, and that prosperity for the vast majority is still well out of reach.

More generally, the experiences of established-population individuals in all three locales suggest that immigrant-origin and established individuals alike are constantly adjusting to a racial terrain to which all parties contribute as both subjects and agents of change. A more panoramic view of their experiences also hints that group size and status are important factors determining the degree to which any given group plays a part in adjusting that terrain. Across Silicon Valley, and especially in the three study locales, newcomers make up a large portion of the population. Their large relative group size puts newcomers in a position to shape multiple aspects of life, including notions of racial identity. The experiences of respondents in all three study locales suggest as much. But group status matters too, as the experiences of Cupertino's white respondents clearly suggest. Asian newcomers, in addition to their large relative group size, are also socioeconomically well off, putting them in a position to challenge entrenched notions of whiteness. It might be said, then, that relative group size and status together determine how symmetrical group change in relational assimilation will be.

As the next chapter shows, the adjustment that established individuals undergo includes shifts in how they draw the lines that demarcate different social groupings. The account of relational assimilation here and in other works suggests that racial lines are important markers in this process. But the next chapter shows that race is hardly an all-encompassing frame defining how established individuals delineate insiders and outsiders.

4   Living with Difference and Similarity

Spend time in any public space in Silicon Valley, and the range of differences associated with immigration becomes abundantly clear.[1] In all directions is a dizzying mélange of languages, social classes, skin tones, legal statuses, sartorial styles, religious symbols, and culinary offerings. Such a mishmash of differences can be found in many areas where immigrants settle in large numbers (Vertovec 2007), yet among the many markers of diversity at play, scholars focus overwhelming attention on ethnic and racial difference (Wimmer 2013)—and with good reason. The way that interviewees articulated the "us" and "them" in their lives comported with social-scientific research that emphasizes ethnic and racial differences as sources of both unity and division (Bonilla-Silva 2006; Omi and Winant 2014; Putnam 2007). In Cupertino and Berryessa, where the busyness of upper-middle- and middle-class life was on full display, respondents saw a particularly "Asian" approach to work, school, and home as interfering with community building. In East Palo Alto, interviewees articulated a set of ethnic symbolic boundaries that centered on access to jobs: these boundaries seemed to exclude African Americans from Latino job networks and to require workers to be bilingual if they were to compete in the local labor market.

But the way established individuals made sense of the most significant ramifications of mass immigrant settlement suggests that observers' focus on race and ethnicity only partially captures the complexity of the lines of unity and division emerging in areas of heavy immigrant settlement like Silicon Valley (Wimmer 2013). A closer examination of respondents' words reveals multiple kinds of symbolic boundaries, the "conceptual distinctions made by social actors to categorize objects, people, practices, and even time and space" (Lamont and Molnár 2002: 168). In essence, symbolic boundaries constitute the everyday ways that respondents distinguished "us" from "them" (Sanders 2002). Symbolic boundaries based on race and ethnicity were paramount in East Palo Alto, Cupertino, and Berryessa. But the symbolic boundaries that established individuals articulated in these contexts were shaped by respondents' extensive exposure to immigration-driven diversity. As immigrants become more settled, and as their second-generation children come of age, immigrant assimilation increases, growing the diversity *within* ethnic groups (Alba, Jiménez, and Marrow 2014; Jiménez, Fields, and Schachter 2015; Crul 2016). Having extensive experience living alongside, attending school with, and working with Latinos and Asians meant that established respondents readily recognized the differences *among* individuals in these groups, and it was these differences that also defined the symbolic boundaries between insiders and outsiders. In particular, linguistic differences and neighborhood tenure constituted especially important symbolic boundaries that cut across ethnic boundaries: for respondents, English speakers and longtime residents constituted the "us" and were juxtaposed against the non-English-speakers and new residents who comprised the "them."

The way established individuals made sense of symbolic boundaries, in conjunction with a growing body of evidence from other settings, suggests that immigration introduces multiple symbolic boundaries (Hannah 2011; Horton 1995; Vertovec 2007; Wimmer 2013; Wimmer 2004). Ethnic boundaries are indeed important, and perhaps preeminent. But they are not all-defining group markers in contexts where diversity exists in such manifold splendor.[2]

ETHNIC BOUNDARIES IN EVERYDAY LIFE

High levels of international migration for the last three decades have transformed metro areas like Silicon Valley to such a degree that self-conscious
articulations of the value of diversity seem passé. Ethnic difference in
regions defined by mass immigrant settlement has an "everyday" (Wise
and Velayutham 2009) or "mundane" (Watson and Saha 2013; also see
Kasinitz et al. 2008) quality. Indeed, respondents regularly offered glowing
assessments of the benefits of diversity as a spur for economic innovation
and an antidote to cultural blandness. But for all their "happy talk" (Bell
and Hartmann 2007) about diversity, the people we interviewed did not
see abundant difference as an unalloyed good. In fact, they were quite adamant that diversity is a double-edged sword that can cut through a sense of
unity. In contrast to their positive comments about immigration-driven
diversity, which often lacked specificity, their observations about the challenges of diversity were more unambiguous. Across all three locales,
respondents noted that diversity was a prime culprit—though by no means
the only one—behind a diminished sense of cohesion among people in
their neighborhood, city, and region. Awareness of the negative effects of
diversity was especially acute among East Palo Alto's African American
respondents who, in addition to remarking on the declining sense of cohesion, readily noted that the diversification of the city by Latino and Pacific
Islander immigrants had drowned out material and symbolic resources for
African Americans, as laid out in the previous chapter.

Their assessment appears to affirm survey research findings showing
that diversity dampens social cohesion, whether that cohesion is measured by organizational membership (Alesina and La Ferrara 2000), trust
(Putnam 2007), census response rates (Vigdor 2004), or support for
redistributive public spending (Eger 2010; Luttmer 2001; Poterba 1997).
These findings are highly contested by scholars, to be sure (Fieldhouse
and Cutts 2010; Hooghe et al. 2009; Kesler and Bloemraad 2010; Letki
2008; Portes and Vickstrom 2011; Abascal and Baldassarri 2015). But
they nonetheless resonate with the assessment offered by established-
population respondents. In East Palo Alto, Cupertino, and Berryessa alike,
respondents offered views of their respective communities as fragmented

by immigration. Strikingly, respondents in the three locales, in spite of their communities' differences in income, crime, and ethnic makeup, came to similar conclusions about immigration-driven diversity's impact on those communities.

Middle- and Upper-Middle-Class Immigrant Striving and Ethnic Boundaries in Cupertino and Berryessa

To hear parents in Cupertino and Berryessa compare their own childhoods to those of their children was to hear them reminisce about a suburban heyday of bustling neighborhoods in which children enjoyed unstructured play outside nearly every day. Now, they said, neighbors kept to themselves, venturing outside only to get into their cars to drive to work or shuttle their children to countless extracurricular activities. They also observed that children spent all of their free time with their faces pressed to a television, tablet, or smartphone screen. Such a shift might be found in any middle- or upper-middle-class suburban landscape, where parents channel ever more time and resources into ensuring that their children hang onto their precarious class status (Cooper 2014; Weis, Cipollone, and Jenkins 2014). Sociologist Annette Lareau (2003) refers to the style of parenting found among the middle and upper middle class as "concerted cultivation": an attempt by parents to prepare their children for the adult world by carefully managing their schedules to include lots of enrichment activities and by treating children as peers. Many of the Berryessa and Cupertino parents engaged in this style of parenting. But they attributed an exaggerated version of concerted cultivation to Asian-immigrant-origin parents, pointing to parents scheduling their children in activities that maximized an academic bottom line (like playing the violin or piano). The established parents we talked to, who mostly followed Lareau's concerted cultivation parenting style, saw newcomer Asian parents as taking a much more controlling approach to interactions with their children, which they contrasted with their own approach. Respondents in both Cupertino and Berryessa said that Asian parents kept their children indoors to do school work or to focus on pursuits perceived as offering an academic advantage. Summarizing the perspective of Cupertino and Berryessa respondents, a longtime high school teacher and coach observed:

I started here in [the late 1960s . . . .] The ethnicity was completely different. It was white and Hispanic. Middle-class white and Hispanic . . . . And it
was not working class but professional type of stuff. And the expectations
were of hard work and you grind in school and work hard in athletics and
that type of thing . . . . Well, [about twenty years ago] there started being an
influx of Asians. And the expectation was more academic and less athletic.
And that's not a dig, it's just that that's the way it happened.

Indeed, established whites identified newcomers' high-powered focus on
academic achievement (the very force that was displacing whites from the
top of the academic racial hierarchy) as the culprit to blame for a declining
sense of community. Cupertino interviewees in particular said that a distinctly Asian pursuit of academic and professional excellence left little
time for the kind of informal socializing that these suburban dwellers
prized. Parents with school-aged children were especially likely to express
frustration, feeling that there were few opportunities for their children to
have the kind of "normal" opportunities for informal play that had characterized their own youth. Consider Denise Miller, the thirty-nine-year-old
white homemaker and former corporate manager who grew up in
Cupertino, already quoted in chapter 3. She was, in many ways, typical in
her concerted cultivation style of parenting. Her children enjoyed quite a
bit of unstructured play (some of it on display during our interview), but
they also had a full schedule of enrichment activities. She noted how a
distinctly Asian, immigrant-origin version of her own style of parenting,
combined with cultural difference, impeded community cohesion to such
a degree that she and her husband were thinking of moving so that their
children could attend public schools outside of Cupertino:

So [the Asian kids] go to the elementary school in the morning and then
after school for two hours the kids are going to language school. And they do
some other cultural activities. They also do tutoring and other things there.
So it's kind of like a full day program. And how that shows up in sixth, sev-
enth, eighth grade when they're still going to those things, then the kids
socially at school are speaking different languages in varying cliques of languages. So if you're not . . . whoever you're hanging out with after school,
whether it's at language school or soccer practice, that's kind of the group
you're with. And so you're seeing a real cultural kind of boundary around
that. So it's a struggle for people. Gosh, if you can't speak the language or get
involved that way or do those really cool dance activities or martial art

activities or whatever, you're kind of left out. Or if you try to do those things but also don't speak the language . . . . It's just a stark difference here, where in places that are a little bit more balanced with different cultures, it kind of shows up differently. But primarily the Chinese population, you're either in or out. And so because this community is tipped into a nonwhite majority, that you're just seeing those things become more prevalent. Actually our kids don't go to a neighborhood school for a lot of reasons. One, there's such a push for academic achievement that it doesn't match our educational goals for how we think a whole child should be developed . . . . And there's just a lot of different traditions obviously for holidays and different things. So just figuring out how to connect for kids with some kind of typical American ways, there's just a lot of differences. Not that that's all bad. That's not why we're going there. It's the academic, it's just the over-the-top academic push.

Charity Hawkins, a white forty-seven-year-old yoga instructor in Cupertino, echoed Denise's observation when she compared Cupertino to neighboring Sunnyvale, a solidly middle-class city:

> I think, my thing is when I lived in Sunnyvale it had more of a community feeling. So I think Cupertino is less that way. And it's interesting if you go and look at high schools and the demographics, it's less Asian in Sunnyvale. I mean there's some mixture but not nearly as many.

Q: Why do you think it is that there's less of a neighborly atmosphere here in Cupertino?

R: Because I think people are so busy working and like our neighbors across the street are Asian and they have piano lessons and they have tutoring and they have all these different functions. And playing outside isn't much of the feeling. They don't do . . . they go to school, they go to all their extracurricular activities and there's very little time to mingle within the community. I mean I know my neighbors but a lot of people around here never speak with their neighbors. Some of them it's a language barrier. That's a lot of it, but a lot of it is people working long, long hours and the kids are booked constantly . . . . I think it's the nature of the, like from what I've learned talking to people from India and from China and different Asian countries, it's very competitive, very, very competitive. And they have this drive in them to excel and to do better. And it's a work ethic and I think, that's a lot of it. It's not as important for them to do sports or do stuff like that. It's more academic. There's a competitive part of them that academics is very, very important.

There is indeed evidence that the "tiger" (Chua 2011) approach to parenting that respondents perceived among Asian parents is indeed popular among Chinese parents. However, research shows that this style is one among many parenting styles, and may not even be the most prevalent style among Chinese-origin parents (Kim et al. 2013). If other styles of parenting exist among Asian parents, respondents did not take note of them. Instead, they saw parenting guided by academic and career competitiveness as getting in the way of community cohesion. Other parents noted that they felt left out of cliques that formed among East Asian and South Asian parents at school. School "pickup" and "drop-off" are potentially a time for parents to connect socially and even instrumentally (Small 2009), but the characteristics of the schools and of the parents who attend determine the shape of those connections. Many of the Cupertino parents we interviewed felt shut out of such networks because of linguistic and cultural differences.

The kinds of social disconnection that respondents described in schools were reflected in neighborhood relations as well. While it was certainly the case that respondents got to know some neighbors and through them became familiar with the immigrant experience (see chapter 1, as well as findings reported later in this chapter), they also described significant disconnections related to ethnic differences. Take, for example, Natalie Hayes, a thirty-three-year-old African American homemaker in Berryessa, introduced in chapter 2. Natalie recalled her own time growing up in Berryessa as full of free play with other kids in the neighborhood. Though hers had been one of the few black families around, she had nonetheless connected with other children and their families precisely because there was an expectation that children would be playing outside. Natalie explained just how different the neighborhood was now and attributed the difference to immigrant settlement:

> Before there was a lot of kids out. We all used to play with each other, we all used to walk with each other. We used to go to each other's houses. We would all go to the same birthday parties, obviously we went to the same school and we all just hung around, whether it was going skating or if it was the Girl Scouts. We were all part of Girl Scouts . . . . And there they used to have a shopping center. So we also had that area to go hang out. It was a pizza parlor, the donut shop, all these good, fun things to do. Now: all gone . . . . You just don't see people any more. Everybody is hidden. It's a hidden neighborhood . . . . I think it's changed because of the cultures of the

people. I think people stay inside more. I think the nationalities also make a difference because their cultures . . . . Like for instance I have friends that say, "When you have a baby, they can't come outside for a month." And I think that a lot of people don't want their children to play outside. They'd rather just have activities for them to do, whether it be piano and that's it. They have things they'd just rather their children do rather than playing outside . . . . I mean there's a more white people on the block, not as many Asian, but now I would probably say maybe 75 or 80 percent Asian rather than what it was before . . . . Because I'm at home I get to see everybody come out . . . [My kids] don't play with any of the ones across the street because they never come outside. I don't even know the children's names. They play with the [third-generation Mexican American] older kids because we've become really good friends with two neighbors. And actually, my next-door neighbor, her children, every now and then they might play with each other but they have such a hectic schedule. Their schedule is ridiculous. Between the private school, the private karate lessons and the Chinese school on the weekends, soccer games on the weekend. I say, "When do you guys ever sit down?"

Cupertino and Berryessa respondents did not have to be raising children to feel disengaged. Even older respondents, whose children were grown and living outside of the home, expressed the same disconnectedness in their neighborhood and city. When asked to describe Cupertino to someone who had never been to the city, Laura Calvin, a white fifty-year-old nurse whose children were in college or beyond, offered the following:

It's not a very cohesive community. I think there are different demographics, which do . . . . And also Cupertino doesn't have one main downtown. I think that also is to its detriment. But I don't think it's a cohesive type of neighborhood.

Q: And what makes it lack cohesiveness?

R: Well first of all, the city planning. I think it was poorly planned city. It kind of sprawls. But also the fact that there is a pretty huge divide as far as the demographics. There's a huge Asian population. But depending on what part of the Asian population, some of the Asian population really has assimilated into culture and then a lot of the Asian population I think tends to stay to themselves. In fact, I know a lot of people even from my work environment who don't live in Cupertino, who commute to Cupertino for their activities just because it is an Asian population.

Laura's comments about the city's fragmentation and Asian assimilation recognize the diversity within ethnic groups, and this recognition has powerful implications for notions of division and unity (a topic I take up later in the chapter). But respondents in Cupertino and Berryessa generally articulated the origins of this fragmentation in broad, ethnic terms, perceiving that distinctly ethnic approaches to school and work got in the way of community. Cupertino and Berryessa respondents cited multiple causes for community fragmentation, but immigration-driven ethnic boundaries were front and center.

Older respondents, who had lived in their neighborhoods for years, if not decades, were especially apt to see a diminished sense of community resulting from the heavy presence of newcomers. They compared the current state of community fragmentation to their early years living in the area. Even when they noted all that was positive about immigration-driven diversity—the range of food choices, the greater potential for innovation, a lack of boringness, etc.—they also articulated notably ambivalent sentiments about this diversity and the disunity they felt it created. Nancy Lott, a seventy-four-year-old white homemaker in Berryessa, had lived in the same immaculately kept home since 1971, just when Berryessa emerged as a residential community. Her long residence in the neighborhood, combined with her rather youthful exuberance, had made her a central organizer of neighborhood activities that she said were now lacking. As Nancy explained:

> In the beginning, when we first lived here, we had a lot of block parties. Maybe every month we had a block party. And we would show movies on the garage doors. We had all kinds of things going and piñatas and all types of things. And then we would have a general, every three months, garage sale, block garage sale. So we did those things. And, of course, that has calmed down since . . . . It's different. It's very different. But it's too quiet, for me, right now. I have one Filipino friend down the block. She's eight years older than I am. She thinks she's getting old. Her culture is just so different than mine. I don't feel that bosom buddy feeling. I have two white lady friends. And I feel more comfortable with them because it reminds me of when I was in high school or something, or college with my . . . being friends. (pause) You can tell it's quiet here . . . . There's three families on this block that have lived here since '71. The other ones are working and we don't have the small children running around back and forth to the different houses. It is a little difficult to communicate. My husband knows a few words in

Vietnamese. And then the people down the block that have lived here since '71, they're Hispanic. I think he's getting very sick . . . . But it's funny that every culture has a different high holiday. When we're having ours . . . now, two doors down, they celebrate Easter, too, and we celebrated Easter. And we both had parties. So there were a lot of cars around. But, of course, next door, the Vietnamese family, they don't celebrate Easter . . . . So everybody's not celebrating the same holidays all the time. And then the fireworks go off on Chinese New Year and they go off on Fourth of July (laughs) . . . . And not everybody gets the [newspaper], of course, because they don't speak English. And the man next door, he gets the Vietnamese paper. So I don't know if he's reading about San Jose or about his own country.

If face-to-face interactions beef up a sense of community (Putnam 2000; Putnam 2007), and newspapers are a key mechanism for creating a remotely shared experience central to larger "imagined community" (Anderson 1991), then Nancy's comments reflect a view that there has been a decline on both fronts. Chloe Campbell, a retired, fifty-eight-year-old white social worker and self-described political conservative in Berryessa, was very clear about her uneasiness with the settlement of Asian immigrants in her neighborhood. Her own discomfort, combined with her sense of a similar sentiment coming from her neighbors, is a recipe for social isolation (Parigi and Henson II 2014). As Chloe put it,

> I've just been here for so long. When we moved in here it was mainly Caucasian and Hispanic in this neighborhood. Then, I guess it was the seventies and really the eighties when all the Asians started moving in. Now, to the point where wow, even grocery stores, or these shopping centers used to be American and they're slowly being Asian, Asian, Asian. So we've seen that over the years. We don't like it. But we've seen it and we deal with and it's fine. The only thing I didn't like about the Asian culture is that they stay to themselves. You don't really know the neighbors around here, mainly because . . . I did know one lady and I went to her door one day. She had a little one and she started crying. And I said, "Oh, I'm sorry." And she said, "No. They just don't like white people."
>
> Q: How did you respond?
>
> R: I said, "Oh." I mean, what are you going to say? I said, "Okay." And a lot of . . . she explained it. She said the grandparents are usually the babysitters so that they don't see white people. So when they see one they cry when they're little. So I said, "Whatever."

There was little question among the people we interviewed in Cupertino and Berryessa that immigration-driven diversity, and the resulting ethnic boundaries, were contributing to a diminished sense of cohesion. But it is important to note that these perceptions were part of a larger ambivalence on the part of respondents about the effects of immigration-driven change. As noted in chapter 1, respondents also got to know many of their immigrant-origin neighbors well, and these connections were a primary means by which respondents became familiar with the immigrant experience. And, as the findings I report later in this chapter make clear, respondents readily form connections with immigrant-origin neighbors especially when these neighbors speak English and have lived in the neighborhood for a long time.

It may very well be the case that the sense of disconnectedness that Cupertino and Berryessa respondents articulated would be found in any middle- or upper-middle-class community, regardless of ethnic and national origin mix (Weis, Cipollone, and Jenkins 2014). As middle- and upper-middle-class parents of all ethnic and national origins work longer hours and shuttle their children to and from countless activities, there is often less time for community building outside the family (Putnam 2000). Respondents' perceptions of what was happening in their local communities might reflect these larger trends. But when asked to account for the diminished sense of cohesion in their communities, respondents of all ethnic backgrounds in these Asian-majority locales pointed to the heightened sense of ethnic difference that results from immigration as a primary cause, even if it was not the only cause.

Ethnic Boundaries in East Palo Alto

Interviews with African Americans in East Palo Alto revealed a strikingly similar view of the immigration's effect on community cohesion. East Palo Alto differs significantly from Cupertino and Berryessa in that the city's historic black ethnic identity is central to how respondents see ethnic boundaries and their impact on community identity. While the visibility of whiteness is relatively new in Cupertino and Berryessa, East Palo Alto's communal identity was built around blackness long before the arrival of a large immigrant population. Respondents' sense, described in the last chapter, that black material and symbolic prominence was on the decline also gave rise to their views regarding diminished community cohesion. While the status of Cupertino and Berryessa as formerly white-majority locales was the unstated demographic and cultural backdrop against which immigration-driven changes came into relief, East Palo Alto's historical and explicit status as Silicon Valley's main black community informed respondents' views of the current state of community solidarity. For all of its struggles with drugs and crime, East Palo Alto residents said that a shared ethnic identity and class status had bonded its residents in powerful ways. Arnold McFadden, a thirty-nine-year-old mechanic, pointed to ethnic boundaries as the source of diminished neighborhood solidarity in much the same way that Cupertino and Berryessa respondents had:

> The neighbors back then seemed to interact a lot more. I think that's primarily because we were of the same race. Now with the change, with the shift and the Latinos being the greater percentage, there's not as much interaction between the neighbors.
>
> Q: Why do you think that is?
>
> A: Just different ethnic backgrounds. If you're of the same ethnicity I think you have more to share, more of a chance to interact when you have the same nationality.

Arnold's comments reflect what we heard again and again from East Palo Alto respondents: according to the city's African Americans, three decades of immigrant settlement has had tangible consequences on community cohesion. In interview after interview, they reported that the city's black population had once served as a network of "fictive kin" (Stack 1997 [1970]) that watched out for the well-being of its members. With the economic and population changes that have come to the city, however, that network had fractured. Melanie Davis, an unemployed twenty-nine-year-old, summarized this view:

> At one point [East Palo Alto] used to be tight knit, I would want to say, but now, no, not at all . . . . Like when I was younger, I used to stay in the Gardens [area of the city], to where everybody in the Gardens knew me, knew my mom. So I couldn't go anywhere or do anything crazy because somebody knew me or somebody would get me and then my mom would get me. . . .

But we all started the same, everybody's parents were the same. I don't know what happened! Within a ten- or fifteen-year bracket it just flipped . . . . To me, basically, a lot of Hispanics came. I'm not going to say that it was a bad thing, but that just flushed EPA. EPA is not the same because my whole street was predominantly all black. My whole area was predominantly all black. If you go to my street now, it's maybe two houses that were those people that were there. So it's all Hispanics. That whole area looks different . . . . All the black people are leaving that was here. It's now Hispanics, Tongan, and Samoans. That's EPA now. That's how it's new because there's no black people here any more.

Even if East Palo Alto's respondents were clear in their view that immigrant settlement had hurt community cohesion, that view was often couched in a set of ambivalent opinions about immigration more generally. Their ambivalence seesawed between empathy for immigrants and their children—empathy that came from relationships with immigrants and second-generation individuals—and a perceived hard truth about the negative impact of immigration on black jobs, unity, and culture. Take, for example, the comments of J. C. Marks, a black, forty-eight-year-old unemployed home health aide who, in one short response to my question about what East Palo Alto would be like without immigrants, touted both the virtues of diversity and the division that it brings about:

It would be beautiful [if there were no more immigration]. It would be peaceful. It would be more togetherness. On one hand. And on the other hand, we would miss a lot of learning experience that we have learned how to get along. I didn't know how to speak no Spanish before my neighbors moved. I know certain words and stuff. I can understand a little bit, now . . . . *Mi amor.* (both laugh) *Buenos dias. Mucha a la gusta*—"I like something very much." If you speaking to me, I can pretty much understand you and answer you. I know a little bit of it. I know my name. I can count a little bit. I can greet you. I can say certain foods. And that's another thing that I learned, how to cook some Spanish food, just by watching some of my neighbor's ingredients that he uses and telling me and stuff. But, if this place was never immigrated, to me in one hand, it worked out. On a positive side, as far as everything mixed together, it can be a plus. But then it also brought the negativity, too . . . . Different nationalities not accepting the other different nationalities. The overflow of different nationalities coming in here—we call it taking over. I think if we had held our ground and stayed here and stood up and paid our bills, they would have never been able to come in and get what you got. I think EPA, if they hadn't immigrated people over here, I think it would still—this is a honest answer—it would still be the way it's like, right now. Because we are our worst enemies. That's the honest . . . I can't lie. That the honest answer. Because, the moral of the story that we talking about, I didn't blame it on anybody else. This is us. And that's real talk.

J. C.'s comments echoed the kind of self-flagellating assessment of black success and failure outlined in the previous chapter, linking the "takeover" as both cause and symptom of blacks' perceived inability to have "held [our] ground" (also see Lee 2002). But regardless of where he and other East Palo Alto respondents placed responsibility, they saw a decline in community cohesion as a result of immigration.

East Palo Alto interviewees also cited more material costs associated with immigration-driven diversity. As noted in the previous chapter, respondents believed Latinos working in service agencies favored their ethnic kin over African Americans, and many saw the same sort of co-ethnic nepotism in the job market. Economic research has focused primarily on the degree of competition between native-born African Americans and immigrants for blue-collar jobs (Borjas 1999; Card 2005). But respondents pointed to service-sector jobs as the competitive prize in the labor market that they navigated. Because of the large Spanish-speaking population, employers prefer workers who can communicate with both Spanish- and English-speaking clientele, leading to a widespread perception that Spanish-speakers thus "hire their own" (Linton and Jiménez 2009). The demand for bilingual workers in East Palo Alto and its environs escalated with a massive economic redevelopment program started in the late 1990s that included razing the city's long-shuttered high school and "Whiskey Gulch," the city's struggling commercial strip, and replacing them with a major retail shopping center and a hotel and business park. Tenants of the shopping center agreed to a policy of "first-source" hiring, whereby East Palo Alto residents had first dibs at jobs there. By most accounts, the employers complied. Yet black respondents who had recently been hunting for a job believed that Latino co-ethnic networks had blunted their chances for success in finding work.

It is important to note that East Palo Alto respondents' articulations about ethnic boundaries revealed more ambivalence than animosity.

Ethnic boundaries were real, in their view, and had real consequences for black respondents. But bonds of affection and sympathy often softened these boundaries. By virtue of a shared class position, black respondents often worked in close contact with large numbers of Latino immigrants, forming close friendships that flowed across ethnic lines. These friendships offered respondents insight into the struggles of the immigrant experience like those presented in chapter 1. African American job seekers in East Palo Alto weighed what they knew from this contact against what they saw as the competitive reality that characterized their job hunt. Jaime Jefferson, a forty-three-year-old black chef from East Palo Alto, was a case in point. Jaime had extensive contact with immigrant and second-generation Latinos. He was conversant in Spanish, a skill that he picked up during years of working alongside Latinos in various area restaurant kitchens. His son was dating a second-generation Mexican American woman. Because he worked in restaurants, he had intimate and frequent contact with unauthorized Latino immigrants. He thus spoke empathetically to me about them to such a degree that he teared up during the interview. Still, as a single father, Jaime's need to find work made him more ambivalent about the co-ethnic networks through which Latinos get jobs. To illustrate, he relayed his recent experience trying to get a job in the kitchen of a recently opened restaurant in East Palo Alto's only large shopping center:

> I do culinary skills, so I knew I was overqualified but I knew I was good for the job, too . . . . So then [the manager] goes, "Oh yeah. I've got everybody I need already. I have my staff. I'm already . . . " And I'm like, "This is an open interview. How do you have the people already?" So I was like, "I put an application in awhile back and I'm just curious. I never got a call. Was there a reason? Or what was the . . . " And he goes, "Like I just told you, I pretty much got everybody I need . . . . " He was Mexican . . . . Every single person in there was Mexican that he was interviewing . . . . And that made me so angry because I knew for a fact that this guy had called 'cause Mexicans, Latins . . . . they really look out for each other. They do. But sometimes they do it to the point to where it's almost like they're creating their own little clique or their own . . . . And I was like, "Wow. He didn't even consider the application, just by my name alone, I'm sure."

Jaime's ambivalence was typical of what we heard in interviews with East Palo Alto residents. As I discuss more fully in the next section, in all three locales we studied, ethnic boundaries were imperfect markers of division and unity. But when it came to competition for scarce resources, ethnic boundaries were nonetheless meaningful, even to people like Jaime who had significant and close contact with immigrant-origin Latinos.

If co-ethnic networks were a first line of exclusion, black respondents saw the demands of a twenty-first-century workplace as a second obstacle between them and their job prospects. Those who were employed in positions that required significant interaction with clients, customers, or medical patients reported that Spanish fluency was a near requirement for getting a job and moving up. A community organizer and longtime participant in efforts to make East Palo Alto more cohesive spoke forcefully about the effect of language on the employment prospects of young black males in particular, going so far as to compare the detrimental effect of English monolingualism to having a criminal record:

> Everything has to be bilingual. It's a prerequisite. So language and cultural differences have had big economic implications on us . . . . One of the things that we've always dealt with in this community like no other is the box on the employment application that says, "Have you ever been arrested?" That box—"Have you ever had a misdemeanor conviction? Have you ever had a felony conviction?" So by checking the box, our community has been severely impacted by that in employment opportunities. You see that, a potential employer looks at it, goes over here (pointing away from the table where we sat). My application doesn't have those areas checked, I might get an opportunity for an interview. Now, the applications for many of the opportunities in the community are bilingual. Can you check that box? What languages do you speak fluently? Can you check that box? And it has the same implications as the incarceration cases and the involvement with the jails. It's an eliminator.

The "mark of a criminal record" (Pager 2003) squelches job prospects for black men, but respondents in East Palo Alto saw monolingualism as potentially just as damaging. Shandra Gallegos, a twenty-six-year-old dental assistant of African American and Mexican descent, described division at work arising from a perception that her employer preferred to promote Spanish-speakers, even over otherwise more qualified workers:

> Well, they prefer for [people moving up] to speak Spanish. And now I think there are some positions that require them to speak Spanish. And some of

us, including myself, feel like that's unfair. Because I think that we're more than qualified to do the job, and now, all of a sudden, we can't move up because we don't speak Spanish. I think that's unfair . . . . They'll ask me if I speak Spanish. Or they'll just let me know because they know that I don't speak Spanish, "Well, we really prefer someone who speaks Spanish." And then it's crazy because in our [office], the people who went to go take the positions couldn't handle it—couldn't handle the position. And then it's like, here we are. One of my other coworkers, she's Palestinian, and we're like the top two people in the [office] who knows everything, who knows all the positions in the [office], and here we are, stuck. We can't move up because this position requires Spanish. And then, when they get in that position, they can't handle it, but we can. So why can't we move up? Because we can't speak Spanish.

These same respondents qualified their descriptions of the negative consequences of monolingualism on their job prospects by asserting that the numerical-majority status of Latinos justifiably makes Spanish-English bilingualism an asset in the labor market. Nonetheless, their sense that Latinos dominated in the job sectors they would like to occupy heightened their perception of ethnic division. When it came to job competition, respondents linked language and ethnicity, seeing the ability to speak Spanish as a component of ethnic identity and thus an ethnic boundary that marked their exclusion.

PARSING BOUNDARIES IN A CONTEXT OF SUPER DIVERSITY

The portrait emerging from the interviews thus far has been consistent with an extensive body of social science research showing an inverse relationship between social cohesion and diversity (Putnam 2007). But to read respondents' views of the symbolic boundaries exclusively in ethnic terms misses important aspects of how they differentiated insiders and outsiders. Ethnic difference was, by far, the most obvious component of diversity introduced by immigration. But in Silicon Valley that diversity has now been around for a long time. The long-settled immigrants and their second-generation children, rather than more recent arrivals, now define the immigrant population in Silicon Valley and other metro areas (Myers and

Pitkin 2009). According to American Community Survey data (2008–2012 estimates), nearly two in five of Santa Clara County's immigrants and nearly half of California's immigrant population arrived in the United States before 1990; more than two in three in Santa Clara County and almost three in four statewide arrived before 2000. Not only is there a substantial long-settled immigrant population, the children of these immigrants, having been born and raised in the United States, are even more firmly planted in American society. The fact that immigrants have been around for a long time, and that there is a substantial U.S.-born second-generation population, creates diversity *within* ethnic groups—in this case, Latinos and Asians—along lines of language, legal status, romantic partner choice, neighborhood residence, and socioeconomic status, among other traits (Alba, Jiménez, and Marrow 2014; Jiménez, Fields, and Schachter 2015; Crul 2016).

That internal diversity powerfully shapes how people distinguish insiders from outsiders. As other research shows, internal diversity raises questions among group members about what it takes to be regarded as an authentic group member (Jackson 2005; Jiménez 2010a; Pattillo 2007; Fields 2016). But intragroup difference also makes ethnic boundaries less significant as a means of dividing insiders from outsiders. German sociologist Georg Simmel (1922 [1955]) noted long ago that individuals in complex societies have multiple group memberships—race, class, gender, neighborhood, profession, etc.—that constitute a "web of affiliations." Later, sociologist Peter Blau and his colleagues (Blau, Beeker, and Fitzpatrick 1984; Blau and Schwartz 1984) expanded this idea to examine how "crosscutting social circles" (Blau and Schwarz 1984) affect group relations. Crosscutting social circles are abundant when groups thought to be distinctive in terms of, say, ethnicity, are similar in multiple other ways, like their neighborhood residence, social class, language, or profession. When there are multiple crosscutting social circles, interethnic-group contact is more abundant, and interethnic-group relations are thus more harmonious (Allport 1954). Much as these insights would predict, when respondents in our three study locales discussed their interpersonal interactions with immigrants and second-generation immigrants, they described boundaries between "insider" and "outsider" that were connected with ethnic boundaries but that also worked independently of them. In particular, linguistic ability and neighborhood residential tenure emerged as important symbolic boundaries that cut across ethnic and racial boundaries, shaping respondents' everyday interpersonal encounters and their perceptions of what unites and divides.

Speaking to and Speaking Past Each Other: Linguistic Boundaries

Shared language is a glue that is necessary, though not sufficient, for creating a sense of peoplehood (Gellner 1983; Weber 1976). Immigrants flock to neighborhoods and jobs where a co-ethnic population provides access to valuable resources and to a cultural home that includes a shared language (Portes and Bach 1985). To the English-monolingual native-born population, however, immigrants' establishment of a cultural home can appear as a cultural invasion that divides populations into linguistic camps (Schildkraut 2005).[3] In the United States, the presence of large, non-English-speaking immigrant populations from Latin American and Asia can feed perceptions that Asians and Latinos are not just failing to learn English, but that they do not *want* to learn it (Schildkraut 2005). These perceptions persist despite social science showing definitive evidence that today's immigrants are learning English faster than in the past, and that U.S.-born generations overwhelmingly speak English (Alba 2005; Fischer and Hout 2006; Rumbaut, Massey, and Bean 2006; National Academies of Sciences, Engineering, and Medicine 2015).

With the growth of second- and even third-generation populations of Latinos and Asians, the divide between English and non-English speakers within these groups can mark important *intra*group boundaries (Alba, Jiménez, and Marrow 2014; Jiménez 2010a; Tuan 1998). While these intragroup linguistic boundaries can create contention about ethnic authenticity within a particular group (Erdmans 1998; Jiménez 2008; Jiménez 2010a), they also define the boundaries that established respondents in Silicon Valley saw when making sense of the groups around them. Regardless of ethnic origin and class status, and across all three study sites, respondents in East Palo Alto, Cupertino, and Berryessa offered accounts of interpersonal interactions in which the ability to speak English, often more than ethnic origin, defined the relevant symbolic boundary between insider and outsider.

The importance of language as a symbolic boundary came into focus when respondents spoke about their interactions with the people who live near them. They were especially likely to cite the role of language in shaping the quantity and quality of interpersonal interactions with neighbors. Respondents across all three study locations sang the praises of bilingualism. But at the same time the interviews captured a resounding chorus of dismay over linguistic division. These linguistic boundaries did not overlap neatly with ethnic boundaries: linguistic boundaries cut through ethnic groups, leaving those who spoke English on one side, and those who did not on the other. This division were relevant in many facets of life, ranging from public interactions with strangers to contact in cooperative settings like schools, workplaces, and public offices. Language appeared particularly divisive to respondents in settings where cohesion was expected. Celebratory events like birthday parties, backyard cookouts, and dinner parties usually have a spirit of inclusiveness, but respondents recalled instances in which non-English-language use extinguished their enthusiasm for these events. Interviewees from East Palo Alto reported attending family parties, like *quinceañeras* celebrated by Latino friends and neighbors to whom they are close, and finding that pervasive use of Spanish often made them feel like partial outsiders. Consider the experience of Derek Jackson, a fifty-six-year-old factory worker. His sons were close friends with several second-generation Mexican Americans. In fact, Derek's living room was lined with school dance photos featuring his sons with these very friends, and often with Mexican American dates. Derek described an occasion when one of his son's friends invited Derek to a barbeque:

> OK, like the blacks, you go over and barbecue, where everybody like to barbecue and sit around and talk mess, in a fun way. Now, I went to a Latino barbecue, and everybody was talking their language, so I felt very uncomfortable, even though I was invited. It was fun, because I was there and I learned something. They want to have fun just as well as I do. I might not have understood what everybody was saying, but the person who invited me, we talked. But I wanted to get to know everybody else. This person introduced me to his family: "This is my family. This is this person." And they're, "How you doing? How you doing?" But as far as the language barrier, that was the only thing that kind of got me down, 'cause I didn't know what they were saying, most of them.

While they recognized that ethnic origin and language use are related, respondents like Derek distinguished between the two when articulating the boundaries most relevant in interpersonal interactions. Indeed, as Derek explained, he had an easy time conversing with the English-speaking Latinos who invited him but had a more difficult time with the monolingual Spanish attendees.

Language can also limit the potential unifying effects of endeavors that scholars might regard as social-capital-building exercises, like volunteering in children's schools, joining a club or organization, or holding a block party (Putnam 2000). In Cupertino and Berryessa, where parents tended to be heavily involved in their children's education, respondents saw linguistic boundaries as far more stifling to participation than ethnic difference. Melanie Peterson, a fifty-one-year-old white nutritionist in Cupertino, frequently volunteered at her sons' schools, as did some immigrant parents. Melanie noted that linguistic differences made it difficult for this engagement to be an effective means of community building:

> You know, it is hard because you can't necessarily get your point across. It's hard when you try to communicate on some level where you're trying to explain how you're going to do something. I was in charge last year of a casino for our grad night and I tried to explain to people how to deal blackjack. OK, well it's hard to explain to people that don't speak English very well how to deal blackjack. It's kind of hard to explain to people that do speak English very well! (laughing) But that's a whole other problem altogether! So there's always a little bit of a frustration level if you don't feel like people are understanding what you're saying and you're not sure how to help them understand it. Then I think it's hard. I think that's one of the reasons that there's a low volunteerism rate in that population, because again I think for them it's hard. Do you want to go be the treasurer of the PTA if you have to stand up in front of people and read a report? Or the president of the PTA if you'd have to stand up in front of people and read a report in English and you don't feel very comfortable reading in English? And I think a lot of times when you look at families who come here, they come here because the husband has a job. And oftentimes a wife doesn't work, might work but doesn't often work. And so [her] English isn't necessarily getting a lot better quickly because she's not in an environment where she's forced to use it on a daily basis.

Cupertino respondents also saw language as something that excluded them from informal networks. When Cupertino parents discussed their involvement in their children's lives, they showed typical expectations for the kind of network formation among parents that develops when children share the same daycare and schools (Small 2009)—and they saw immigrant-origin parents' use of a shared language, as part of a co-ethnic community, as a form of exclusion. Take, for example, the comments of Lori Brewer, the white, forty-year-old banker introduced in previous chapters. Like other respondents, Lori's views about the large immigrant settlement in Cupertino were ambivalent. She was sympathetic to the challenges that came with the immigrant experience, but she also expressed frustration that the dense co-ethnic networks and use of a foreign language that help immigrants adjust effectively excluded people like her. The following comments showcase her ambivalence:

> It's been a real learning experience for us. Every year there are less and less Americans going [to my children's school] and I'm actually pissed off about that because, to me, [native-born] people are being shallow. I mean I feel like they complain. I hear a lot of people complain about all these Indians and Asians here invading us. And they make negative comments about it. And I will admit, I've made those comments too because we get left out, we really do. I mean when they're in their own culture and they feel comfortable with each other, it's only natural they're going to hang together. They're not going to necessarily think, "Oh wait. And what about [Lori]? How's she feeling? Maybe we should invite her to come play with us or her kids." They're not thinking that. And they're not doing it maliciously; they're in their box. And so they're comfortable, they're in their comfort zone and I'm sure it must be hugely scary. I would be freaked out if I moved to China or India where people spoke a totally different language. And they teach English in school in China and India. So it's not like they don't understand how to speak the language. I get it. It makes sense. To go [to] some completely foreign land, scared to death, you don't know the area, you worry about crime, you worry about your kids and everything making friends, being comfortable. So it totally makes sense. So I've just had to be more assertive, which may not necessarily work with some people because then all of a sudden I'm this assertive woman in their face saying, "Let's play." But it's been challenging, it really has been. And there's been moments where I've felt lonely and left out and I feel like, "Why aren't my kids getting invited to birthday parties or whatever?"

Cupertino respondents underscored the importance of language to symbolic boundaries when they distinguished *between* the different Asian subgroups that predominate in the city. While respondents tended to homogenize these groups in discussing academic achievement, they disentangled them when explaining what makes different people sociable, for instance saying that South Asian Indians were generally more sociable than East Asians, partly because of the former's ease with English. For people like Lori, whose best friend was an Indian immigrant, the density of co-ethnic networks sometimes made it difficult to connect with newcomers of any national origin. These difficulties were only compounded when linguistic differences blocked off potential entry points, as was the case with East Asians. A teacher at one of the area high schools put it like this:

> Of the Asian kids, there are very few who don't [speak English]. We just don't have a lot of kids who are Asian and whose parents were born here. We just really don't. And so apart from the very occasional Latino that we get and the white kids, that's the population. So they have that other variable that separates them. There is a difference in the way the kids group themselves between the kids who have been here long enough so that they're completely bilingual and they're totally comfortable. I think the measure is how well they speak English. The ones who are more recent tend to hang out together and you'll hear them speaking Chinese around campus. I would say the Indian kids—I don't perceive that I have as many Indian kids with second language issues when I read their papers.

As this teacher suggests, language is an important marker of difference among the groups included in the broad category of "Asian."

Across the Valley in Berryessa, respondents viewed the situation in much the same way. Take Clint Honda, a sixty-two-year-old retired engineer of Japanese descent in Berryessa. A war veteran with a gritty demeanor, Clint had close friends from a range of backgrounds, suggesting that ethnic origin was hardly a barrier to how he chose companions. As he explained, language was the primary hurdle to forming friendships with people closer to the immigrant generation:

> I believe that when just about any other ethnic group might come in, a new immigrant into this country, I would think it's going to be natural to gravitate to your own kind, so to speak, 'cause you feel comfortable. But once you've lived here awhile, and hopefully tried to assimilate, then you should

feel comfortable enough to start to expand your socialization process out-side of your own little ethnic group and make new friends of other nationali-ties . . . . Generally speaking—I'm thinking of [nationals]—Chinese nationals, Vietnamese, East Indians—this is going by greater population—Filipinos, Mexicans. (laughs) . . . . OK, whereas myself, I go to a neighbor-hood bar after dinner on Friday, Saturday, after dinner I'll go have a few beers. I'm sitting with friends that are Mexicans, a couple blacks . . . . And there might be a young Vietnamese guy that shows up now and then. But the point is, we're together. We're laughing and joking and talking to each other. We're mixing. We're not a new immigrant group . . . . Whether it's Chinese, Vietnamese, or East Indians . . . . when they socialize, they stay amongst their own nationality, I presume because of the comfort zone that . . . And to me that stems from insecurity. We all have insecurities to varying degrees. But I presume for various degrees of insecurity that they just want to stay together and that's their comfort zone. But not really mingle with other nationalities outside of their comfortable. They can speak their own language. The have their own culture here in the U.S., in this country here. But like I say, my grandparents, when they came here, they didn't speak any English. But they learned to speak English 'cause they wanted to assimilate. And they wanted their children, which would be my parents, to assimilate as quickly as possible into the American culture. So why can't they?

Clint's comments were more openly critical of immigrants' level of assimilation—which he associated with speaking English—than most other respondents' were. But the distinction he identified between his Mexican-origin and Vietnamese-origin friends on the one hand and immigrant-origin Asians on the other has more to do with the cohesive power of language than the dividing force of ethnic origin. Regine Cooper, a forty-two-year-old black cosmetologist from East Palo Alto, similarly explained how linguistic bound-aries defined the differences within her friends' families:

And not learning how to speak the language—I have friends whose parents still don't know how to speak English. They've been here ten, fifteen, twenty years. I've got a neighbor across the street from me. She's been here since I was at least nine. And she doesn't know how to speak English. I think it cuts people off from a lot of the opportunities they could have here for being stubborn or not.

Regine's wide experience interacting with Latinos precluded her from painting all Latinos with the same brush. Instead, she recognized significant linguistic differences among Latinos, and that those differences determined the formation of networks that reached across the black ethnic boundary. For most respondents, but especially for the young people we interviewed, the idea of clear-cut ethnic groupings appeared out of step with their reality. Growing up amid the multiple kinds of diversity introduced by immigration had forced them to grapple with a set of groups defined only in part by ethnic origin. Consider the case of Taylor Hopkins, a white nineteen-year-old college student. Taylor's boyfriend had Asian ancestry (his family was from Latin America, but was of Asian origin), and her best friend was an established-population woman of Taiwanese and Chinese ancestry, who spoke only English. Taylor went through a litany of boundaries that obtained in Cupertino, ultimately settling on linguistic boundaries as the clearest marker of group distinctions:

> I think that it would be much easier to communicate with everyone [if there were no immigrants] because everyone would basically be the same. I think there would be a lot less division among the people so that would be kind of nice in a sense.
>
> Q: What kind of division do you see?
>
> R: Division by language, division by the cliques that races form, division by status, people that think they're better or less than other people. I think it would just flow a little bit easier. Not better necessarily, just easier . . . .
> I think that a lot of the Persians are very rich, or that's what I perceive them to be. In terms of attitude I don't see much. I think some Asians have this elitist attitude too, either in school because they're incredibly intelligent, or outside of school because like when people don't understand them they get frustrated and they think that we should understand them even though . . . .
> I think sometimes by Asians, the white people are looked down upon. But sometimes they're not. Not as much as division in status as there is language and culture.

Ryan Jordan, a recent college graduate from Berryessa introduced in the previous chapter, also cited linguistic distinctions as the most obvious distinction between the native- and foreign-born. Having grown up in Berryessa with its large Asian-origin populations, Ryan saw the differences among people of Asian origin, including linguistic differences, as more than academic: they determined his feelings of closeness to the people around him. He offered recent experiences as a student at a University of California campus to illustrate:

> I guess the two main friends I made on that [dorm] floor were white . . . . We ended up living together in a house with one other person from our floor who is from Fremont, [Mike]. He's Asian American, but his family's been here a long time. And then another guy, [Ray], who's white . . . . if someone's born and raised in California, it's pretty easy to relate to them even no matter how—not always no matter how their family raised them, but just living in California, having that shaped [a] shared experience makes it easier to be friends with than someone who comes over at a later age. It's really mainly because of language . . . . [Someone was] doing a survey for their Asian American studies class. . . . I asked them, "Are you asking about Asian students who come here, or do you mean Asian American in terms of having emigrated here, or do you mean Asian American in terms of having an Asian background somewhere in your family history, but you've been here for generations?" 'Cause it's one thing I didn't have a clear understanding of, who is Asian American and who's Asian? In my mind, if you were born here you're American but also you are Asian American. Some people would think of them as just Asian. But I think of anybody who's here, now, as American.

As chapter 1 highlights, when established individuals have frequent contact with immigrant-origin individuals, they become more familiar with the contours of the immigrant-origin experience. Ryan's comments illustrate the way that such familiarity can include a nuanced view of the attributes that characterize diversity within ethnic groups, especially when components of that diversity, like language, allow non-ethnic-group members, like Ryan, to find commonality.

Linguistic differences were sometimes an elusive and situational marker of intergroup boundaries, especially for the youngest respondents. Growing up in a context of mass immigrant settlement, these respondents lacked a historical frame of reference to a time when immigrants were fewer in number. Having grown up alongside first- and second-generation newcomers, they readily recognized internal differences at work in other ethnic groups. This recognition informed their conception of symbolic boundaries. Chanita Jones, a seventeen-year-old black high school student from East Palo Alto, was active in her school's cheerleading squad. Her two best friends were also cheerleaders. One was a Mexican immigrant who had come to the United States at a young age; the other was

Mexican/black biracial. But when her friends used Spanish to communicate with one another, linguistic boundaries became a defining obstacle to intergroup interaction:

> Because most people [at school] seem to be closer to their own race, especially not trying to be racist, but Mexicans. Because you know they like to talk their native language and they like to talk Spanish and for you to not be in that loop, it would be like ... especially when you're with her or him and then they're with their own friends of their racial background, it's kind of like weird. You feel like the oddball out because they're up there talking Spanish and you're like, "Ummmm, yeah ... " (confused tone) And I just ... feels weird. So I think most people I'm closest probably are going to be the same racial background.

Q: Do you remember a particular instance where a group of Mexican students were talking in Spanish and you felt ...

R: Oh heck yeah! All the time! I would just be talking to my Mexican friend and just out of nowhere a friend would come by and say something in Spanish and I'd just be like, "Uhhh what?" I don't know what they're talking about.

While linguistic boundaries can be a source of exclusion for the established population when there are many newcomers present, it is important to note that linguistic exclusion is undoubtedly a more powerful marker of exclusion for the newcomer population. English may not be the official language of the United States, but thirty-one states have declared English their official language, and bills are regularly introduced in the U.S. Congress to do the same at the federal level. While these laws and legislation are largely symbolic, the role that English plays as a source of exclusion for immigrants and the second generation is very real. Lacking the ability to speak English is, on its own, associated with a host of negative social and economic outcomes (Akresh and Frank 2011). As the next chapter will make clear, respondents endorsed the importance of English as a core feature of American national identity. Indeed, language was a dimension of assimilation where the direction of expected adaptation was abundantly clear: people who did not speak English needed to learn the language for maximum access to opportunities and institutions in the United States.

That view guided how the established population made sense of symbolic boundaries. In a context of heavy immigrant settlement that included many non-English speakers, linguistic differences became so important that they bisected ethnic boundaries to become one of the symbolic boundaries that really mattered.

Coming and Going: Neighborhood Residential Tenure

Ethnic boundaries were further complicated by the symbolic boundaries that respondents drew based on how long individuals had lived in their neighborhood. Silicon Valley is a place of mass immigrant settlement. But the immigrants are hardly newcomers. As stated earlier, well over one third of the region's immigrant population has been in the United States for more than two decades, and more than two thirds have been in the United States since before 2000. Having spent a long period in the United States, these immigrants settle into neighborhoods, often becoming homeowners and long-term residents of neighborhoods (Myers and Pitkin 2009). If language is an important symbolic boundary defined by a spe cific behavior, neighborhood tenure captures multiple kinds of attributes associated with immigrant assimilation. But respondents, either implicitly or explicitly, pointed to neighborhood tenure as an important marker defining insiders and outsiders, one that, like language, often cut across ethnic boundaries.

The importance of neighborhood tenure emerged prominently in the portion of the interviews in which respondents explained what makes someone an outsider. They often complained about neighborhood turnover and the seeming insularity of recently arrived immigrant households. In the process of offering these laments, respondents noted their connection to neighbors who had stayed put for a long time, including long-settled immigrants. While language was a key boundary for all respondents regardless of age, neighborhood tenure appeared as a concern among middle-aged and older homeowners because they had often lived in their respective homes for many years, if not decades. Karen Morse, a white seventy-one-year-old retired physical therapist, was a case in point. She had an unusually high level of engagement in her Berryessa neighborhood. Most weekday mornings she could be found roaming the streets near her home with a garbage bag and a long-arm grabber tool, plucking litter from the sidewalk and street. In addition to keeping the neighborhood clean, she was active on several citizen commissions sponsored by the city government. Her explanation of her relationship with her neighbors, including a woman from the Philippines and another from Vietnam, highlighted neighborhood tenure as an important symbolic boundary:

> If they're not home, we watch their house. There's not as much borrowing back and forth, I don't . . . in the old days you'd borrow something and then you'd give it back. Still, between [Van] and I, if we need something we borrow back and forth. I tutored her kids for a while. Now they're getting bigger and they don't need tutoring. And so it's pretty much just the immediate neighbor . . . . [My other neighbor, Maria,] they go back and forth to the Philippines and [Van] is from Vietnam. And her mom and I guess her brother, they live in Iowa. I'm not sure how long [Van] . . . they've lived here a long time. So she's been here a long time . . . . [Maria] has been here a long time too. She's raised up her two boys and now they're married. So that's an interesting question because that's like the relationship with these people who have been here a long time, so that we're closer than say the families that moved [in more recently].

Karen's view of long-residing neighbors found echoes in how East Palo Alto and Cupertino interviewees drew symbolic boundaries around neighborhood tenure.

Home ownership is a norm in Cupertino, where according to the 2010 US Census, 64 percent of units were owner-occupied. Consider the case of Ronda Hellman, a sixty-two-year-old, white homemaker in Cupertino. She and her husband were the original owners of the home that they had lived in for more than three decades. She was something of a matriarch in her neighborhood, often watching out for children who wandered into the street and alerting neighbors when there was suspicious activity in the neighborhood (a very rare occurrence in Cupertino). She stockpiled toys in her front room for the children in the neighborhood, but especially for the daughters of a Fijian immigrant of Indian ancestry for whom Ronda served a fictive "grandma." Her closest friend on the block was an Indian woman who had lived across the street for more than twenty years. The two organized block parties, attended family functions at their respective homes, and housesat for each other if one or the other was away for a few nights. Her neighbor from India was part of one of the few immigrant-headed households on the block that could claim significant tenure in the neighborhood.

My interview with Ronda, like those with other Cupertino residents, made it clear that having lived in the neighborhood for a long time was a significant factor in her feelings of isolation. As Ronda explained:

> Well there's only two of us who are original owners: [a family around the corner] and us. Most of these houses have turned over at least three times. And, generally speaking, when they turn over the second or third time, either Chinese have moved in or East Indian. And I have a lot of East Indian friends, I really like them. And my best friend was [later-generation] Chinese [American] up here (pointing up the block) . . . . And [their] daughter, [Jenny] . . . I used to go to their house after school because mom and dad worked. But anyway, [the Chinese American mother] was my best friend for years . . . . But the people that are here now just really don't have an interest in interacting with the neighbors. And as I said, it's fine. I've lived here so long I've got lots of friends. I don't need to do that. It's just that it's sad for me for the little kids because the kids [used to] have so much fun in this neighborhood, and consequently the adults did too. But it just has really changed.

Ronda's espousal of the virtues of diversity that punctuated the interview did not stand on principle alone. She and her husband had traveled throughout the world, and they looked for opportunities locally to enjoy the kaleidoscope of ethnically themed festivities that take place throughout Silicon Valley. Her response to my question about whether there was anything about ethnic diversity that she did not particularly like captured the importance of time in the United States and neighborhood tenure, apart from ethnic origin:

> I don't like the fact that it's not a community as such. It's not the community I'm used to. I don't know how you would change that either. As I said, [my best friend, who is Indian], we've done things together for twenty-three years. [Her daughters] see me on the street, it's "Hi" and I get a big hug. And they're twenty-six and twenty-three now. But it's just different. And she's very fond of my kids, especially my daughter. She thinks my daughter is wonderful.

Q: Why is it that you think some people are not as interactive?

A: Because they have so many of their own community and their own kind here and I think they're comfortable. And comfort just . . . they have enough things that I think are pushing them emotionally and economically that when they relax they want to really relax and maybe they don't relax around us as much or something.

As Ronda pointed out, the relationship she has with her friend and neighbor of twenty-three years was distinguished more by time in the neighborhood than by ethnic origin.

In most respects, neighborhood tenure emerged as an important basis for distinguishing between residential insiders and outsiders. However, the low class standing of most East Palo Alto residents intensified the differences between insiders and outsiders. The majority of residents rented (54 percent, according to 2010 U.S. Census data). Rent was expensive in the city in spite of rent control, and it was thus not uncommon for Latino immigrants to crowd into a single dwelling in order to reduce housing costs. Lingering over East Palo Alto's residential instability was a foreclosure crisis that reached its peak during the time we conducted fieldwork (LeVine 2014). Residential turnover, combined with the transiency that came with crowding in the single-family units, exacerbated a sense of neighborhood disunity, while also highlighting for respondents the importance of neighborhood tenure as a social boundary. East Palo Alto interviewees, all but one of whom were black, were far more likely to report close ties with black neighbors, but they also noted that Latino neighbors who had "been around forever" were central members of their neighborhood network. Take, for example, Molly Taylor, a fifty-four-year-old black warehouse worker. During our interview, Molly's next-door neighbor, a second-generation Mexican American woman, stopped by to bring Molly peaches from her tree. The visit sparked a conversation once the interview resumed about the changed demographics of her neighborhood, but also on Molly's closeness to her Mexican American neighbor:

> We've been here thirteen years. Oh, I've seen, since we've been here, the majority of Mexicans have moved in here . . . . Well, right in this little block, about six black families. The rest are Mexicans. Yeah. They're the ones coming over here buying all these houses. . . . But they do fix up the house. They do fix—not all of them, but—they fix up the house. . . . [My Mexican neighbors] were there when we moved here. So they've been there awhile, probably over twenty [years] . . . . But we get along good with my neighbors. We do. You should look out for your neighbors, each other, you really should. That's a good thing. When they're going on vacation they ask us to watch their house. And we do the same thing. Which is good. And every time they go . . . Christmas time, they always give you a Christmas gift. And we do the same. My mom, they do the [same gift exchange with another family] and

us. And we always give them a present, too, which is nice. They started doing this, so we . . . and they're nice people. They really are. We look out for each other.

The relationships that formed between long-time Latino residents and respondents went beyond neighborly niceties. As described earlier in the chapter, East Palo Alto respondent Jaime Jefferson saw his struggles to find work as a function of his exclusion from Mexican ethnic networks. However, while his job search was defined by ethnic boundaries, these took a back seat to other symbolic boundaries in his description of his relationships in his neighborhood. His comments about the nature of his connection to his Mexican-immigrant neighbors highlights the distinction between ethnic origin and residential tenure as markers of symbolic boundaries:

> I went to [my neighbor's] *quinceañera* . . . . We went over there and ate with the rest of them in their back yard. That's pretty much it. Well, there's a girl that stays—but I been knowing her all my life so wouldn't call her neighbor. She's more like family . . . . I have my Latin neighbors across street, they always come and bring me Latin dishes and stuff like that. And I can go swimming at their house anytime I want without asking. I pretty much know most of my neighbors and I have a general basic relationship with them, some of them a little closer than more [people] that been on the street just as long as I have. Last week [my Latin neighbors cooked] . . . some kind of salsa made with shrimp and it was delicious. It had cucumbers and everything in it. I forgot [the name]. But anyway, it was good—tamales, enchiladas. Their dad marinates chicken and he grills it. It's really good. Just the typical Latin dishes, though, the traditional ones that they bring me. I'm a cook, too. I barbecue. If I made baby-back ribs—their mom loves baby-back ribs. I make barbecue sauce. She's always like, "Did you make any barbecue sauce?"

In three locales as ethnically and socioeconomically disparate as East Palo Alto, Cupertino, and Berryessa, the similar level of importance respondents placed on neighborhood tenure when drawing symbolic boundaries might seem somewhat surprising. After all, social scientists interested in neighborhoods largely look to ethnic background as the defining frame through which to view unity and division, segregation and integration (Crowder, Hall, and Tolnay 2011; Massey and Denton 1993; South,

Crowder, and Chavez 2005). But the findings I report from Silicon Valley appear less surprising in light of research about how residents of other settings draw symbolic boundaries. Other ethnographic research shows that the newcomer/established-resident divide often trumps ethnic distinctions, much as it does in the three Silicon Valley locations we studied. Whether established residents were black and white and newcomers were black (Woldoff 2011), or established residents were native- and foreign-born, and newcomers were recently arrived immigrants (Horton 1995; Watson and Saha 2013; Wimmer 2004), living side-by-side for a long time facilitated solidarity, often regardless of ethnic background, especially when a newcomer population catalyzed that solidarity.

Of course, self-selection likely accounts for why individuals who have spent a long time in the neighborhood know each other and get along well (Schachter 2015). Individuals who do not particularly like a neighborhood, whether because of its changing demographics or for some other reason, may move out. Immigrant-origin families who are most socially integrated and economically successful are the very ones most likely to stick around. Much as self-selection is an inherent part of the international migration process, it is also a part of neighborhood dynamics (Feliciano 2006). That selection, however, did not factor into how the people we interviewed made sense of the lines that unite and divide in their neighborhoods. Their much more locally rooted perceptions instead came from the kinds of characteristics that allowed people to get along in daily life. Chief among those characteristics were language and neighborhood tenure.

CONCLUSION

The dizzying changes resulting from mass immigrant settlement centrally include ethnic change in places like Silicon Valley. In some ways, respondents' accounts of these changes, and of the symbolic boundaries that result, reflect the fears of scholars and pundits that ethnic difference may damage social cohesion. Cupertino and Berryessa interviewees tied a sense of diminished community to a distinctly immigrant-origin Asian approach to work and home life, which they saw as focusing an amped-up work ethic on academic and career advancement to the exclusion of community building. Respondents in East Palo Alto articulated a similar degree of community dissolution, but it differed in kind. Black respondents from East Palo Alto lamented that the heavy Latino presence diminished the sense of a distinctly black community. They saw their exclusion from immigrant ethnic networks that determine hiring, and the now-prized place of bilingualism, as an instantiation of ethnic boundaries.

However, ethnic boundaries, while significant, represent only one dimension of the multiple symbolic boundaries that immigration brings about. Many other kinds of immigration-related diversity factored into respondents' rendering of the symbolic boundaries that mattered to them (Hannah 2011; Horton 1995; Vertovec 2007; Watson and Saha 2013; Wimmer 2004). The long-term settlement of the immigrant population (Myers and Pitkin 2009) and the rise of the second generation have led to manifold diversity within ethnic groups. This within-group difference factored into how respondents conceptualized symbolic boundaries. In all three study locales, respondents explained how the ability to speak English and length of neighborhood residence were key symbolic boundaries that could cross ethnic distinctions in defining insiders and outsiders. Ethnic boundaries mattered, to be sure. But in places like Silicon Valley, these boundaries were only one among many kinds of symbolic boundaries that mattered.

This is not to say that growing differences among people within a given ethnic group are washing away ethnic differences between groups. Far from it. But these intragroup differences muddy the ways that individuals define insiders and outsiders in daily life. The view of established individuals suggests that the give-and-take character of relational assimilation involves more than ethnic boundaries. Immigration and newcomer assimilation contribute to the complexities of groups that occupy any social context. As characteristics like language, legal status, romantic partner choice, and residential locale become more differentiated among people of a particular ethnic origin, the web of crosscutting group memberships also grows more complex (Blau, Beeker, and Fitzpatrick 1984; Blau and Schwartz 1984). That is certainly the case in Silicon Valley, where ethnicity, English proficiency, and length of residence are important crosscutting characteristics, and where established individuals recognized the importance of the latter two kinds of group membership in their everyday interactions with newcomers. Such commonalities meant not just that newcomers and established individuals interacted more; those bases for interaction also became the bases upon which they drew symbolic boundaries. Indeed, the large population of newcomers whose ethnic ancestries differed from those of respondents' meant that respondents were almost forced to recognize symbolic boundaries that were not ethnic in nature in order to find community in the places they lived, worked, and played.

The intersecting nature of multiple symbolic boundaries also helps explain the coexistence of perceptions of competition (Blumer 1958) and cooperation (Allport 1954) in Silicon Valley and in the research on immigration more generally (Schachter 2016). Scholars often characterize the relationship between established and newcomer groups as one of either competition or cooperation. In Silicon Valley, accounts of group competition reinforcing ethnic boundaries emerged prominently from interviews. But so did accounts of cohesion across ethnic boundaries. While respondents prominently cited ethnic boundaries as markers of group division, their renditions of everyday contact revealed how the interplay of other, crosscutting symbolic boundaries can reduce the importance of ethnicity as a basis for competition. Perceptions of ethnic group boundaries were hardly absent from the scene. But respondents' sustained interpersonal interactions with newcomers highlighted how the diversity within groups, marked in Silicon Valley by language and neighborhood tenure, can be a basis for intergroup cooperation—and that this cooperation can coexist with a sense that members of other groups nonetheless represent competition.

The established population's participation in relational assimilation may thus involve comparisons that result in flexible perceptions about which boundaries are most important. If relational assimilation involves adjustment on the part of the established population, then making ethnic origin the sole determinant of group membership in a place as ethnically diverse as Silicon Valley could well place established individuals in a lonely spot. It would be hard for whites and blacks in particular to feel any connection to the people around them if ethnic differences were all that mattered. Emphasizing nonethnic categorical distinctions, like language and neighborhood tenure, may be a necessary adjustment to living a place where immigration introduces so much ethnic difference.

There is yet another kind of difference entailed in relational assimilation that reaches beyond the confines of Silicon Valley: notions of American national identity. How respondents made sense of what it means to be American in view of the large newcomer population around them is the topic of the next chapter.

5 Living Locally, Thinking Nationally

Along with the ambivalence that tinged how established-population inter-viewees made sense of living in a place so heavily characterized by immi-grants, respondents still believed that they lived in a special region. They saw Silicon Valley as the navel of the global technological industry—a region whose ethos leaned on disruption, innovation, and breaking (and rebreaking) the mold, more than on tradition and history. And they believed that Silicon Valley's special quality was amplified by its being in California, a state they saw as leading the rest of the country on several fronts. But for all their expressions of regional and state pride, their view of political inclusion and exclusion emanated not just from living in Silicon Valley or California, but also from being members of the American nation: a group of individuals united by a shared claim to political autonomy and a culture that captures the essence of their political peoplehood (Cornell and Hartmann 2006). As the previous chapters have shown, immigration overturns, stretches, and shifts respondents' notions of ethnic and racial identity, culture, and symbolic boundaries. This more local effect that relational assimilation has on individuals' notions of race and ethnicity parallels an effect on their ideas about the nation as a whole. Living amid so many newcomers virtually forced respondents to sort out what it means to be American. That sorting out was a central feature of their participation in the process of relational assimilation, and understanding it may also shed light on broader changes in conceptions of American national identity that have taken place in recent decades.

Respondents' sorting out of what it means to be American takes sociologist Christian Joppke's (1998) observation that immigration is a "challenge to the nation-state" and plays it out on an individual level. According to most academic accounts, the challenge that Joppke identified manifests in protests, acts of violence, legislation, and court cases (Haney-López 1996; HoSang 2010; Linton 2007; Newton 2000; Sánchez 1997), or in the voices of prominent individuals—politicians, political elites, leaders of social movements, et cetera (Joppke and Torpey 2013; Smith 1997). But focusing on "big events" and "loud people" misses how experiences with immigration may also directly challenge individuals' conceptions of the nation-state as they go about their daily lives. As sociologist Jon Fox and his colleagues (Fox and Miller-Idriss 2008; Fox and Jones 2013; also see Hobsbawm 1990) have pointed out, the nation "is not simply the product of macro-structural forces; it is simultaneously the practical accomplishment of ordinary people engaging in routine activities" (Fox and Miller-Idriss 2008: 537).[1] The individuals who make up the nation might draw on the legal and rhetorical framings provided by policies and prominent individuals to make sense of immigration's challenge to the nation-state (Calhoun 1997). But they do not necessarily draw on wholesale application of those framings: their individual experiences and perceptions of daily life are equally potent in shaping their views of American national identity.

That was certainly the case for the established Silicon Valley individuals we interviewed. Respondents showed striking similarities across all three study locations in how the presence of a large immigrant population stimulated both more restrictive and more open conceptions of what it means to be a member of the American nation. As they worked through the complex give and take that is relational assimilation, respondents explicitly evaluated both "soft," cultural components of membership in the American nation, and "hard," legal conceptions of membership. Where the soft notions were concerned, the outlines of national membership were mostly blurry with one critical exception: speaking English. Among the people we interviewed, from staunch assimilationists to ardent multiculturalists, speaking English stood as the preeminent symbol of Americanness. The presence of immigrants intensified that belief. Aside from speaking English, there were few other commonly held informal criteria for national belonging. In fact, interviewees were open to multiple ways of expressing an American identity, including those derived from an ethnic origin.

They were less clear about whether the formal, hard criteria of legal national membership should be equivalent to American identity. In a time of mass unauthorized immigration, they saw legal status as an important threshold for accessing the rights and privileges that come with formal political belonging. However, their personal connections with unauthorized immigrants or with individuals who had unauthorized parents led respondents to prioritize behavior over legal documentation in their conceptualizations of national belonging. Working hard, playing by the rules once in the United States, raising a family, and speaking English were criteria that interviewees believed ought to earn anyone a legal place in the nation. The way respondents articulated national identity indicates that immigration does indeed challenge the nation-state. But that challenge may come just as much from how the current members of the body politic adjust their ideas about the bounds of American identity as a result of their everyday contact with immigrants, as it does from the immigrants themselves.

"SOFT" AND "HARD" CITIZENSHIP

A look at any world map shows a globe divided into discrete nation-states. Citizenship is the formal status of belonging to a nation-state and comes with a set of rights and responsibilities. In liberal democracies that purport to protect individual rights, citizens can, for example, vote for their political leaders, access the welfare state, and receive state-sponsored protection from harm.[2] Citizenship comes with responsibilities too. Citizens are expected to protect the nation-state when called upon, pay taxes to fund the state's functions, and to abide by the laws of the land. While these rights and responsibilities constitute the "hard," legal side of the citizen-state relationship, there is also a "soft" component that has to do with the symbolic elements of membership, such as language, observance of certain holidays, and sometimes ethnicity and race. This softer side of citizenship tends to be enforced more by social norms than by legal codes, though the two can be mutually reinforcing. For example, not long ago attributes that today serve as informal criteria for membership, like race, formed the legal basis for inclusion and exclusion in the United States and other countries (FitzGerald and Cook-Martín 2014; Haney-López 1996). An overlap between soft and hard notions of citizenship still exists. Speaking English, as I will show, remains a central component of cultural conceptions of American identity, and at the same time English proficiency is also a hard requirement for gaining U.S. citizenship.[3] For respondents, however, the cultural importance of speaking English far outstripped its importance as a legal requirement for citizenship.

But focusing on the distant portrait of nation-states offered by a global map misses the important ways in which the individual members of a nation work out, in daily life, their own understanding of soft and hard notions of national membership (Fox and Miller-Idriss 2008). When migrants cross borders and settle in the receiving country, as millions have done in the United States, the process of transformation they undergo is not merely social, but political. Integration, as sociologist Roger Waldinger pointed out, involves the transformation of "foreigners into nationals" (2007). That transformation on the part of immigrant newcomers fundamentally implicates the established members of the nation, like the established population individuals we interviewed. They stand in judgment of who can be a national insider, and who ought to remain on the outside. But as the foreigners become nationals, they can transform the national character. That transformation is clear in the way that Silicon Valley respondents made sense of the nation in a context so heavily defined by immigrants.

The Language of Citizenship

If respondents perceived any particular challenge as paramount to national identity, it was language. The linguistic diversity that immigrants bring to Silicon Valley is palpable. According the American Community Survey, half of the foreign-born population in Santa Clara County, and more than one in five total residents, spoke English less than "very well" in 2011, and the Valley's residents collectively speak more than one hundred different languages. The mix of Spanish, Vietnamese, Mandarin, Tagalog, Korean, Tamil, and Hindi that respondents heard as they went about their lives amounted to linguistic white noise to their monolingual English aural sense. And yet for the people we interviewed, English was the only key in which it was possible to sing the national tune. Political psychologists have shown that national identity revolves around key symbols in which individuals are emotionally invested. Adherence to those symbols can form the basis for attitudes about policy such that any group that violates those symbols is viewed more negatively and their fitness to be members of the nation is questioned (Citrin and Sears 2014; Masuoka and Junn 2013; Schildkraut 2010; Sears 1993). Like Americans as a whole, the people we interviewed—regardless of age, ethnic and racial background, socioeconomic status, or city of residence—said that speaking English was the central symbol and behavior around which American identity revolves (see Schildkraut 2005).

Respondents articulated these views not only in response to questions that prompted them to "think nationally," but also independently, without any such prompting. When they referenced the need for immigrants to "assimilate," "Americanize," or "blend in," we followed up by asking them what that would entail in concrete terms. Almost invariably, the responses began and ended with speaking English. Consider, for example, John Robertson, a retired, sixty-three-year-old white electronics technician and proud political conservative from Berryessa. John was one of the few working-class white respondents we interviewed, and his view of the relationship between immigration and American identity squares with the sense of threat expressed by working-class whites in the United States and abroad (Gest 2016). John's sternly stated convictions fit with his towering stature and booming voice. After a long stint as a technician in the military during the Vietnam War, John spent the majority of his career working in the various electronic assembly plants in Silicon Valley. Among his former colleagues were many Vietnamese and Filipino immigrants, two groups that predominated in electronics assembly jobs (Pellow and Park 2002). His experience working alongside these immigrants, and living in a neighborhood where East Asian immigrants resided in large numbers, informed his view that being American and speaking English went hand-in-hand. For John, speaking English was more than a tool of communication; it signaled a commitment to being American that too many immigrants lacked:

> I think the sad thing is it seems to me so many people come here from wherever. But they don't seem to want to come to America to become an American. They want to take care of all the economic advantages one has to living in America. But when they come down to say—'cause the number one thing in my mind, and why I believe our nation became as great as it did— we decided long ago a common language would be a good thing. And I'm afraid I'm seeing that today because, again, I have a dog that I take for a walk. And as you walk down the street the elderly Asian population, much to their credit, seems to like to exercise. And they do it by going for walks. You can always nod your head and smile and wave, and you'll get an acknowledgment back. But don't ever try to have a conversation. And it isn't that they're being rude. They can't speak English. I can't speak whatever language they are. So you feel like, "This isn't good."

John's views align with survey research showing that people who describe themselves as American in the strongest of terms tend to have stricter ideas about the content of American identity (Theiss-Morse 2009). But to chalk up John's opinion to his strong American identity and political conservatism ignores the robust consensus among respondents, regardless of political orientation, that language plays a key role both in *being* American and *being in* the United States.

The full-throated emphasis that respondents placed on English language use as the core of American national identity was just as likely to come from staunch supporters of multiculturalism. The tenets of multiculturalism have become institutionalized in the United States. Diversity is celebrated, even if only superficially, by schools, corporations, religious congregations, retailers, and even major sports franchises (Berrey 2015; Dobbin 2009; Skrentny 2014). Nathan Glazer's observation that "We are all multiculturalists now" (1997) is an apt description of where respondents from all three study locales stood on issues of diversity. But even the most avid multiculturalists we interviewed thought it was possible to take linguistic diversity too far. Take, for example, Lynn Brown, a white fifty-one-year-old software developer from Berryessa, who was a supporter of diversity in both word and deed. Having grown up in a mostly white town in another state, Lynn could not imagine living in a homogenous place as an adult. She routinely hauled her daughters to local ethnic festivals and celebrations, and she reveled in the immense diversity that abounds in Silicon Valley. But like other multiculturalists we spoke to, she was hesitant to include linguistic difference as a wholly positive form of diversity. The following answer to a question about language and whether she would support an English-only law highlights how everyday experiences with people who spoke a language other than English led her and other multiculturalists to grapple with the importance of language:

> I really, really admire my friends who have held on to their traditions. I'm so jealous of anybody who can speak two languages, (laughs) any other language. I can't speak anything other than English. And I think it's great that these families try their best to hang on to their language. And I think it's important to hang on to your cultures as well. But I gotta admit that there have been times that I wish people would . . . I don't know. (sigh) While I'm thinking about it I'm like, "Even why do I even wish that?" An example I would give is that you can walk into a break room at [the high-tech company where I work] and you'll have your little group of Chinese people sitting and eating lunch speaking Chinese. You'll have your little group of Indian people sitting, eating their lunch, speaking Indian. And you go around, and at times I would like to just say, "Speak English." But then the other side of me says, "If I were from another country I would never want to forget the language." Especially the language, but also other things, the cultures too, and stuff . . . . Plus it's good for the country . . . . I think that's a good idea [to make English the official language]. I think, just like I said, that when people come here I think for them to lose their language would just be a crime. For us to not have a language to me is a crime, too. It's so much a part of who we are that I do believe that there should be an official language in the U.S., and that it should be English. It doesn't mean that I don't think people should learn other languages. And anybody who knows another language, I think they should do everything in their power to retain it. But I do believe that the schools should be teaching in English. But along the same lines, a lot of people are saying that kind of thing because they don't want to have to do ballots in six different languages, and they don't want to have to have English as a second language in the schools. They don't want to have to support these other languages. I don't agree with that. I believe we should have English as a second language in schools. I believe that ballots should be done in multiple languages. But I do feel like the

primary language, in schools especially, should be English. Anything that has to do with government, laws, laws should be written in English. Political speeches should be done in English. It should be the primary language of the country.

For all Lynn's ambivalence, the practical and symbolic value of English emerged clearly from her comments. So too did the value of English ring out in comments from respondents in East Palo Alto, who were often the most ardent supporters of multiculturalism. Recall that the city had been a hotbed of Afrocentrism in the 1960s and 1970s, and the spirit of that movement lived on in respondents' expressions of pride about living in such a diverse city. Still, East Palo Alto respondents' equation of being American with speaking English, and their frustration about people who did not speak English, pushed up against that sense of local pride. Felicia Brown, a black, thirty-year-old full-time student from East Palo Alto, worried about the effect of immigration on jobs and even connected her daughter's failing health to the immigrant influx. Even so, like other East Palo Alto respondents, she still saw the outlines of American culture as essentially inclusive of the traditions that immigrants brought with them. And on the issue of language, her beliefs about the importance of English to American identity were entirely typical:

> I think that the immigrants should adapt to American culture because we're not coming to them, they're coming to us. And we was here for how many years now and been doing the same thing? Now like you call 411, to ask one to hear Spanish, two to hear English. Why we do we have to do that now? It's like things are changing because we're trying to fit with them. But if they're immigrants why are we changing our lifestyle for them? So why don't you just make them American and teach them how to become an American basically. Make it easier on us Americans because that's who we are and that's where we came from. So for an immigrant to come over we've got to learn their language—I think that's really wrong.

In spite of the racial, class, and political differences among John, Lynn, and Felicia, all three came to the same conclusion as other respondents about the instrumental and symbolic importance of English to American identity. Moreover, they were not merely parroting the politically charged discourse spouted by politicians and activists (Smith 1997). Instead, they drew from personal experiences that illustrated to them the importance of English to being American.

The near-sacred position of English in American national identity became especially clear when respondents framed non-English languages as a threat to the position of U.S.-born individuals as "hosts" to immigrant "guests" in their midst. They adopted a model of language adjustment seemingly taken from the pages of straight-line assimilation theory, wherein immigrants and their descendants become more like their monolithic host society (Gordon 1964). Respondents said that their regular exposure to non-English speakers gave them the sense that this presumably natural order of assimilation had been turned on its head. Nothing made respondents feel more like outsiders than being unable to communicate because the other party did not speak English. Interviewees made sense of these situations by drawing on frames of national identity. For example, Joanne Lockhardt, a white, forty-six-year-old cosmetologist in Cupertino, described her experience growing up in a predominantly Mexican American neighborhood in San Jose, where most of her neighbors were U.S.-born. Joanne held up Mexican Americans as something of a "model minority" compared to the Asian Americans in her current neighborhood, because the former spoke English well and thus seemed socially warmer (Fiske et al. 2002). As she explained:

> I do worry that people won't want to become American. That they want to come here and have their own country here. That offends me. I don't know that it's a worry, it offends me. If you don't want to become American then stay in your own country.
>
> Q: What about it offends you?
>
> A: Because to me it ignores my right to have a home. You have a right to have a home. I have a right to have a home. And if your home is in India and then do all things that are Indian. If you're home is in the U.S., then certainly I think you should—and again this I can't divide what's my selfishness and what's reality. But then I think you should embrace the American culture. It offends me that you would water down my culture so that you can maintain what you left. That's just the reality. If you leave your home . . . and I'm not talking about within your own home. But if you leave your homeland, then leave it. Then come here, celebrate privately, like I grew up some people had their own private celebrations. But again it's the language. Embrace my language so that we still are one. I guess that's the other thing, so that we're one country.

For Joanne and other respondents, being "one" meant speaking English. The experience of feeling left out of contexts where a language other than English predominates is not at all uncommon in Silicon Valley. Interviewees did not see these experiences as instances of mere social exclusion, but rather as violations of a central tenet of the assimilation bargain that new-comers would adopt the language of the American people: English. They saw this linguistic threat as ever-present, popping up where they lived, worked, shopped, played, and worshipped. As Jamie Jefferson, from East Palo Alto, put it,

> My personal experience—very frustrating sometimes. I've gone to place and I'm like, . . . You go to certain restaurants, certain places—even like Target or somewhere—and you go and you talk to that person at the register, if they ring up—sometime you don't speak at all—but you might like, "Well, do you know where the . . . " And that person be like, "I'm sorry. Um . . . " And they don't really, literally understand what you're saying. And you're like, "You have a job. You're working. You're in America."

As in other respondents' accounts, such everyday encounters frustrated Jaime partly because they made communication difficult, complicating otherwise routine tasks. But even more, encounters like these were also everyday violations of what mattered most to being American. In his com-ment, Jaime implied that individuals should speak English not because they were in a particular region or state, but because they were "in America." Speaking English was not something that respondents saw as the exclusive domain of a particular ethnic group, but rather as emblem-atic of their position as Americans. Indeed, as others have shown, there is near unanimity in the view of Americans of all ethnic and racial back-grounds that English is essential to being American (Citrin and Sears 2014; Hutchings and Wong 2014; Schildkraut 2010).

American Identity as Linguistic Addition, Not Subtraction

Interpersonal experience also softened the edges of otherwise rigid beliefs about the relationship between English proficiency and American identity. If interviewees believed that speaking English and being American went hand in hand, they also believed that retaining a non-English language had tremendous value. As the previous quotes hint, respondents did not see the importance of English as zero-sum. Much as they viewed other dimensions of culture as potentially offering valuable additions to the larger American culture, they tried to strike a balance between what they believed was beneficial about multilingualism and the potential costs of having too much linguistic diversity. John Lockhardt, a forty-four-year-old white computer programmer from Cupertino (and husband of Joanne, whom I quoted earlier), offered comments that echoed his wife's ambivalence about legislation that would make English the official language:

> So I'm kind of torn when it comes to those kind of bills. And largely I fall onto the no side because I feel like it's not really going to fix anything. If you strip all the different languages out of official documents, you're not really encouraging anyone to learn English. You're just denying them services that they would normally have. So it's not going to solve anything. It's just going to make people's lives worse. But I do think that, on the other extreme, where people feel like there should be multiple languages for everything and we should bend over backwards to accommodate all these different cultures, that doesn't encourage the right thing, either. I tend to fall on the side of, when it comes to you show up in an emergency room, yeah, there should be different languages on everything. When you go to apply for city services, yeah, assuming, in fact, you are a citizen and you pay taxes and such, you're entitled to these things and OK, maybe your English is pretty poor, you should be able to fully understand what you're trying to do. And I think that's reasonable. I think there is a happy medium there somewhere. I tend to think that people who want to do English only, they're trying to turn that clock back fifty years, and you just can't do that.

Respondents tried to balance their belief in English as the American cultural core with a pragmatic view of the value of speaking more than one language, especially in a region so central to the global economy. Fred Nugent, a white, fifty-seven-year-old software engineer living in Cupertino, grew up near the U.S.-Mexico border, where immigration is a perennial issue. He was staunch in his belief that speaking English was central to living in the United States and being American. But his mother's experience growing up in Chicago also persuaded him of the value of speaking another language alongside English:

I remember my mom saying that in Chicago, when she was growing up, there'd be different neighborhoods. The Italian neighborhood's over here. The Polish is over here. But they're still in America, but they have their identities . . . . If you're living in America I would think it would be important to adapt to the laws, the language. If you don't speak English, to learn English. Maybe some of the culture—how to be polite or impolite. Understand there's things in different cultures about like lining up to buy a ticket or something. You just don't cut in front of people—things like that. But I think it's important they maintain their language with their children. Any child can grow up with more than one language it's gonna be valuable. It's a valuable trait.

Bilingualism is not merely valuable to professionals, who often interact with overseas colleagues and clients. Because Silicon Valley attracts immigrants, there is also a demand for service sector workers who can communicate with a non-English-speaking clientele. Recall from chapter 4 that established African American individuals in East Palo Alto saw their lack of Spanish proficiency as a mark against them in their quest for service sector jobs—but rather than rejecting bilingualism, they viewed it as a hard but valuable skill. Thus, they saw eye-to-eye with their more well-to-do Silicon Valley counterparts in appreciating the instrumental advantage of speaking more than one language. The job search question was paramount for Melanie Davis, a black, twenty-nine-year-old resident of East Palo Alto. She, like all too many East Palo Alto residents during the time we conducted the interviews, was unemployed. Perhaps not surprisingly, her view of language maintenance was filtered through her view of the economic benefits of speaking Spanish, which had become especially clear at a job she had applied for shortly before the interview:

Q: Do you ever wish you spoke another language?

R: Yes! Yes! I want to learn Spanish. That's something I need to. That's not a want, that's a need that I have to have . . . . Because that's my community. If I want to evolve, I need to evolve with my community and that's what my community is. A lot of these jobs right now, like for example I just went to school for medical assistant. I tried to apply right here at the local community thing. The first thing is not experience, it's are you bilingual? And I'm like, "No." And they're like, "Oh OK." I still went ahead with the interview but I know that right here, you pushed me out because the next person that came in automatically knows that because that's her first language. So I need to have that up under my belt to do anything I think within California, if I want to do anything, that's just something that is a necessity. That's a necessity for real.

But Melanie was nonetheless unflinching in her belief that English should prevail. Shortly after offering comments about the value of bilingualism, she was asked whether she would favor a bill making English the official language of the United States:

> I thought English was the language, so English needs to be the language! I mean that's what you come here speaking is English. If you want a job you speak English to get that job. You go to the grocery store, you speak English. You go to the post office, you speak English. That's just what you do for everyday life here. But that lets you know how everything is changing. If we had to sit here and learn a different language when we've been here already and we've got to learn a different language?! For real?! (exasperated tone) That don't even sound right to me! (laughing)

Respondents' call for bilingualism was not an idealistic or politically liberal interpretation of the way things ought to be: it came from their strong sense of the way things are. Respondents based that sense on their experience with bilingual immigrant and second-generation individuals. Indeed, respondents from across the interview sample seemed to endorse what sociologists Alejandro Portes and Rubén Rumbaut (2001) call "selective acculturation," which includes immigrants and their second-generation children maintaining their native tongue alongside English as a strategy for making it in American society. Some established individuals offered real-life examples of selective acculturation as representing their ideal. Lori Brewer's in-laws were from Israel; she used their example to argue that while English is extremely important, learning it does require squashing the use of another language:

> I think you can blend in very well and still maintain. My in-laws have blended in well and yet they speak English, they write it, they are citizens. They've learned how to drive and do taxes and everything else. They've bought property. They've done everything else. They schooled their kids here et cetera. And yet they still have their culture, they have their friends. They have other friends who are not of their culture. They do business with all different people. They don't just do business with their culture. So what

I don't like is this one lady who lived next door to me. She didn't feel this way. She actually loves America, loves English—took English classes before she moved here from China. And she told me one of her friends that she met at school told her, "You don't have to learn English. You can keep speaking Chinese. You can go to Chinese doctors. You can go to a Chinese bakery, you can go to a Chinese grocery store. You can do all these things and you don't even need to learn English." And I just think that's wrong. I don't agree. I wouldn't go to France and keep speaking English. No one is asking anyone to give up their culture or their beliefs or adhere to our standards. But I do think that it's ridiculous to print the DMV handbook in twelve different languages or the voter handbooks. If you are voting in this country you should be speaking the language. So that's just my thing.

It might seem schizophrenic to insist on English's centrality to American identity, while at the same time stressing the importance of speaking more than one language. Those views appear more compatible in the context of the symbolic value that Americans as a whole place on English as well as of the simultaneous labor market demand for people who speak more than one language—both of which owe to the presence of a large immigrant population. On the one hand, Americans desire unity, and language is an obvious source for such unity because it is so fundamental to both routine and nonroutine activity. When linguistic difference leads to a breakdown in communication, it strikes an almost visceral chord echoed not only in Silicon Valley, but also nationally. Using a nationally representative sample of Americans, political scientist Deborah Schildkraut (2010) showed that there is virtual consensus that speaking English is core to making someone a true American. And yet this belief exists alongside a pragmatic understanding that in a context defined by immigrants, many of whom speak no English, speaking more than one language is of the utmost utility. Both the symbolic ideal and the pragmatic reality came into focus because respondents lived, worked, attended school, and did business with people born in other countries.

Everything Else Is Fuzzy: Nonlinguistic Dimensions of American Identity

Respondents centered their conception of American national identity around English language use; they saw other aspects of culture as only loosely connected to American identity. In this, they seemed to be living out Glazer's (1997) observation that everyone has seemingly adopted a multicultural worldview. When they did consider the content of American culture, instead of explicitly identifying traits like race, ethnic origin, or religion as representing American identity, respondents were far more likely to cite behaviors, like the observance of national holidays and speaking English, as defining features. This view reflected a liberal civic tradition of national self-understanding in the United States. Modern notions of American civic identity hold that anyone, regardless of race, ethnic origin, religion, gender, or sexual orientation, can achieve American citizenship and claim membership in both a legal and cultural sense. That liberal conception is one among competing and generally more restrictive American civic traditions (Schildkraut 2010; Smith 1997). For much of American history, legal and cultural membership in the nation was reserved mostly for white men. Indeed, legal exclusion of women (Nakano Glenn 2009), minorities (Haney-López 1996; Motomura 2006; Ngai 2004), and nonstraight people was inscribed in law (Lewin 2009). Only recently has there been a fuller realization of the American founding principle that citizenship be available regardless of these group markers. Nonetheless, the United States is quite different from other countries, many of which base their national self-understanding on explicitly ethnic conceptions (Brubaker 1992; Brubaker et al. 2007; Shin 2006; Tsuda 2003).

The people we interviewed echoed a view of the United States as a nation built on a civic foundation of citizenship. They were not merely taking this tradition and applying it to their immediate context of heavy immigrant settlement; their notions of Americanness drew on those contexts. Respondents generally struggled to define the specific outlines of the symbols and practices that made up American culture partly because of their belief that immigration introduces new symbols and practices into the mix. Some saw trying to define American culture, apart from the English language, as impossible. When they mused about what it takes to be American, they often ended up in this place of flexibility. Yvonne Winston, a black forty-three-year-old medical billing examiner from East Palo Alto introduced in chapter 3, highlighted the way that what she and other respondents saw as the ill-defined nature of American identity made that identity highly malleable. The clarity of English as a core criterion, and the opaqueness of everything else, was apparent when she said:

> America is not one culture, it's not society of people. It's multiculture. And why should people from other countries be stripped of their culture because they are now living in America? I mean you have your beliefs as an individual and you have your cultures that you have practiced since you starting understanding, having the ability to understand. Now, if you come up to America, I don't think it should be taken away. I think it should be respected. But as well, respect someone else's because that's what it's about, multiculture . . . . And I think English should be the first language. And if it means you learn, you have to learn. My aunt did. My aunt didn't know English; she spoke French. She had to learn how to speak English when they moved out here to EPA. And she did and was a teacher. So what's wrong with it? I see nothing. I think it's just better character because you never know where you might be that you might need to communicate with someone and no one can speak but those two languages. So English should stay the first language.

Few labeled their concept of American culture as flexible per se. They were more likely to describe American culture as difficult to pinpoint, unless it had to do with speaking English. For example Cindy Reid, a white, forty-five-year-old software engineer from Cupertino, reflected on what she saw as the right balance between immigrants maintaining the ethnic culture they brought with them and blending into life in the United States. But her reflection led her to a dead end in trying to specify exactly what it was immigrants would blend into:

> I think it's better to maintain the traditions if they want to. (laughing) If they want to. Why does everyone want to be all the same? I enjoy learning about the different traditions. Not so much as something to believe in or not, or whatever, but it's interesting and something to talk about and then it leads to more discussion and you learn something more. That's only how I know some of the comments I've told you, like how the Indian parents told me, "We have to keep going to school here because if we don't go back . . . " But they've told me about the different days on Diwali and this and that. I don't have them all straight in my head but there was one where the husband had to do something. Serve the wife for the day. I remember saying, "Well that sounds really good!" We don't have that one! Yeah, because what's American? How can you say you have to be the American one? How do you know what that is? I don't know what that would be. So I would say maintain [traditions].

For Cindy, opining about whether immigrants should blend in or maintain some cultural distinctiveness was an almost pointless exercise precisely because American culture was so difficult to define.

Rather than specific celebrations, types of music, or styles of dress, respondents offered behaviors having nothing to do with ethnic origin as emblematic of Americanness: being assertive, questioning authority, carrying oneself with confidence, and working hard. Eric Nicks, a white, fifty-nine-year-old retired project manager from Berryessa, was adamant that speaking English is central to American identity. But he also cited less tangible, behavior-linked elements in his version of American identity:

> We have a culture here. And we have a way of doing things, just like any other country does. And it just seems to me if you're gonna live in this country, if you're gonna be a member of this society, a citizen of this country you need adapt to that country's culture and attitudes and heritage and stuff. And it's all right to maintain some of yours. There's nothing wrong with that . . .

> Q: What would you say are the most significant or the most important elements of the American way of life that you think people should adapt to?

> R: Well, your attitudes about how you go about living your life. We have the freedom to make our own decisions, to decide what kind of jobs we want to get. If we want to go to school to learn a trade, if we want to go to college to learn a profession, you have that opportunity. It's not always gonna be easy, necessarily. It's not gonna be given to you. But you have the opportunity if you want to pursue it. And if you want to work at it you can achieve your goals. The government isn't going to come in and prohibit you from becoming a plumber, a carpenter, or a doctor, or whatever you want to be. You have that decision. You have that right. And nobody can really stop you from pursuing it.

For many respondents, being American was a state of mind emanating from a set of principles related to individualism—a state of mind that, to varying degrees, was present among some of the immigrants with whom respondents interacted. Although the people we interviewed almost never held out group markers, like race, ethnicity, and religion, as an indicator of Americanness, some stated that they could tell who was American by merely how they carry themselves. A generally confident comportment combined with an assertive style of interpersonal interaction was said to symbolize Americanness in its truest form. Andy Zulfan, an engineer from Berryessa quoted in chapter 2, was married to a woman with some Filipino ancestry. His description of how her ancestry combined with her "all-American" demeanor illustrated the kind of fine-grained distinctions that respondents made between behaviors they identified as American and those that were not.

> [My wife is] half Filipino but she's 100 percent American to me. So cultur-ally she's 100 percent American . . . . Well, I think most of the people here that are foreign students or whatever, were born not in the U.S., they're not really Americans in culture yet. I think in a generation or two probably should see a little bit more of that . . . . So I could tell you an Asian woman that I know through work, and she was born in the exact same city I was born [on the East Coast]. And she's all American. How she acts, how she expresses herself is different from another person who looks identical to her from an Asian ethnicity perspective. So I can't say if I meet them on the street I'd know right away because there are people who still can be shy when you first meet someone and then open up later. But I'd say half the time yes, that it may not take very long before I sort of categorize them in terms of what kind of culture they have and stuff.

Whiteness is, to be sure, a signifier of Americanness across the United States. From the perspective of newcomers, race may play a central role. Sociologists Natasha Warikoo and Irene Bloemraad (2015) showed that immigrant-origin youth describe American identity in explicitly racial terms, often viewing their nonwhiteness as a barrier to national belong-ing. But respondents almost never explicitly made ethnic and racial crite-ria synonymous with Americanness in the interviews. Nor does such a linkage register nationally. Schildkraut (2010) showed that fewer than one in ten people in the United States believes that being white should be part of being American. Indeed, our respondents balked at the idea that phenotype was a telltale sign of someone's national membership.

The time period during which respondents came of age inflected how they understood American culture and its contours. Young and old, respondents agreed that what it takes to be American is elusive and hard to define—but younger respondents were more likely to arrive at this conclu-sion as a first response rather than as a last resort. Growing up in the midst of so much diversity and in an age of multiculturalism renders American culture as a blend of ethnic cultural elements (Hochschild, Weaver, and Burch 2012). The dynamism of this American culture makes it difficult to articulate in concrete terms, and so young respondents turned to their friends and acquaintances as illustrations. Kyle Zell, a white, sixteen-year-old high school student in Berryessa, typified how young people saw American culture as a you-know-it-when-you-see-it phenomenon:

> Our [American] culture is the absence of culture. They have a distinct culture and every other country has a very distinct culture except us, because we're a blend of all the cultures. And that blend creates a very unique culture that a lot of people just don't see. They think it's just all wild and free. But I disagree. It's the only cultural idea in the world. I think it's much better to live here and experience the mixture and go to one town and see incense on the wall and Indian food lined up on a buffet. And another town and go to get a bento box than it is to go to France and every corner there's a bakery or a restaurant and they're all the same . . . . It definitely helps if they speak fluent English with as little accent as possible. What else? It would be easier if they did better at school. If they do better at school, they have more of a chance of getting a better job and getting a high position where they can be accepted by all their peers and colleagues. They could also eat American food I guess instead of just strictly their own diet . . . . Well, all my friends have been born here, but a lot of their parents don't speak English and I think their parents have trouble really being accepted by other people because they don't speak fluent English.

Respondents' views provide some support to arguments that as today's young people replace older people in the ranks of American adults, a new racial order will emerge (Hochschild, Weaver, and Burch 2012). This argument is premised on the fact that today's youth are more diverse than ever and are thus more likely to hold accommodating attitudes about diversity and people different from themselves. Yet this greater openness is not evenly distributed across the entire population of young people. National surveys show that young people on the whole exhibit less racist attitudes than do earlier cohorts. But young whites are still far less likely to perceive racial injustice and to endorse measures to remedy racial injustice than are young minorities. Moreover, among whites, the differences between age cohorts are actually quite minimal: today's white youth generally have attitudes about race that are about the same as their parents' (Clement 2015; Cohen 2011; Hutchings 2009). But our findings from Silicon Valley suggest that nationally representative data may not capture variation in context and thus may miss important nuances. The young people we interviewed, regardless of ethnic or racial background, had navigated contexts defined by immigration-driven diversity their entire lives, tinting the lens through which they viewed what it means to be American. As a result they were more accommodating than their parents, and possibly more accommodating than their white peers in other regions. Among the people we interviewed, younger respondents were not only more likely than older respondents to define American culture as having many sources, they also expressed a greater degree of comfort with that cultural admixture. When parents compared their own childhood to that of their children, and children compared how they were growing up to what they knew of their parents' childhood, it became clear that immigration-driven change was a key distinguishing feature between cohorts. Take, for example, Justin Nicks, a white, twenty-three-year-old recent college graduate living in Berryessa. During the long drive from the Bay Area to his college in Southern California, he spoke with his father Eric (quoted earlier) about the changing demographics of the United States. The conversation brought to light different cohorts' distinct experiences of national identity. As Justin recounted:

> But to me what it's added to the national culture is a lot of, again, diversity but diversity not just ethnically but of experience. That we're not just a homogenous nation any more. My dad was telling me as we were driving through the Central Valley the other day, because actually it was quite a culture shock to come over the hill from LA into the Central Valley. So I asked him, "Well, I get that this is the Central Valley but this is also California. What must the heartland be like? What is Iowa like?" He says, "Well, I can't tell you now because I haven't been there for a while. But thirty years ago when I took a road trip through there it was homogeneously white. It was only white. That was the only thing you'd see." And, so I mean, the ethnic difference is obviously visible and obviously there. But I think a lot of these immigrants who come, and not just the people who physically come but then their children and the generations that follow them, they bring a lot of different perspectives. They just bring a lot to add I think. And I say that fully aware that I'm coming from a very specific enclave in the U.S. But that's my thinking.

Like other respondents, Justin recognized that California, and the Bay Area in particular, might not resemble the rest of United States in the scale of its diversity. But it was nonetheless clear that young respondents' local experience shaped their ideas about what it means to be a member of the American nation, in all of its variation. For them, the contours of American identity, however opaque, were not handed down from elites who define what it means to be a national insider (Smith 1997). Instead, they worked out those contours in a context defined by their own experiences with immigrants and second-generation individuals. Their closeness with second-generation youth showed them how the cultures that immigrant groups bring with them mix and meld with a culture that existed before the arrival of large numbers of immigrants (National Academies of Science, Engineering, and Medicine 2015; Crul 2016). Much as the immigrant second generation may have an advantage because of a cultural flexibility that comes from navigating between an immigrant household and the rest of American society (Kasinitz et al. 2008), established-population youth experienced a similar flexibility because of the presence in their lives of a large immigrant and second-generation population. The cultural dynamism that they observed among their second-generation friends informed their notion of American culture as defined explicitly by its ability to shift in response to contributions that immigrants make to it (Schildkraut 2010).

Of course, the presence of immigrants hardly guarantees that individuals will adopt more expansive notions of what makes someone an American. U.S. history is replete with instances in which the presence of immigrants produced stricter notions codified in immigration laws. The Chinese Exclusion Act of 1882 barred Chinese immigration, and the Immigration Quota Act of 1924 restricted Southern and Eastern European immigration and barred Asians, who were already ineligible for citizenship, from immigrating at all (Haney-López 1996; Zolberg 2006). Domestic policies further encoded whiteness as the core of American identity through Jim Crow laws in the South, and Jim Crow–like policies applied to Mexicans in the Midwest and West (García 1996; Katznelson 2005; Stevens 1976). But the civil rights movement ushered in new conceptions of what it meant to be American, which were reflected in subsequent public and private policies (Alba and Nee 2003; Dobbin 2009; Skrentny 2002; Skrentny 2014). This new notion of American national identity embraced immigration as a foundational myth of the national origin (Jacobson 2006) and diversity as a feature of the American nation (Alba and Nee 2003; Schildkraut 2010). This more expansive notion of American identity was part of an ideology of multiculturalism embodied in respondents' views about what being American entailed. And yet, the cultural outlines were perhaps so expansive that respondents had a hard time defining them. It was not that a firm belief in multiculturalism obscured their view of the outer bounds of American national identity. Instead their personal experience with immigrants and their knowledge of the immigrant experience, in combination with this ideology, stretched their conception of the American cultural core beyond its historical limits.

THE "HARD" SIDE OF CITIZENSHIP

Personal contact with newcomers also stretched respondents' conceptions of the hard, legal side of national belonging. As roughly 8 percent of the Silicon Valley's total residents are unauthorized immigrants (see table 1), the realities of immigration and even unauthorized immigration were part of daily life for respondents who had frequent contact with these immigrants or their children. The prevalence of the unauthorized population in Silicon Valley informed respondents' conceptions of the meaning of citizenship.

Political scientist Aristide Zolberg (2006) argues that the American nation has designed itself historically through how it sets criteria for immigrant admission and citizenship. The current policy design features of the nation, in contrast with those from the first two centuries of the American state, exclude explicit reference to racial identity as a criterion for citizenship. In 1965 Congress passed the Hart-Celler Act which, among other provisions, lifted quotas set by the Immigration Quota Act of 1924, granting visas more equitably across the globe. But those changes in immigration law did not account for existing immigration patterns, mainly from Mexico. Even as hemispheric and per-country caps for the first time limited Mexican migration, economic integration, the high demand for unskilled work, and economic uncertainty in Mexico continued to attract migrants northward to the United States—now mostly as unauthorized migrants. Meanwhile, the United States moved ever more forcefully to militarize the border, making the northbound crossing more expensive and dangerous. Because of the danger and cost of crossing, migrants began settling permanently north of the border (Cornelius 2005; Massey, Durand, and Malone 2002). As a result, the number of unauthorized immigrants climbed to a high of more than twelve million in 2007. Since that time, the unauthorized immigrant population has declined by about one million, and there is now net negative migration from Mexico, which had previously been the largest source country of both authorized and unauthorized immigration (Pew Research Center 2015a). It is little surprise, then, that the issue of unauthorized migration has dominated the political discourse on immigration in the United States, and that media coverage on immigration has focused squarely on unauthorized immigration (Chávez 2001; 2008). This focus has been intensified by passage of high-profile laws limiting unauthorized immigrants' access to a host of public resources and authorizing local police to detain individuals for violation of immigration laws (Golash-Boza 2012). No group has been constructed as more of an outsider in recent years than unauthorized immigrants, and particularly unauthorized Latin American immigrants (Chávez 2008). The contemporary case of unauthorized Mexican immigration is a clear example of how immigration policy constructs the category of "illegal" upon which the larger discourse on immigration relies (Ngai 2004).

Unauthorized immigrants are not the only category of noncitizens in the United States. Of the foreign-born population in the United States, roughly 42 percent are naturalized citizens, 27 percent are legal permanent residents, another 5 percent are temporary immigrants (such as people on student and work visas), while roughly 26 percent are unauthorized (National Academies of Science, Engineering, and Medicine 2015: 119). This spectrum of legal statuses, ranging from naturalized citizen to unauthorized, corresponds to a range of rights conferred by the U.S. government. But while the state makes fine-grained legal distinctions based on differences in immigration status, the discourse surrounding immigration offers a binary framing of the issue that paints a clear distinction between unauthorized immigrants and everyone else. The current design of the nation, and the corresponding discourse, leaves millions of unauthorized immigrants in the United States without any possibility of citizenship. But that official design only partially reflects respondents' vision—based on interpersonal experience—of what it means to be a member of the nation-state. While the people we interviewed saw the hard side of citizenship through the binary frame of "legal" and "illegal" immigrants, they did not necessarily subscribe to the binary implied by these discursive and bureaucratic definitions. Instead of uncritically adopting formal legal status as the basis for membership, respondents invoked both "soft" and "hard" aspects of citizenship to redefine it in a way that upheld everyday behavior as more important than legal documentation. Citizenship, for respondents, was more about deeds than papers.

The Part of "Illegal" They Understand

While there was no feature of hard citizenship as definitive in establishing American identity as the "softer" notion of English proficiency, legal status came close. Like Americans nationwide, respondents argued that coming to the United States without legal documentation was wrong (Newport and Wilke 2013). Legal status, according to respondents, conferred not just the legally inscribed privileges of citizenship, like voting and access to social services. It also included rightful access to the opportunities that the United States offers. Respondents' comments on this topic might be best characterized as economic nationalism—the idea that the state provides certain economic benefits, and only its legal members ought to be entitled to those benefits (Fox and Miller-Idriss 2008). This attitude was especially prevalent among lower-income African American respondents in East Palo Alto, who saw unauthorized workers as competition for low-wage jobs. Though one quarter of the adult (twenty-five years of age or older) unauthorized population in Silicon Valley has a bachelor's degree or more (Migration Policy Institute 2015), unauthorized immigrants are primarily low-wage workers. Poor African Americans saw economic opportunities as a zero-sum situation in which unauthorized immigrants often won out over African Americans, and they were adamant that certain economic opportunities should be reserved for individuals who are here legally. Those who had fallen on hard economic times were especially likely to voice such a view. We conducted the interviews during the worst portion of the Great Recession, when the unemployment rate in East Palo Alto hovered at around 20 percent and the foreclosure crisis had hit the city hard.

Those economic circumstances made some respondents feel especially vulnerable, inspiring their economic nationalism. Take Melanie Davis, the black twenty-nine-year-old unemployed single mother from East Palo Alto introduced in the last chapter. As we talked on her mother's front porch, she stared steely-eyed at the cars and neighbors passing by on a relatively busy Saturday morning in the neighborhood. The mix of black and Latino individuals moving back and forth was a constant reminder to Melanie about how much the population in East Palo Alto had changed and how that change had affected opportunities that she and others believed should be reserved for national insiders. Her lack of economic mobility was a lens through which she made sense of unauthorized immigration:

> Yeah, sometimes because they're just letting people in just to be letting them in. Everybody they can just get a pass to do anything. But black folks don't get a pass. We don't get anything easy . . . . Just on getting a job. Just getting a job and say you didn't speak English or if you couldn't read like that, you wouldn't get that job. But I know a lot of these people here that have jobs around here probably can't read English, but they have a job. You know? Just because they're going to do it for that pay . . . . I feel as though they just are taking a lot of jobs from everybody else. Not saying that black people are lazy and wouldn't do the job but if that job was available to them, they would take it. But the jobs will never be available. It's already gone.

Derek Jackson, the fifty-six-year-old factory worker also introduced in the last chapter, echoed Melanie's comments, stating:

> With immigration here . . . 'cause we letting a lot of people in here that want to use American society, the American government as a crutch. "I ain't got to work a day in my life, but I'm going to get paid for being here." But as an American, you can't really get paid for being here. You got to work! (laughs) That's serious. You got to work! So, if they keep letting a lot of foreigners in here, and all they going to do . . . . They get food stamp, welfare money, as quick as the American person himself. 'Cause the U.S. allowed it. The government allowed that. I think that's kind of bad. I would rather see us being strong. Help us Americans get on our feet versus someone from another country get on their feet before you do. I don't like that. I don't like that at all.

As chapter 3 highlights, poor black respondents often felt that they were outsiders looking in at ethnic networks that primarily benefited Latinos. Legal status added a layer of clarity to who was an insider and who was an outsider. Survey research shows that blacks tend to have softer views of immigration than whites along an array of measures, and the opinions of poor blacks appear even more accommodating when compared to those of poor whites. Moreover, whites are more likely to see immigration as a threat to their racial group than are blacks (Hutchings and Wong 2014). But in East Palo Alto, black respondents like Melanie and Derek positioned themselves not as members of a racial group facing unfair competition, but instead as national insiders who were entitled to the rights and responsibilities that came with legal citizenship.

Melanie and Derek were not alone in how they saw things. Not only did other black respondents in East Palo Alto echo their comments, but survey experiments in other contexts have revealed very similar findings. Sociologist Maria Abascal (2015) showed that when African Americans are presented with information about a growing Latino population, they exhibit more attachment to an American national identity, mirroring the findings from East Palo Alto.[4] There is some irony in this stance: after all, African Americans' legal citizenship has never guaranteed them access to the full rights of citizenship. Black history is largely a history of a struggle for rights to which they were entitled, but which they were denied by systematic racism (Bonilla-Silva 1997). While respondents did not say so explicitly, the presence of unauthorized immigrants may have seemed an offensive reminder of the lingering institutionalized racism that denies black citizens access to the full rights of citizenship on equal footing with whites (Coates 2015). Thus, for some, the view that unauthorized immigrants were accessing resources intended for America's neediest was not just unfair in the abstract: it came at their personal expense. But crucially, poor black respondents in East Palo Alto did not identify the group most threatened by unauthorized immigration in racial terms (or at least did so only implicitly). Instead, as Melanie's and Derek's comments suggest, the more important aspect was their position as members of a national group—as Americans.

Middle- and upper-middle-class respondents in Berryessa and Cupertino relied on a similar framing in positing unauthorized immigrants' legal status as marking a clear boundary between national insiders and outsiders. Like poor blacks, these middle- and upper-middle-class respondents believed that unauthorized immigrants often unfairly access opportunities and resources that ought to be reserved for people who are citizens. But Berryessa and Cupertino interviewees were living in better economic circumstances and were often the primary beneficiaries of services that unauthorized immigrants provided. Legality was thus a panoramic rather than microscopic lens through which they made sense of the rights of national insiders versus outsiders. None of the middle- and upper-middle-class respondents saw unauthorized immigration as exacting personal consequences for them. To the extent that they saw unauthorized immigration as a cost, that cost was being borne by an economic and political system to which they felt they had contributed. In their eyes, unauthorized immigration thus violated a civic republican notion of citizenship that focuses on participation for the sake of the collective. While welfare was perhaps the most obvious sore spot, these respondents also cited other taxpayer-funded institutions. Take, for example, how Larry Smith, a white, fifty-year-old corporate executive from Berryessa, articulated the effects of unauthorized immigration on public education:

> I think illegal immigration, especially in California, is a huge concern. Just practical, budget-wise, I think it's huge. Issues like that. Yeah, I'm concerned about trying to keep it all afloat . . . . Well, I just think if you're in the system and you're supporting the system, that's how it was designed to work. I'm not saying that it's a good system or a bad system, but that's the way the system was designed. If you have a lot people who are using the system who aren't really part of it, that's not how it was designed to work. So that's kind of concerned me.

Using a similar civic-republican logic, Noel Keats, a white, forty-seven-year-old administrative assistant in Cupertino, noted how her husband's experience trying to rectify a speeding ticket made clear the cost of unauthorized immigration to taxpayers:

> And every single person before him was there on a traffic violation and did not have a license [except for two]. All the rest of them said they were not eligible to get a license, which means they're not legal here. Because if you're here legally you can apply for a driver's license.[5] And so they all had to pay their fine for their moving violation. And they all asked for extra time and [my husband is] completely convinced that they'll never see them again and they'll never pay their money . . . . I mean those people are taking resources,

court time, judge, it's all money that they're not supporting because they're not doing what the rest of us are. So yeah, stuff like that concerns me.

Immigration laws and the discourse surrounding unauthorized immigration offered respondents a frame for making sense of who is entitled to the benefits and resources of political membership and who should be excluded. The difference between East Palo Alto respondents' emphasis on the personal cost of unauthorized immigration and Berryessa and Cupertino respondents' more impersonal take likely boiled down to differences in class status: East Palo Alto residents were directly vulnerable to economic competition with unauthorized immigrants, while their counterparts in Cupertino and Berryessa were vulnerable only in the sense that unauthorized immigrants might use public resources to which middle- and upper-middle-class individuals feel like they are the major contributors (Hainmueller and Hopkins 2014). And yet for all parties there was a clear conclusion: unauthorized status is a clear line distinguishing who can rightfully access the resources and opportunities that belong to national insiders (Waters and Kasinitz 2015).

"That Catch-22 type thing": Being a Human, Being American, and Softening the Edges of Hard Citizenship

Respondents' connections to the immigrant experience muddied what might otherwise have been a wholesale application of a legal framework that clearly delineates "illegal" from "legal" immigrants. That law-based framework is regularly presented and reinforced in political discourse. There can be little doubt that political leaders have an amplified voice that frames what it takes to be considered a true national insider (Smith 1997). And political leaders can raise the importance of issues like immigration among their followers. For example, in late 2005 a Republican-led House of Representatives passed a draconian immigration bill that would have, among other measures, made being in the United States without legal authorization a felony. That act sparked a wave of immigrant-rights protests and counterprotests that, together, lifted the importance of immigration as an issue among rank-and-file Americans (Saad 2014). And, during the 2016 presidential campaign, Donald Trump kicked off his candidacy by framing Mexican immigration as a serious threat to the United States. He reiterated those sentiments throughout the campaign, and into his time as president. In spite of overwhelming evidence that there was net negative Mexican migration at the time (Gonzales-Barrera 2015), Trump's rhetoric made immigration a central issue.

But the interviews showed that respondents' everyday experiences with immigrants had powerfully shaped their views and that these views did not fall in line with the framing implied by immigration laws and political rhetoric. Respondents' notions of political membership were defined by a set of everyday behaviors unrelated to legal documentation, like abiding by the law, paying taxes, and working hard. These supposedly American behaviors, respondents said, were not the exclusive dominion of citizens or even of legal residents—and those behaviors, respondents argued, should give currently unauthorized immigrants access to the rights and responsibilities of legal members of the political community. Take for example Michael Thomas, a black, forty-nine-year-old food-service worker. Michael worked alongside immigrants daily and knew well the challenges associated with legal status. Michael noted:

> [Illegal immigration is] like a toss up. I'm almost for the build a wall so they just can't travel anywhere you want to and just come over here. And then I'm like, nah that's kind of jack because with the cartels and stuff going over to Mexico, they killing people off like flies over there. So it's really hard. It's a real toss up question right there. As a human, you don't want to see other humans just getting killed off for money. But at the same time, you still want your way of life and you don't want just anybody to be able to come in your country. So it's that catch-22 type thing—being a human, being an American. And it's just hard. That's really a hard question. I do truly wish they had some kind of regulated it some kind of way a little bit better. But now I'm like, "How would you do it?" You don't have an idea. So that's really a hard question. I can understand why somebody want to run to America because, especially when you getting paid. My buddy, [Ronaldo], he's going back to Mexico. All he wanted to do is work here for four months and he can live for a whole year in Mexico and live good.

Michael's position as an American national inclined him to emphasize the importance of legality. He was far from a proponent of "open borders"—he more than flirted with favoring a border wall. But his personal relationship with an unauthorized Mexican immigrant brought forth a stance rooted in his belief that human rights are not contained within nation-state borders (Soysal 1994).

Even in places like Cupertino, where there are fewer unauthorized immigrants, personal connections to unauthorized immigrants outweighed a strictly legal framing of membership. Young people in Cupertino often described the city as being an upper-middle-class "bubble," with very few poor people and few unauthorized immigrants. But unauthorized immigrants were not entirely absent from the scene. Because most of the young people from Cupertino go away for college, their experiences outside the Cupertino bubble complicated their views about immigration. Consider the case of Kevin Baker, a white, twenty-year-old college student who grew up in Cupertino. During most of his childhood, his best friend was an East Asian immigrant who came to the United States with his family at a young age, but who, along with his parents, had overstayed his visa. For the previous two years, Kevin had attended a top-tier University of California campus, where he became close friends with a second-generation Mexican immigrant whose parents were unauthorized. His relationship with these individuals was a window through which he viewed citizenship:

> Well for a long time I was very opinionated because I would have considered [my neighbor] to be my best friend. So I would say, "Oh I have a best friend who is an illegal immigrant." I mean they're just people. They're really just people. And I understand that you can't let every single person into the country but there's a real need to be compassionate with the situation there . . . . And understand where people are coming from but a lot of the . . . I mean like I said, I can take both sides. I understand where people are coming [in wanting to pass restrictive immigration laws] from but I don't agree with it. And the fact that also going back to my friend at UCLA, the Mexican American girl, she was legal but her parents weren't. And so you see a lot of . . . I mean if your best friend is illegal and your other good friend, her parents are illegal, you're going to see a lot of the compassionate side of things. That these people are really just trying . . . really, they're good people. They're good people and they're trying to do good things. So a reactionary, "Send everyone back to Mexico" to me is just wrong.

Much like Michael, Kevin prioritized human rights over rights defined by laws of citizenship because of personal connections with people who were unauthorized or whose parents were unauthorized. Others premised their view that unauthorized immigrants ought to be brought into the legal fold partly on their informal observation that many unauthorized immigrants are well settled in the United States. Dennis Hayes, a black, sixty-seven-year-old retired nonprofit executive from Berryessa, shared the following:

> And you're talking about people that have been here ten, fifteen, twenty years some of them. Well if they're here, they have kids that have grown up here, then let them have their citizenship, let's get the kids into college. Like now, a lot of those kids you go to the public high school and they get straight As and you see in the paper a dozen situations. Then they try to go to college and they can't get scholarships because their parents aren't legal or they aren't legal. But yet they've grown up here, went from kindergarten through high school. Why shouldn't they be able to go to school here and make a contribution educationally to our society?

Dennis's observation squares with demographic research. According to a Pew Hispanic Center Report, the median length of residence for an unauthorized immigrant in 2013 was thirteen years (Passel et al. 2014). And because they have been in the United States for so long, many unauthorized immigrants have put down social and economic roots: they have U.S.-born children, own homes, and attend colleges and universities (National Academies of Science, Engineering, and Medicine 2015). Dennis's view was more than just academic, though. His experience growing up in Southern California and his decades-long career in nonprofits were also bases for his belief that unauthorized immigrants ought to be given a chance to become full political members of the American community.

> Well, I think through association and witnessing and living in [Southern California] and knowing a lot of people who were immigrants and some of them illegals. I worked in adoptions for a long time and I had several legal immigrants who adopted so I had the paperwork, the green cards, I was able to deal with them. But in the neighborhood I lived in as I grew up, it was a mixed neighborhood of Latino and black. So a lot of illegals were there working. Lot of legal immigrants were there and even then, their children were friends of yours so you heard the stories and you knew about them and you knew about some of the hardships and you knew somebody's relative who got shipped back off to Mexico and everybody was upset and crying. And you're there crying with them. So it's through experience really.

For Dennis and other respondents, personal contact with unauthorized immigrants rendered legal notions of citizenship too crude a framework to capture their experiences with immigrants who exhibited the behavior that they saw as hallmarks of good citizenship. Take for example, Mike Cabrillo, a twenty-one-year-old college student of Mexican and Portuguese ancestry. Many of his white friends assumed that he shared their opinion that unauthorized immigrants ought to be kicked out of the country. But he offered a more inclusive framing based on his connection to individuals whose lives were directly affected by unauthorized status.

> They just think that I'm on their side, that we'll kick these guys out because they're taking my job. It's like, "No! I don't think that at all." They don't understand that I know their point of view, I know the illegal immigrants . . . . Well, not necessarily know but I understand their point of view. I've had friends whose family were illegal immigrants. And so I know the limbo that they're in, being in the U.S. and trying to find a job and trying to support their family.

Personal connections with unauthorized immigrants or people who have unauthorized immigrant family members increased the likelihood that established individuals would privilege the informal, behavioral components of citizenship over the legal components. Supporting one's family and striving to get ahead are soft components of citizenship that respondents saw as behaviors desirable in fellow national insiders.

The people we interviewed in Silicon Valley did not necessarily stand out in their conceptualizations of citizenship in an age of mass unauthorized immigration. Survey research regularly shows that current immigration laws are widely out of step with most Americans' views. While Americans consistently report that they would like more border security, they also favor a policy that would legalize immigrants who are currently unauthorized, provided that those immigrants pay back taxes, learn English, and pass a criminal background check (Newport and Wilke 2013). And, as respondents' comments suggests, survey research in other settings shows that individuals exhibit more accommodating views of immigration when they have contact with immigrants (Ellison, Shin, and Leal 2011).

Note, however, that in spite of their concerns about human rights, respondents still believed that the United States must maintain territorial control at its borders. As a number of scholars have noted, greater emphasis on human rights has become an international norm seen in a range of institutions, from education to supranational structures (Meyer, Bromley, and Ramirez 2010; Soysal 1994). Some have claimed that these norms are trumping nation-state-bounded notions of political membership (Soysal 1994). For the people we interviewed, though, nation-state-bounded membership mattered. They felt no pressure to conform to international human-rights norms. And respondents firmly believed that the border matters. But they also reasoned that unauthorized immigrants who live inside U.S. borders and who are well versed in the soft side of citizenship should be brought into the fold and become part of the national "us" in the form of citizenship.

CONCLUSION

If relational assimilation results in new notions of race and ethnicity operating at the local level, it also yields new ideas about what it means to belong to the nation a whole. Perhaps no dimension of relational assimilation better embodies its give-and-take nature than conceptions of national identity. The frames implied by prevailing policies and political rhetoric might suggest that respondents would be reluctant to let personal contact with newcomers inform their views about what it means to be a national insider. In some ways, there was far more "give" than "take" implied by respondents' views of what makes someone American. Across the board they gave out a vision of American national identity that strongly aligned with the one offered by dominant policy and political frames, in which speaking English is the linchpin of national belonging. They also believed that unauthorized immigrants unfairly take advantage of public services that should be enjoyed only by national insiders. Poor African American interviewees in East Palo Alto were especially likely to argue that access to jobs and welfare for unauthorized immigrants violated important distinctions between national insiders and outsiders. Middle- and upper-middle-class respondents in Berryessa and Cupertino described unauthorized immigration as a more diffuse threat, saying that unauthorized immigrants were unfairly using resources that middle- and upper-middle-class Americans, like themselves, funded.

At the same time, respondents' view of American national identity also displayed tremendous "take" as they absorbed and incorporated their experiences and contact with immigrants. Even though they were unflinching in calling out English as the core of American identity, the importance they placed on language had a multicultural hue: they believed that English could stand alongside non-English languages in an individual's linguistic repertoire. Interactions with unauthorized immigrants smoothed the edges of the hard notions of citizenship too. Rather than founding their views of citizenship on legal bases, respondents privileged human rights and behavioral components of citizenship related to working hard, playing by the rules once in the United States, raising a family, and speaking English. Interviewees agreed that individuals who followed these less formal criteria for membership, as the immigrants whom respondents knew personally had, should be entitled to the legal dimension of citizenship because they acted like good citizens. Also notable is what respondents did not offer as criteria for national belonging. Being an American, according to their articulation, had little to do with race, ethnicity, or religion. Indeed, they offered a distinctly civic notion of Americanness; one that did not depend on ascribed characteristics.

These findings show how seeing assimilation as a relational process helps explain changing conceptions of the American nation more generally. There can be little doubt that popular notions of American identity have historically expanded to include previously excluded groups, ultimately elevating immigration to stand as a core part of the American national myth of origin (Jacobson 2006). There can also be little doubt that there is tremendous consensus about the core aspects of what it takes to be considered American (Hainmueller and Hopkins 2014; Schildkraut 2010). But the gradual expansion of that consensus may not be only a function of immigrant groups exerting influence once they have become assimilated into an American mainstream (Alba and Nee 2003; Orum 2005). That change may have also emerged from the most generationally established members of American society expanding some aspects of their understanding of American identity, while contracting others, all in response to their interactions with immigrants.

Conclusion

The changes that immigration is bringing to the United States affect more than the cityscape; they also appear in how established individuals, who were born in the United States to U.S.-born parents, make sense of contexts being reshaped by a newcomer population made up of immigrants and the children of immigrants. The findings from the preceding chapters, in conjunction with what is widely known about immigrant assimilation, show that the adjustment made by established individuals to immigrant-rich contexts bears some resemblance to newcomer assimilation. Just as newcomers adjust to new ethnic, racial, cultural, national, political, and economic contexts, so too do generationally established individuals adjust to the significant imprint that immigrants are making on these settings. Newcomer individuals are ambivalent about this adjustment, often lamenting what they lose even as they celebrate what they gain (Alba and Nee 2003; Bodnar 1985; Jacobson 2002). Likewise, established respondents see immigration-driven change as a mixed blessing that includes losses and gains. Immigration-driven change adds diversity, they say, but often too much; it drives innovation and economic growth, but it also creates competition in schools and the labor market; it is a source of friendship and romantic partners, but it can also be a source of disunity. And just as newcomers adjust almost unintentionally to their new environment, the established population finds itself required to adapt to immigration-driven change.

If immigration makes established and newcomer individuals strangers to each other, assimilation is the process by which strangeness gives way to familiarity. But according to both scholarly theories and popular lore, immigrants are the strangers, the established population (usually U.S.-born whites) are the familiar, and the onus for making these parties less strange to each other falls squarely on the newcomers. Indeed, some observers bluster that immigrants will never assimilate, reinforcing the idea that it is up to newcomers to change themselves to blend in to their monolithic new environment (Buchanan 2006; Coulter 2015; Krikorian 2008). More thoughtful theorizing by scholars notes that change takes place among both newcomer and established populations (Alba and Nee 2003; Massey and Sánchez 2010; Orum 2005; Bean, Brown, and Bachmeier 2015; National Academies of Science, Engineering, and Medicine 2015). But almost without exception scholarly research has focused on how newcomers adjust and the factors that lead them to make themselves more familiar and acceptable to an established population that sits in judgment.[1]

That conventional approach does not fully appreciate the full impact of immigration, however, or consider how much the processes of adjustment for newcomers and established individuals not only mirror each other, but also implicate one another. Perhaps more than any other academic work, Richard Alba and Victor Nee's (2003) "new assimilation" theory pushed the idea that multiple groups participate in and are changed by assimilation. Alba and Nee took stock of both historical and contemporary waves of immigration to craft an assimilation story that accounted for the potentially mutual nature of assimilation. They argued that immigrant groups might begin their time in the United States outside the mainstream, but that across generations and through individual and collective strategies, those groups join the mainstream, changing its character in the process. Alba and Nee offered evidence that intergenerational socioeconomic advancement among past waves of immigrants brought with it changes to the linguistic, ethnic, racial, and religious dimensions of the mainstream. Additionally, an ideology of multiculturalism and an associated value of diversity make key American institutions more open to participation from minorities, including the large numbers of newcomers among them (see Alba and Yrizar Barbosa 2015). In this account, significant changes to the mainstream happen at a slow pace, appearing generations after the arrival of an immigrant population.

The interviews we conducted with established individuals in Silicon Valley showed that immigration may change a mainstream or its various racial and class segments not only down the road in some yet-to-be realized future, but also in the here and now, by shaping the experiences and transforming the outlooks of its current occupants. For our established respondents, that transformation took place because they lived in areas with a large newcomer presence and had contact with newcomers in multiple realms of life. The resulting interweaving of diversity and various immigrant narratives into their lives changed their view of what constituted "normal." As newcomers made the places in which they settled more culturally comfortable for themselves with food, artistic representations, festivals, religious customs, and holidays that reflected their ethnic origins, established individuals saw the definition of "mainstream" expanding to normalize a strong ethnic identity. Because the immigrant points of origin of established individuals, if they had any at all, were too far back for them to feel a strong attachment to an ethnic ancestry, they found it difficult to attain this marker of "normalcy."

Newcomers also forced established individuals to adjust to atypical inflections of racial categories. With newcomers adopting "ethnic" strategies to get ahead in school, established whites found themselves adjusting to inflections of whiteness that rendered it a more visible, less-than category where academic achievement was concerned. And as they navigated the labor market, established poor blacks found that blackness had become less visible and that it was being driven further down a perceived racial status hierarchy where symbolic civic representation and material resources were concerned.

The social and economic assimilation of newcomers also altered how established individuals determined who was an insider and who was an outsider in their world. Respondents drew distinctions between the more assimilated insiders who had lived in their neighborhoods for a long time and who spoke English, and less assimilated outsiders, who were more recently arrived in the United States. These distinctions cut across ethnic boundaries, even as those boundaries remained salient. Such adjustments extended beyond the local community to the national community as well. As they became familiar with newcomers struggling with English, and in some cases with precarious legal status, respondents were forced to readjust the lens through which they saw Americanness itself. English-language use came into clearer focus as the nation's cultural core, but other potential cultural dimensions of American identity were blurry. In particular, knowing people who were unauthorized or whose parents were unauthorized led established individuals to uncouple legal status from other kinds of behavior that could make anyone American.

The sum total of these findings turns conventional notions of assimilation on their head. Whether established respondents represented a monolithic mainstream or various racial and class segments of U.S. society, they were far from an unchanging backdrop against which immigrant assimilation unfolded, whatever conventional assimilation accounts may suggest. Instead, the findings in this book, considered together with well-established research, suggest that established individuals are taking part in a *relational form of assimilation* that involves both newcomer individuals and the most generationally established members of the receiving society. For newcomers, assimilation plays out as a story of an often uncomfortable adjustment in relation to the languages they speak (Rumbaut, Massey, and Bean 2006), their legal status (Gonzales 2015; Menjívar and Abrego 2012), their social class (Agius Vallejo 2012), ethnic and racial identities (Waters 1999), their romantic partnerships (Vasquez-Tokos 2017; Wang 2012), their residential location (Brown 2007; Lichter et al. 2010), and their gender roles (Hondagneu-Sotelo 1994). But the transformation of newcomers is just one side of a two-sided coin of assimilation. On the other side of that coin is an assimilation taking place among the most generationally established. The deliberate and incidental adjustments made by newcomers often change the very contexts they are adjusting to—and the established individuals must make their own adjustments in response. Mobility in terms of education, income, occupation, and neighborhood residence provides opportunities for newcomers and established individuals to come into contact with one another. The initial contact yields an intense period of mutual adjustment. But over time, and across generations, these back-and-forth adjustments become less apparent and less frequent, as a working consensus around ethnic, racial, and national belonging develops—until in hindsight it becomes clear that the initial consensus has changed quite dramatically.

THE CONTOURS OF RELATIONAL ASSIMILATION

Assimilation may be relational, but it is not necessarily symmetrical: the different groups involved will change in different ways and to varying degrees. Silicon Valley possesses a special set of characteristics that make assimilation appear more symmetrical than it is likely to be in other places. But examining a context where the newcomer population is especially large and where established individuals from across the racial and class spectrum live, work, and play alongside them throws the established population's adjustments into vivid relief. Thus, for those who wish to understand other contexts, the primary usefulness of this study comes from the insight it generates about the *process* of relational assimilation rather than its discussion of the parameters driving relational assimilation in general. Still, those findings hint at the factors that may be most important in determining how relational assimilation plays out in other contexts. These factors include the group combinations involved; relative group size, status, and power; and prevailing institutional arrangements.

Group Combinations in Relational Assimilation

Relational assimilation involves individuals from various kinds of groups, but chief among them are the newcomer and established populations. Recall from the introduction that the established population in the United States is overwhelmingly white. Thus, relational assimilation taking place between an established population and an immigrant-origin group is generally happening with whites on one side and nonwhites on the other. But this is far from the only possible combination. As this and other research on assimilation has shown, a shared class standing can bring different ethnic and racial configurations of established and newcomer groups together, including African Americans and Caribbean immigrants (Tran 2015; Waters 1999); African Americans and a Vietnamese second generation (Zhou and Bankston 1998); and Mexican Americans and Mexican immigrants (Gutiérrez 1995; Jiménez 2010a; Ochoa 2004). Relational assimilation may also include only newcomer groups. In metro areas with very large immigrant populations and very small established populations, first- and second-generation immigrants may only rarely come into contact with established individuals, such that newcomers' only relevant outgroup contact is with other newcomers of different ethnic and racial backgrounds (Crul 2016). In a study of second-generation immigrants in Los Angeles, for example, sociologists Jennifer Lee and Min Zhou showed that native-born whites were not a reference point for a Chinese American and Vietnamese American second generation that primarily came into contact with other Asian groups and Latinos (Lee and Zhou 2015). Likewise, the second generation in New York, as studied by Phil Kasinitz and his colleagues (2008), experienced a mixing and melding of cultures originating in immigrant-origin groups from various ethnic backgrounds, resulting in an ethnically flecked notion of what it means to be a New Yorker (also see Kasinitz, Mollenkopf, and Waters 2002).[2]

The interviews we conducted in Silicon Valley, in combination with these studies from other metro areas with large immigrant populations, suggest that local mainstreams are shaped by the particular combinations of group interaction that take place there: what it means, culturally, to be a resident of Silicon Valley, an Angeleno, or a New Yorker is in large part defined by the interactions among and between these regions' newcomer and established groups.

Power and Symmetry of Change in Relational Assimilation

Not all parties have equal ability to dictate the terms of the back-and-forth adjustment that is relational assimilation. In fact, symmetry in relational assimilation is likely rare. The everyday interactions through which relational assimilation works are shaped by power differences among different ethnic, racial, and national-origin groups. The interviews we did in Silicon Valley hinted at the group-level factors most likely to matter: size and relative status.[3] Certainly size is important. The large number of newcomers in the places we studied meant that they could exert tremendous influence on local culture and institutions. Recall from chapter 1 that newcomers wove their ethnic culture so densely into the cultural fabric of the region that interviewees described having a strong connection to an ethnic culture as a *requirement* of local belonging. And African Americans in East Palo Alto believed that the size of the Latino population conferred on it a degree of power that forced institutions to meet the needs of newcomer Latinos. These are instances in which the newcomer population, because of its overall size, helped define the local mainstream culture and institutions.

Status matters as well. Individuals from specific groups, because of the size and class standing of the group, may have the power to shape the local inflection of racial categories. Chapter 4 showed how the meaning and status of whiteness in Cupertino (and to some degree in Berryessa) had been flipped on its head in relation to academic achievement. In this instance the population of Asian newcomers, because of its large relative size and elevated class standing, had the power to shape locally held norms about race and achievement and to integrate those new norms into local institutions. The result was a change in the definition and status of race categories and how they operated in daily life that profoundly affected whites, the racial group generally sitting in a superordinate status position.

It is important to bear in mind that populations (established or newcomer) do not simply leave their imprint at will, even when they are large and occupy a high-status position. If relational assimilation is a back-and-forth volley of adjustment and readjustment, there are dimensions of life in which the established population's return volley is overpowering, especially when there are well-entrenched norms to which established individuals attach great significance. Such is the case with the English language. Recall from chapter 4 that respondents across Silicon Valley defined symbolic boundaries according to English-language ability: those who could speak English fluently were insiders; those who could not were outsiders. And chapter 5 clearly illustrates that, for all their willingness to offer flexible definitions of American culture, respondents in all three cities were unbending in their view that the English language is *the* American cultural nucleus. Respondents' abundant contact with newcomers and exposure to non-English languages did little to blunt their perspective. If anything, it sharpened it.

The Institutional Structuring of Relational Assimilation

Neither relative group size nor group status is enough to determine the degree of symmetry in relational assimilation. Institutional arrangements also play a key role in dictating these terms. In the contemporary United States, changes in norms of racial inclusion and legal protections against racial, linguistic, and national-origin discrimination have made institutions generally more open to societal changes originating with immigrant groups (Alba and Nee 2003). In Silicon Valley, this institutional support can be seen in school- and city-sponsored festivals celebrating different ethnic cultures. That institutional support, along with the large immigrant population, made ethnic culture an abundant part of respondents' accounts of their daily life. If the norms and laws of the land are stacked against an immigrant group, however, that group's power to influence the terms of assimilation will almost certainly be diminished, regardless of group size and status. No clearer example of this exists than in U.S. immigration policy, which defines an entire set of immigrants as "illegal." That status colors the experiences of those who carry it in ways that are detrimental to their ability to be full participants in American society (Bean, Brown, and Bachmeier 2015; Gonzales 2015). And, when those in charge of the immigration enforcement institutions stringently enforce immigration policies, the exclusionary edges of that status become sharper, making illegality even more damaging to newcomer assimilation. Moreover, policies offer a frame through which individuals decipher insider and outsider status in everyday life. As chapter 5 showed, the idea of illegality weighed heavily on respondents' view of the fitness of today's immigrants to access opportunities and recourses in the United States.

There are myriad other historical examples where key institutions tilted the balance of influence, sometimes in favor of immigrants, but also against them. Colonization in places like South Africa and the Americas allowed migrants, though few in number, to quickly establish a superordinate position and set up institutions for their own economic, social, and political benefit (Lieberson 1961; Marx 1998). There are also contemporary instances in the United States and other countries where newcomers make up a large share of the population but still exert limited influence because legal and social institutions prevent such influence. In a number of California cities, for example, the Latino newcomer population makes up a plurality of residents, but still lacks cultural and political clout, partly because of the large unauthorized population among them. Internationally, the asymmetry between group size and group influence is abundantly apparent in Persian Gulf countries, where migrant workers often make up a large majority of the work force but have virtually no ability to determine their own social and political fortunes because they lack labor protections and have essentially no way of gaining long-term legal status (Ruhs 2013).

This is not to say that newcomers can have no influence over key institutions. Some immigrant groups, because of their status, are in a better position to leave an imprint on social, political, and economic institutions in ways that tip the symmetry of relational assimilation in their favor. As sociologist Anthony Orum (2005) argued, immigrant groups have greater influence when members establish themselves in positions of power and when these groups organize to make group claims. Indeed, organized protests (Voss and Bloemraad 2011; Zlolniski 2006), the establishment of ethnic occupational niches (Roediger 1991; Waldinger 1996), and political machines (Golway 2014) are all ways in which immigrant groups, past and present, have exerted influence and power through institutions.

Relational Assimilation as Change and Continuity

As relational assimilation unfolds over the long term, a consensus emerges around which racial, ethnic, and national groups of individuals belong, and which do not. But this agreement does not necessarily overturn entrenched lines of division. Some have argued that the most durable racial dividing line in the United States remains the one between blacks and everyone else (Lee and Bean 2010), and relational assimilation appears to do little to change that. In Silicon Valley, African Americans' encounters with relational assimilation reflected the national dynamic that placed them at the bottom of the racial hierarchy, a fact that for some black respondents was painfully obvious. Their interpretation of the world around them lends some support to the idea of a black/nonblack divide, wherein Asian and Latino assimilation, relational as it may be, does not alter this deepest fissure in the American racial landscape (Lee and Bean 2010).

And when Asians and Latinos engage in relational assimilation with whites, the importance of group size and status still puts whites in the driver's seat in determining the symmetry of that assimilation. Even in regions where minorities are the numerical majority, the status of whiteness might be shaken—as it has been in some aspects of Silicon Valley life—but it is not stirred into a dynamic fundamentally different from the system of race relations built up over generations (Bonilla-Silva 1997). The history of race relations throughout the United States adds up to an American society today in which whiteness still largely defines social, political, and economic belonging. And so to the extent that group size, group status, and institutional arrangements confer power on groups to tilt the symmetry of relational assimilation in their favor, relational assimilation often tilts in the favor of whites. Still, as the experiences of the established whites in Silicon Valley show, viewing assimilation—whether conceived as relational, straight-line, or segmented in nature—as a process dictated only by whites too easily paints over important ways in which immigration can destabilize the social order, including what it means to be white. The situation in Cupertino is a clear example of that destabilization. Larger national trends hint at it too. The extent of white dominance might appear most obviously in the kinds of jobs that individuals get. If whiteness unequivocally ruled the labor market roost, then there would be very few nonwhites in the best paid and most prestigious jobs, whatever immigration-driven demographic change might be taking place. But the opposite is happening. Asians, and to a lesser degree Latinos, are finding their way into the best jobs (Alba and Yrizar Barbosa 2015). Whites still disproportionately occupy those jobs, but the changing racial composition of the people in them suggests that whites are all but forced to make room at the top, opening up the elite to select nonwhites today, much as established whites had to make room for Southern and Eastern European newcomers in the past (Alba 2009; Alba and Yrizar Barbosa 2015).

Group combinations, group power (conferred by group size and status), and institutional arrangements are only some of the factors that are likely to shape how relational assimilation plays out in different contexts. They are, however, a starting point from which to understand how these important factors might shape the relational assimilation that is taking place in everyday life across the United States.

NOT JUST A SILICON VALLEY THING: IMMIGRATION AND
CHANGING AMERICAN SOCIETY

The basis for regarding assimilation as a relational process, with all of the
potential axes of variation just mentioned, arises from a study done in a
very particular time and place. The introduction described in detail the
range of ways in which Silicon Valley can be considered an outlier relative
to the rest of the country. For one, Silicon Valley simply has more immigrants: the share of the population that is foreign-born in Silicon Valley is
more than three times what it is in the entire United States; more than
half of Silicon Valley residents are newcomers, compared to about one-
quarter in the United States as a whole. Silicon Valley's immigrants also
tend to be higher skilled, with high-skilled immigrants outnumbering the
low-skilled by two to one, while the ratio is roughly even nationwide.
Silicon Valley immigrants are more likely to be naturalized citizens, and
although unauthorized immigrants make up a larger share of Silicon
Valley's total population than in the entire United States, because of the
large overall number of immigrants the unauthorized are slightly under-
represented as a share of the immigrant population. While Latin America
is the main source for immigration in the United States as a whole, more
Silicon Valley immigrants are from Asia than anywhere else. And while
the United States has yet to become a majority-minority nation, Silicon
Valley reached that milestone in 1999.

The fact that Silicon Valley stands out so much from the rest of the
country begs the question: What can be gleaned from this study to make
sense of other contexts? Even if the findings reported in this book are not
generalizable in a statistical sense, there is good reason to think that variants of what we discovered in East Palo Alto, Cupertino, and Berryessa
might be found in other places. The immigration-driven demography of
the United States makes the prevalence of relational assimilation a near
certainty, most especially in "global" regions like Silicon Valley. As sociologist Saskia Sassen (1991) argues, "global cities" are home to industries that
connect similarly situated cities around the world. Without a doubt,
Silicon Valley's technology industry ties the region to many other parts of
the globe. Migration is central to those ties. Much the same can be said of
metro regions throughout the United States that serve as global hubs for

innovation (Seattle), financial services (Chicago, New York), entertainment (Los Angeles, New York), energy (Houston), and trade (Miami). The insights generated from studying the established population in Silicon Valley are highly transportable to these other large, global cities.

But the insights likely have relevance beyond these places. Like many global regions, Silicon Valley can be divided into racial and class subregions that have very different characteristics (see table 1). Specific findings from one or another of these locales may well also apply in other places that have experienced similar immigration-driven population shifts. Take East Palo Alto, which is hardly unique in changing from a black-majority to a Latino-majority city. Other neighborhoods and cities that have undergone similar changes include Harlem (New York City), New Orleans, South Central Los Angeles, Watts, Southwest Detroit, and the Independence Heights and Sunnyside neighborhoods of Houston (to name a few). Existing research on "black-brown" relations suggests that these locales feature a mix of conflict and cooperation highly reminiscent of what we uncovered in East Palo Alto (Telles, Sawyer, and Rivera-Salgado 2011). Similarly, a number of wealthy neighborhoods and cities have seen the same pattern we observed in Cupertino, with tremendous growth of an Asian-immigrant population that now lives alongside established whites: San Marino, California; Irvine, California; West Windsor Township, New Jersey; North Potomac, Maryland; Lexington, Massachusetts; Sugar Land, Texas; and Tysons Corner, Virginia (to name a few).[4] In these places—where immigrants are anything but the "tired," "poor," "huddled masses" of Emma Lazarus's famous poem—there is good reason to believe that the dynamics we uncovered in Cupertino are playing out as well (see, for example, Chowkwanyun and Segal 2012; Spencer 2015).

However much or little the population of other locales resembles that of Silicon Valley, there can be little doubt that some form of relational assimilation is taking place throughout the United States, precisely because immigration now touches virtually all parts of the national map. Perhaps no one has done more to paint a picture of what immigrant-driven diversity looks like in this country than demographer William Frey. He describes a "diversity explosion" (2014) in which the United States' nonwhite population has grown tremendously in absolute terms, and also relative to whites, as a result of the growth of the newcomer population.

Yet this nationwide growth of the minority population should not obscure the tectonic immigration-driven changes taking place in smaller geographies. Much of the action is in central cities. According to Frey's analysis of 2010 U.S. Census data, among central cities that make up the nation's one hundred largest metropolitan areas, on average, just 41 percent of the population was white, 26 percent was Latino, 22 percent was black, and 8 percent was Asian (Frey 2014: 158). There is also significant action in the suburbs that surround these central cities. Most whites, blacks, Asians, and Latinos now live in the suburbs (Frey 2014: 163). And, according to Frey, "In 36 of the 100 largest metropolitan areas, minorities represent at least 35% of the suburban population, approximately the same as their share in the national population. Within those areas, 16 have majority-minority populations, up from just eight in 2000" (2014: 159). "Global neighborhoods," where whites, blacks, Latinos, and Asians are all well represented, have been growing in number in the last three decades, mirroring the immigration-driven diversity of the metro areas in which they are nested (Logan and Zhang 2011). These demographic trends mean that in metro areas across the nation, white and black established individuals are coming into contact with Latino and Asian newcomers, and it is very likely that the dynamics that will come into play are more similar to than different from those in Silicon Valley.

Perhaps the most apparent immigration-driven demographic changes have taken place in the South and Midwest, regions that before two decades ago scarcely had a newcomer population at all. These "new destinations" include cities, towns, and even rural areas that have been profoundly affected by the settlement of large numbers of immigrants. Between 1990 and 2010, eight of the ten cities with the fastest-growing Latino population, and seven of the ten cities with the fastest-growing Asian population, were in the South or Midwest (Frey 2014: 55). The significance of immigration-driven demographic change in new destinations is not just due to the small number of immigrants who lived there to begin with, such that the arrival of a few immigrants make for impressive proportional growth. Immigration has also produced a sizeable absolute presence of Latinos and Asians in several places. For example, in 1990, Nashville, Indianapolis, and Charlotte each had a Latino population that equaled roughly 1 percent of each city's population. But in 2013, Latinos were 10 percent, 10 percent, and 13 percent of the respective population of these cities. Small Midwestern and Southern cities are also home to large numbers of Latinos as a result of immigration. In Muscatine, Iowa, for example, nearly 17 percent of the population was Latino in 2010; Latinos made up nearly half of the residents of Siler City, North Carolina, in 2010; and roughly the same proportion was Latino in Garden City, Kansas. The rise of global neighborhoods of the sort so apparent in the most diverse metropolitan areas is also evident in other, historically less diverse locales. Between 1980 and 2010, diverse neighborhoods within metro regions across the nation grew in numbers far larger than might be expected based on a reading of overall population change at the regional level (Zhang and Logan 2016).

A large body of research documents newcomers' adjustment in popular immigrant destinations like Los Angeles (Lee and Zhou 2015; Bean, Brown, and Bachmeier 2015) and New York (Kasinitz et al. 2008). There is also a growing corpus of research examining the newcomer experience in the newer Midwestern and Southern gateways. This research reveals a mixed bag that includes both welcome and open hostility (Lay 2012; Marrow 2011; Winders 2013; Ribas 2016); local policies that are both accommodating and exclusionary (Varsanyi et al. 2012; Gulasekaram and Ramakrishnan 2015); and economic mobility is accessible for some but stalled for others, especially the unauthorized (Hernández-León and Lakhani 2013; López-Sanders 2009; Tran and Valdez 2015). Less clear is how established populations are adjusting to the settlement of large immigrant populations in these new gateways. Because of the small working-class white population in Silicon Valley, our interviews may offer a more limited clue about the specific contours of the adjustment in the new gateways. There is evidence that immigration pushes whites, regardless of class standing, to favor more punitive immigration policies and to support a Republican party that has, for the better part of the last two decades, supported a far more restrictionist immigration policy platform than has the Democratic party.[5] Those views are especially strong among poorer and less-educated whites (Abrajano and Hajnal 2015; Gest 2016). Given the large numbers of working-class whites in the Midwest and South, the relative class standing of whites likely structures the racial and class axes of relational assimilation in the new gateways in ways that our sample of Silicon Valley interview respondents did not capture.

But if demography shapes destiny, the situation in Silicon Valley tells of the processes that form the specifics of that destiny. Some of the same processes that we uncovered among Silicon Valley's established population may very well be emerging across the United States, even in unlikely places. In 2014, *The New York Times* reporter Damien Cave (2014) traveled Interstate 35, which stretches from Laredo, Texas, in the south to Duluth, Minnesota, in the north, to understand how immigration shaped life in the cities and towns that dot the interstate. At the conclusion of the thirty-eight-day journey, Cave identified the kinds of rifts in churches, downtowns, schools, workplaces, and city halls that might be expected in places with large newcomer populations. He also noted that established individuals spoke about the permanent presence of newcomers with a tone of resignation. And he reported that many established individuals were adjusting, if sometimes begrudgingly. As newcomers set down roots, and as their second-generation children enter adulthood, contact between established and newcomer individuals is virtually inevitable, and views of difference and similarity; notions of the cultural norm; and even institutions are, in the words of a woman from Farmers Branch, Texas, "evolving" (Cave 2014). That evolution, which immigration produces locally and which reverberates across the national scene, is not smooth for newcomers—nor is it smooth for established individuals, as interviews in Silicon Valley showed. It varies by the race and class of newcomers who arrive, and by the race and class of the established individuals they encounter (Gay 2006; Marrow 2011; McDermott 2011). And what comes of that evolution still includes racial and class demarcations of insiders and outsiders. But the dynamics of the evolution can only be understood, in all of their complexity, by considering how both newcomers and established populations are adjusting, by studying assimilation as a relational process.

TAKING STOCK OF THE NATIONAL SCENE: WHERE ARE WE AND WHERE ARE WE HEADED?

Looking ahead, what comes of that process will likely include significant changes in local experience with and notions of race and ethnicity, as well as adjusted ideas about what it means to be American. This is not to say that the process will be smooth, or even that future descendants of the post-1965 immigrants who become part of the established population will enjoy full access to all facets of American life. Just as immigration is part of the DNA of the United States, so too is ambivalence about the changes that immigration brings. Today, resistance to immigration takes the form of an inflexible federal policy that blocks the mobility of an entire class of immigrants—those without legal documentation (Gonzalez 2015)—and even hampers the mobility of these immigrants' U.S. citizen children (Bean, Brown, and Bachmeier 2015). Some state and local policies have made things decidedly unwelcoming for unauthorized immigrants by denying them driver's licenses, forbidding them access to public universities, empowering police to target people believed to be unauthorized (mostly based on skin color and language), and preventing unauthorized immigrants from renting housing, to name a few (Gulasekaram and Ramakrishnan 2015; Varsanyi et al. 2012). Moreover, legal status remains in the minds of many Americans not just a defining legal line, but also an important social distinction that separates insiders and outsiders. And even when immigrants appear to be well integrated socially and economically, race persists as a durable dividing line (Schachter 2016). There is also, of course, a virulent strand of anti-immigrant political rhetoric and policy that inflames what might otherwise be latent negative sentiment about today's newcomers (Hopkins 2010). There is no clearer example of the activation of xenophobic views than Donald Trump's successful run for president. Trump's campaign was built on anti-immigrant fearmongering and draconian, if vague, immigration policy proposals. In spite of abundant evidence that unauthorized immigration was on the decline (Gonzales-Barrera 2015), and that immigrants were assimilating (National Academies of Sciences, Engineering, and Medicine 2015), Trump's loud pronouncements of the perils of immigration inspired a very visible anti-immigrant backlash among his rank-and-file supporters. Trump's efforts to make good on his campaign promises will, at the very least, spread fear in newcomer communities. At worst, that fear will be coupled with policies that exact severe costs to immigrants, the country that depends on their labor, and the families that become forcibly divided by borders.[6] But the notion that costs caused by such policies will be restricted to newcomer communities is dubious. For all of the ambivalence expressed by established individuals about the immigration-driven changes to which they adjust, the lives of established and newcomer individuals are deeply entwined in neighborhoods, workplaces, schools, and even families. Thus, the pain caused by draconian rhetoric and policies will be felt not just by those most directly targeted, but also by all people—newcomer and established—living in regions whose character is defined heavily by immigration.

There is a flip side to what is often seen as a purely negative response to immigrant newcomers. The mingled sense of gain and loss that emerges from Silicon Valley reflects the ambivalence that characterizes the United States as a whole. Federal laws that leave more than eleven million people in unauthorized status hardly have the support of the American people. Indeed, consistent majorities of Americans, regardless of political party identification, favor giving people who are unauthorized a pathway to legal residency and indeed citizenship if they meet certain requirements (Pew Research Center 2015b). That share has increased since the 2016 presidential election (Kopan and Agiesta 2017). A majority of people in the United States see immigrants as having a more positive than negative impact on U.S. society (Pew Research Center 2015a). Policies can reflect this more accommodating view of immigrants. While comprehensive immigration reform was stalled in Congress, President Barack Obama signed executive orders that deferred deportation action for individuals who arrived as children (in 2012) and for unauthorized adults who have U.S.-born children (in 2014).[7] And while some state and local governments have taken a decidedly punitive stance toward unauthorized immigrants, a number of others have taken the opposite approach, promoting efforts to integrate immigrants into the social and economic fabric. Consider California, the largest state in the union and home to more immigrants than any other state. Just two decades ago California was an emblem of an anti-immigrant backlash. Throughout the 1990s, California voters passed a series of initiatives meant to make the state less hospitable for unauthorized, and even legal immigrants.[8] But today, California is arguably the most welcoming state in the union. It offers unauthorized immigrants access to in-state tuition and driver's licenses, funds K-12 schools to serve all students, including the unauthorized, has a domestic workers' bill of rights (which benefits an occupation dominated by unauthorized women), bilingual education, state-sponsored healthcare access for all unauthorized children, and funding for naturalization assistance (Ramakrishnan and Colbern 2015).

California is not alone. Across the nation, states, counties, and cities have rolled out the welcome mat for immigrants. For instance, Welcoming America, a national network of state and local governments that promotes a welcoming reception for immigrants, has sixty-six mostly municipal governments as members. Member governments span the United States, and include a substantial number of local governments in the Midwest and South, regions of the country that often conjure images of intolerance.

The existence of more welcoming policies represents the kind of institutional change that, according to Alba and Nee (2003), eases the pathway for immigrants and their descendants to enter a mainstream. But institutions are made up of individuals, and institutional changes thus come about because the individuals who are part of them alter how they see and do things. In some instances, that entails using the institutions to restrict access to the mainstream. But it can also mean that the individuals already in the institutions adjust how they see the world and implement changes according to that new view (see Marrow 2009), allowing once-excluded groups to become part of key institutions (Alba and Nee 2003). The experiences of the people we interviewed in Silicon Valley depict the latter form of change. Respondents' interactions with immigrants had a profound influence on how they understood what it meant to belong culturally, ethnically, racially, and legally. The individual changes attested to in the interviews we did in Silicon Valley are likely taking place throughout the United States and may ultimately scale up to institutional changes that, on balance, will make way for even greater newcomer influence in all walks of life (Marrow 2011; Alba and Foner 2015).

Amid the ambivalence there is a certainty that immigration will shape America's racial, ethnic, and generational destiny. Projections of future U.S. racial composition must be met with caution, partly because they often fail to consider how people with multiple ancestries will choose to identify (Alba 2016). Even with this caveat, though, America's population is almost assuredly becoming much less white, a trend commonly cited by scholars, pundits, and journalists alike. Much less appreciated is the fact that America's racial and generational profiles will continue to be important crosscutting axes. As I pointed out in the introduction, today's established population is overwhelmingly black and white. But as the first and second generations of the mostly Latino and Asian post-1965 immigration wave give way to their grandchildren and great-grandchildren, the ranks of the established population—one that is U.S.-born of U.S.-born parents—will be much less white (Alba and Yrizar Barbosa 2015; Jiménez, Park, and Pedroza forthcoming). Most evidence suggests that the segment of the established population that descends from the post-1965 immigration wave will enter jobs, inhabit neighborhoods, and take on ethnic and racial identities that are different from those of their second-generation parents and first-generation grandparents (Alba 2009; Alba and Yrizar Barbosa 2015; National Academies of Science, Engineering, and Medicine 2015). If the past is any indicator, these new entrants to the established population will also be less likely to speak the language of their immigrant grandparents, will have a fuzzier understanding of their grandparents' immigrant experience, and will be more likely to marry into families whose immigrant origins are rooted in the even more distant past (Waters 1990; Alba and Nee 2003).

The multigenerational process of assimilation for the post-1965 wave of immigrants is not the only way that American society will change. As the grandchildren and great-grandchildren of the post-1965 immigrants come of age, they will be part of the established population that will play host to the next waves of immigrants. Like their forebears, this new established population will find that contact with the next wave of newcomers will force them to adjust to contexts once again being reconfigured by immigration. Immigrant newcomers and established individuals will be strangers to each other. And America will be again remade through a bumpy process that ultimately makes them more familiar.

Notes

1. I use "race" when referring to a group of people defined by shared physical traits and whose place in a hierarchy is defined by notions of worth, power, and morality. I use "ethnicity" when referencing a group of people who make claims to a shared ancestry, history, and culture. Though there are groups defined both in racial and ethnic terms, the concepts are nonetheless distinct in how they operate (Cornell and Hartmann 2006).

2. See Alba and Nee 2003 (chapter 2) for a summary of critiques of Park's view of assimilation. Also see Allport (1954: 261).

3. As Julie Park, Juan Pedroza, and I (forthcoming) show, the third-generation descendants of the post-1965 wave of immigrants are relatively young, with an average age of about nine.

4. Nikesh Patel, Sean Podesta, and Alexandra Ornelas helped author this section.

5. The "Silicon Valley" moniker originated from the title of a 1971 series of articles for the trade publication *Electronic News*.

6. Based on the author's analysis of Current Population Survey data, 2009–2013.

7. Lee and Bean (2010) treat Latinos as a separate race group in their analysis.

8. In spite of these population changes, African Americans are overrepresented in local government. During our fieldwork in the city, three of the five

members of the city council, as well as the police chief, were African American. The superintendent of schools was Latina. African American respondents made no mention of these issues; however, several key informants, many of whom were heavily involved in local politics, mentioned them.

9. According to KQED News's analysis of 2010 U.S. Census data, there were eighty-nine black men per one hundred black women in East Palo Alto, suggesting that these informants may be right (Kukreja and Green 2016).

10. This figure is based on 2010 ACCRA Cost of Living Index, where 100 is the composite national average and the San Francisco-San Mateo-Redwood City score is 164, indicating it costs 64 percent more to live in the region compared to the U.S. average.

11. Several interview respondents believed that airports in China are adorned with advertisements for Cupertino public schools. Though factually dubious, these claims speak to Cupertino's popularity as a destination for Chinese and Indian immigrants.

12. Whereas most Californio families lost their land in legal disputes, the Berryessa family managed to prevail in a case that the U.S. Supreme Court ultimately settled (Sawyer 1922).

13. We compensated each respondent forty-five dollars in cash as an incentive to participate in the study.

14. Based on the author's calculations. Source data are drawn from 2009–2013 American Community Survey, Five-Year Estimates.

CHAPTER 1: THE (NOT-SO-STRANGE) STRANGERS IN THEIR MIDST

1. Logan and Zhang (2011) counted as "multiethnic" "metropolitan regions where in 1980, 1990, 2000, and 2010 at least two minority groups were present at or above their average national level, and the third group was present at or above one-half of their average national level" (15). Their analysis excluded the Washington, DC, and Miami metro areas. The rise of these global neighborhoods coexists with stubborn segregation across generations, especially for African Americans (Sharkey 2013).

2. These regions of the country have also experienced significant, though more recent, immigration-driven change (see, for example, Marrow 2011; Massey 2008). Respondents in this study did not mention knowledge of these changes, however.

3. Some students attend these schools through a voluntary interdistrict transfer program mandated by court-ordered desegregation in the mid-1980s (Bischoff 2011).

4. My own observational research in one of the area's high schools confirms as much.

5. See Wright, Ellis, and Parks (2005) for a critique of this conceptualization. Rather than viewing spatial assimilation processes as structured by an urban core/suburban ring dynamic, they argue that any metro area has a constellation of neighborhoods that define its dynamics of race and place.

6. Lee and Bean (2010) use the San Jose-Sunnyvale-Santa Clara metropolitan area for their analysis.

7. All of the dating relationships described by respondents were heterosexual; only two respondents were openly gay.

8. The Catholics we interviewed told of immigrant priests (often from the Philippines or Vietnam) in their churches. The hierarchical nature of the Catholic church means that priests are often assigned to overseas parishes. Given the large population of Asians in Silicon Valley, the region is a popular landing spot for newcomer Asian priests, allowing them to serve both the "mainstream" and newcomer members of the parish. Still, most respondents saw the presence of these clergy as a distant form of contact with newcomer individuals, as the priests' roles were largely limited to leading the Catholic Mass and they did not develop particularly close personal connections with respondents.

CHAPTER 2: SALSA AND KETCHUP—CULTURAL
EXPOSURE AND ADOPTION

1. Waldinger and Lichter (1996) show Russian Jews in Los Angeles to be a notable exception in their continued social distinctiveness.

2. Historically, some African Americans with light skin "passed" as white to enjoy the legal and social benefits that came with being treated as white. As historian Allyson Hobbs (2014) has shown, some of the benefits incurred by passing were offset by isolation from a black community.

CHAPTER 3: SPOTLIGHT ON WHITE, FADE TO BLACK

1. Findings reported in this chapter also appear in Jiménez and Horowitz (2013).

2. According the American Community Survey data (2008–2013; Five-Year Estimates), the Asian advantage in income and education holds in every U.S. region.

3. Eight of the twenty-five elementary schools that scored highest on California's Academic Performance Index are in the Cupertino Union Elementary School District (California Department of Education 2013). The Fremont Union High School District, which serves Cupertino residents, has two high schools

244   NOTES TO PAGES 130-213

ranked in the state's top fifteen based on average SAT scores (*Los Angeles Times* 2013).

4. After the completion of the interviews, several high-profile shootings of unarmed black men by police raised the topic of anti-black racism in national discourse.

5. See Bischoff (2011).

6. This line of reasoning was the basis of Stanley Lieberson's (1980) classic book comparing European immigrant groups and African Americans.

7. There is evidence that Asians today face soft quotas at elite colleges and universities. Indeed, one study shaded that Asians admitted to Ivy League schools had higher GPA and SAT scores than members of other groups, even after accounting for other factors relevant to admissions (Espenshade, Radford, and Chung 2009). Aware of these hurdles, newcomer Asian-origin individuals compensate with a hypercompetitive effort to excel (Kasinitz et al. 2008; Lee and Zhou 2015).

CHAPTER 4: LIVING WITH DIFFERENCE AND SIMILARITY

1. Portions of this chapter's findings also appear in Jiménez (2016).

2. See Winant (2015) and Wimmer (2015) for a spirited debate about the centrality of race relative to other categories of difference in social science research.

3. A number of commentators have offered lengthy normative articulations of these fears (see, for example, Buchanan 2006; Huntington 2004).

CHAPTER 5: LIVING LOCALLY, THINKING NATIONALLY

1. For similar arguments, see Brubaker et al. (2007) and Hobsbawm (1990)

2. This is, of course, an ideal type. There are many notable instances in which the state inflicts harm on its citizens, an act that is seen as being in direct contradiction to liberal democratic principle.

3. There is an exception to the English-language requirement for applicants over the age of fifty-five who have been permanent residents for fifteen years, and for applicants fifty years and older who have been permanent residents for twenty years.

4. Abascal's (2015) experiment also included whites and found that when whites are presented with information about a growing Latino population, they show greater investment in a white identity.

5. Beginning on January 1, 2015, unauthorized immigrants in California could legally apply for a driver's license.

CONCLUSION

1. For one notable exception, see Dominguez and May-Jareigo (2008) and Crul (2016).

2. There are historical parallels to these studies. Varzally (2008), for example, shows how Asians, Latinos, blacks, and some white ethnics together formed a collective "nonwhite" population in Los Angeles during the early twentieth century.

3. In a similar vein, Allport (1954) predicted that the status of contact between members of different racial groups was an important determinant of the resulting attitudes.

4. This listing of cities is courtesy of Natasha Kumar Warikoo, who compiled a list of all cities where the median household income is above one hundred thousand dollars and where a growing or stable Asian population was at least 20 percent of the total population in 2010. Warikoo identified thirty-four such cities.

5. There are notable exceptions, of course. Many Republican leaders, including George W. Bush, Jeff Flake, Lindsey Graham, and John McCain, have favored more welcoming policies for immigrants than those supported by their Republican colleagues.

6. For a detailed ethnographic account of what families experience when they are divided by the migration experience, see Dreby (2010).

7. For full details of these executive actions, see www.uscis.gov /immigrationaction.

8. Three measures constitute the core of the anti-immigrant and anti-Latino turn in California: Proposition 187 (1994), which targeted unauthorized immigrants; Proposition 209 (1996), which ended state-sponsored affirmative action; and proposition 227 (1998), which did away with bilingual education. In 2016, California voters passed Proposition 58, which reinstated bilingual education.

Works Cited

Abascal, Maria. 2015. "Us and Them: Black-White Relations in the Wake of Hispanic Population Growth." *American Sociological Review* 80(4):789–813.

Abascal, Maria, and Delia Baldassarri. 2015. "Love Thy Neighbor? Ethnoracial Diversity and Trust Reexamined." *American Journal of Sociology* 121(3):722–82.

Abrajano, Marisa, and Zoltan L. Hajnal. 2015. *White Backlash: Immigration, Race, and American Politics*. Princeton, NJ: Princeton University Press.

Abrego, L. 2008. "Legitimacy, Social Identity, and the Mobilization of Law: The Effects of Assembly Bill 540 on Undocumented Students in California." *Law and Social Inquiry* 33(3):709–1071.

Agius Vallejo, Jody. 2012. *Barrios to Burbs: The Making of the Mexican-American Middle Class*. Stanford, CA: Stanford University Press.

Akresh, Ilana R., and Reanne Frank. 2011. "At the Intersection of Self and Other: English Language Ability and Immigrant Labor Market Outcomes." *Social Science Research* 40(5):1362–70.

Alba, Richard. 1990. *Ethnic Identity: The Transformation of White America*. New Haven, CT: Yale University Press.

———. 2005. "Language Assimilation Today: Bilingualism Persists More than in the Past, but English Still Dominates." Washington, DC: Migration Policy Institute.

———. 2009. *Blurring the Color Line: The New Chance for a More Integrated America*. Cambridge, MA: Harvard University Press.

————. 2016. "The Likely Persistence of a White Majority." *The American Prospect.* January 11, 2016. http://prospect.org/article/likely-persistence-white-majority-0.

Alba, Richard D., and Nancy Foner. 2015. *Strangers No More: Immigration and the Challenges of Integration in North America and Western Europe.* Princeton, NJ: Princeton University Press.

Alba, Richard, Tomás R. Jiménez, and Helen B. Marrow. 2014. "Mexican Americans as a Paradigm for Contemporary Intra-Group Heterogeneity." *Ethnic and Racial Studies* 37(3):446–66.

Alba, Richard, Philip Kasinitz, and Mary C. Waters. 2011. "The Kids Are (Mostly) Alright: Second-Generation Assimilation: Comments on Haller, Portes and Lynch." *Social Forces* 89(3):763–73.

Alba, Richard D., John R. Logan, Brian J. Stults, Gilbert Marzan, and Wenquan Zhang. 1999. "Immigrant Groups in the Suburbs: A Reexamination of Suburbanization and Spatial Assimilation." *American Sociological Review* 64(3):446–60.

Alba, Richard, and Victor Nee. 2003. *Remaking the American Mainstream: Assimilation and Contemporary Immigration.* Cambridge, MA: Harvard University Press.

Alba, Richard, and Guillermo Yrizar Barbosa. 2015. "Room at the Top? Minority Mobility and the Transition to Demographic Diversity in the USA." *Ethnic and Racial Studies* 39(6):917–38.

Alesina, Alberto, and Eliana La Ferrara. 2000. "Participation in Heterogeneous Communities." *Quarterly Journal of Economics* 115(3):847–904.

Alexander, Jeffrey C. 2006. *The Civil Sphere.* New York: Oxford University Press.

Allport, Gordon W. 1954. *The Nature of Prejudice.* Cambridge, MA: Addison-Wesley.

Almaguer, Tomás. 1994. *Racial Fault Lines: The Historical Origins of White Supremacy in California.* Berkeley: University of California Press.

Anderson, Benedict. 1991. *Imagined Communities: Reflections on the Origin and Spread of Nationalism.* New York: Verso Press.

Anderson, Elijah. 2011. *The Cosmopolitan Canopy: Race and Civility in Everyday Life.* New York: W.W. Norton.

Appiah, Kwame A. 1997. "Cosmopolitan Patriots." *Critical Inquiry* 23(3):617.

Aronson, Joshua, Michael J. Lustina, Catherine Good, Kelli Keough, Claude M. Steele, and Joseph Brown. 1999. "When White Men Can't Do Math: Necessary and Sufficient Factors in Stereotype Threat." *Journal of Experimental Social Psychology* 35(1):29–46.

Bachmeier, James D., and Frank D. Bean. 2011. "Ethnoracial Patterns of Schooling and Work among Adolescents: Implications for Mexican Immigrant Incorporation." *Social Science Research* 40(6):1579–95.

Barreto, Matt, and Gary Segura. 2014. *Latino America: How America's Most Dynamic Population Is Poised to Transform the Politics of the Nation.* New York: Public Affairs.

Bean, Frank D., Susan K. Brown, and James D. Bachmeier. 2015. *Parents without Papers: The Progress and Pitfalls of Mexican American Integration.* New York: Russell Sage Foundation.

Bell, Joyce M., and Douglas Hartmann. 2007. "Diversity in Everyday Discourse: The Cultural Ambiguities and Consequences of Happy Talk." *American Sociological Review* 72(6):895–914.

Berman, Michael. 2002. "Race, Ethnicity, and Inter-Minority Suburban Politics: East Palo Alto, 1950–2002." MA thesis, Department of History, Stanford University.

Berrey, Ellen. 2015. *The Enigma of Diversity: The Language of Race and the Limits of Racial Justice.* Chicago: University of Chicago Press.

Blau, Peter M. 1977. *Inequality and Heterogeneity: A Primitive Theory of Social Structure.* New York: Free Press.

Blau, Peter M., Carolyn Beeker, and Kevin M. Fitzpatrick. 1984. "Intersecting Social Affiliations and Intermarriage." *Social Forces* 62(3):585–606.

Blau, Peter M., and Joseph E. Schwartz. 1984. *Crosscutting Social Circles: Testing a Macrostructural Theory of Intergroup Relations.* Orlando, FL: Academic Press.

Bloemraad, Irene. 2011. "The Debate over Multiculturalism: Philosophy, Politics, and Policy." Washington, D.C.: Migration Policy Institute.

Bloemraad, Irene, Anna Korteweg, and Gökçe Yurdakul. 2008. "Citizenship and Immigration: Multiculturalism, Assimilation, and Challenges to the Nation-State." *Annual Review of Sociology* 34:153–79.

Blumer, Herbert. 1958. "Race Prejudice as a Sense of Group Position." *Pacific Sociological Review* 1(1):3–7.

Bobo, Lawrence D. 2011. "Somewhere between Jim Crow and Post-Racialism: Reflections on the Racial Divide in America Today." *Daedalus* 140(2):11–36.

Bobo, Lawrence, and Ryan A. Smith. 1998. "From Jim Crow Racism to Laissez-Faire Racism: The Transformation of Racial Attitudes." In *Beyond Pluralism: The Conception of Groups and Group Identities in America,* edited by Wendy Freedman Katkin, Ned C. Landsman, and Andrea Tyree, 182–220. Urbana: University of Illinois Press.

Bodnar, John. 1985. *The Transplanted: A History of Immigrants in Urban America.* Bloomington: University of Indiana Press.

Bonilla-Silva, Eduardo. 1997. "Rethinking Racism: Toward a Structural Interpretation." *American Sociological Review* 62(3):465–80.

———. 2006. *Racism without Racists: Color-Blind Racism and the Persistence of Racial Inequality in the United States.* New York: Rowman and Littlefield Publishers.

Borjas, George J. 1999. *Heaven's Door: Immigration Policy and the American Economy.* Princeton, NJ: Princeton University Press.

Brannon, Tiffany N., and Gregory M. Walton. 2013. "Enacting Cultural Interests: How Intergroup Contact Reduces Prejudice by Sparking Interest in an Out-Group's Culture." *Psychological Science* 24(10):1947–57.

Brown, Susan K. 2007. "Delayed Spatial Assimilation: Multigenerational Incorporation of the Mexican-Origin Population in Los Angeles." *City and Community* 6(3):193–209.

Brubaker, Rogers. 1992. *Citizenship and Nationhood in France and Germany.* Cambridge, MA: Harvard University Press.

———. 2001. "The Return of Assimilation? Changing Perspectives on Immigration and its Sequels in France, Germany, and the United States." *Ethnic and Racial Studies* 24(4):531–48.

Brubaker, Rogers, Margit Feinschmidt, Jon Fox, and Liana Grancea. 2007. *Nationalist Politics and Everyday Ethnicity in a Transylvanian Town.* Princeton, NJ: Princeton University Press.

Buchanan, Patrick J. 2006. *State of Emergency: The Third World Invasion and Conquest of America.* New York: Thomas Dunne Books.

Calhoun, Craig. 1997. *Nationalism.* Minneapolis: University of Minnesota Press.

California Department of Education. 2013. *API Reports.* http://api.cde.ca.gov/Acnt2011/2010Base_DstApi.aspx?cYear=&allcds=4369419&cChoice=2010ApiD.

Camarillo, Albert M. 2007. "Cities of Color: The New Racial Frontier in California's Minority-Majority Cities." *Pacific Historical Review* 76(1):1–28.

Card, David. 2005. "Is the New Immigration Really So Bad?" *The Economic Journal* 115(507):300–23.

Cave, Damien. 2014. "On Immigration, the Hard Lines Start to Blur." *The New York Times,* June 20.

Charles, Camille Z. 2006. *Won't You Be My Neighbor? Race, Class, and Residence in Los Angeles.* New York: Russell Sage Foundation.

Chávez, Leo R. 2001. *Covering Immigration: Popular Images and the Politics of the Nation.* Berkeley: University of California Press.

———. 2008. *The Latino Threat: Constructing Immigrants, Citizens, and the Nation.* Stanford, CA: Stanford University Press.

Chowkwanyun, Merlin, and Jordan Segal. 2012. "How an Exclusive Los Angeles Suburb Lost Its Whiteness." *The Atlantic: City Lab,* August 27.www.citylab.com/politics/2012/08/how-exclusive-los-angeles-suburb-lost-its-whiteness/3046/.

Chua, Amy. 2011. *Battle Hymn of the Tiger Mother.* New York: Bloomsbury Publishing.

Citrin, Jack, and David O. Sears. 2014. *American Identity and the Politics of Multiculturalism.* New York: Cambridge University Press.

Clement, Scott. 2015. "Millennials Are Just about as Racist as their Parents." *Wonkblog: Washington Post*, April 7. www.washingtonpost.com/blogs /wonkblog/wp/2015/04/07/white-millennials-are-just-about-as-racist-as-their-parents/.

Coates, Ta-Nehisi. 2015. *Between the World and Me*. New York: Spiegel and Grau.

Cohen, Cathy J. 2011. "Millennials and the Myth of the Post-Racial Society: Black Youth, Intra-Generational Divisions and the Continuing Racial Divide in American Politics." *Daedalus* 140(2):197–205.

Cooper, Marianne. 2014. *Cut Adrift: Families in Insecure Times*. Berkeley: University of California Press.

Cornelius, Wayne A. 2005. "Controlling 'Unwanted' Immigration: Lessons from the United States, 1993–2004." *Journal of Ethnic and Migration Studies* 31(4):775–94.

Cornell, Stephen, and Douglas Hartmann. 2006. *Ethnicity and Race: Making Identities in a Changing World*, 2nd ed. Thousand Oaks, CA: Pine Forge Press.

Cortese, David. 2013. Personal Communication.

Coulter, Ann. 2015. *Adios, America! The Left's Plan to Turn Our Country into a Third World Hellhole*. Washington, DC: Regnery Publishing.

Crowder, K., M. Hall, and S. E. Tolnay. 2011. "Neighborhood Immigration and Native Out-Migration." *American Sociological Review* 76(1):25–47.

Crul, Maurice. 2016. "Super-Diversity vs. Assimilation: How Complex Diversity in Majority–Minority Cities Challenges the Assumptions of Assimilation." *Journal of Ethnic and Migration Studies*. 42(1):54–68.

Cutler, Kim-Mai. 2015. "East of Palo Alto's Eden: Race and the Formation of Silicon Valley." *TechCrunch*, January 10, 2015. http://techcrunch.com/2015 /01/10/east-of-palo-altos-eden/.

De Graauw, Els, Shannon Gleeson, and Irene Bloemraad. 2013. "Funding Immigrant Organizations: Suburban Free Riding and Local Civic Presence." *American Journal of Sociology* 119(1):75–130.

Di Leonardo, Micaela. 1984. *The Varieties of Ethnic Experience: Kinship, Class, and Gender among California Italian-Americans*. Ithaca, NY: Cornell University Press.

Dobbin, Frank. 2009. *Inventing Equal Opportunity*. Princeton, NJ: Princeton University Press.

Dreby, Joanna. 2010. *Divided by Borders: Mexican Migrants and their Children*. Berkeley: University of California Press.

Duster, Troy. 2005. "Race and Reification in Science." *Science* 307(5712):1050–51.

Eck, Diana L. 2001. *A New Religious America: How a "Christian Country" Has Now Become the World's Most Religiously Diverse Nation*. New York: HarperCollins.

Eger, Maureen A. 2010. "Even in Sweden: The Effect of Immigration on Support for Welfare State Spending." *European Sociological Review* 26(2):203–17.

Ellis, Mark, Richard Wright, and Virginia Parks. 2004. "Work Together, Live Apart? Geographies of Racial and Ethnic Segregation at Home and at Work." *Annals of the Association of American Geographers* 94(3):620–37.

Ellison, Christopher G., Heeju Shin, and David L. Leal. 2011. "The Contact Hypothesis and Attitudes toward Latinos in the United States." *Social Science Quarterly* 92(4):938–58.

Erdmans, Mary P. 1998. *Opposite Poles: Immigrants and Ethnics in Polish Chicago, 1976–1990*. University Park: Pennsylvania State University Press.

Espenshade, Thomas J., Alexandria W. Radford, and Chang Y. Chung. 2009. *No Longer Separate, Not Yet Equal: Race and Class in Elite College Admission and Campus Life*. Princeton, NJ: Princeton University Press.

Feagin, Joe R. 1994. *Living with Racism: The Black Middle Class Experience*. Boston: Beacon Press.

———. 2010. *Racist America: Roots, Current Realities, and Future Reparations*. New York: Routledge.

Feliciano, Cynthia. 2006. *Unequal Origins: Immigrant Selection and the Education of the Second Generation*. El Paso: LFB Scholarly Publishing.

Ferguson, Ronald F., Jens Ludwig, and Wilber Rich. 2001. "A Diagnostic Analysis of Black-White GPA Disparities in Shaker Heights, Ohio." *Brookings Papers on Education Policy* (4):347–414.

Fieldhouse, Edward, and David Cutts. 2010. "Does Diversity Damage Social Capital? A Comparative Study of Neighbourhood Diversity and Social Capital in the US and Britain." *Canadian Journal of Political Science* 43(2):289–318.

Fields, Corey D. 2016. *Black Elephants in the Room: The Unexpected Politics of African American Republicans*. Oakland: University of California Press.

Fischer, Claude S., and Michael Hout. 2006. *Century of Difference: How America Changed in the Last One Hundred Years*. New York: Russell Sage Foundation.

Fiske, Susan T., Amy J. C. Cuddy, Peter Glick, and Jun Xu. 2002. "A Model of (Often Mixed) Stereotype Content: Competence and Warmth Respectively Follow from Perceived Status and Competition." *Journal of Personality and Social Psychology* 82(6):878–902.

FitzGerald, David S., and David Cook-Martín. 2014. *Culling the Masses: The Democratic Origins of Racist Immigration Policy in the Americas*. Cambridge, MA: Harvard University Press.

Foner, Nancy, and Richard Alba. 2008. "Immigrant Religion in the US and Western Europe: Bridge or Barrier to Inclusion?" *International Migration Review* 42(2):360–92.

Fox, Cybelle. 2012. *Three Worlds of Relief: Race, Immigration, and the American Welfare State from the Progressive Era to the New Deal*. Princeton, NJ: Princeton University Press.

Fox, Jon E., and Demelza Jones. 2013. "Migration, Everyday Life and the Ethnicity Bias." *Ethnicities* 13(4):385–400.

Fox, Jon E., and Cynthia Miller-Idriss. 2008. "Everyday Nationhood." *Ethnicities* 8(4)536–76.

Frankenberg, Ruth. 1993. *White Women, Race Matters: The Social Construction of Whiteness*. Minneapolis: University of Minnesota Press.

Frey, William H. 2014. *Diversity Explosion: How New Racial Demographics Are Remaking America*. Washington, DC: Brookings Institution Press.

Fryer Jr., Roland G., and Paul Torelli. 2010. "An Empirical Analysis of 'Acting White.'" *Journal of Public Economics* 94(5–6):380–96.

Gans, Herbert J. 1979. "Symbolic Ethnicity: The Future of Ethnic Groups and Cultures in America." *Ethnic and Racial Studies* 2(1):1–20.

———. 1992a. "Comment: Ethnic Invention and Acculturation, a Bumpy-Line Approach." *Journal of American Ethnic History* 12(1):42–52.

———. 1992b. "Second Generation Decline: Scenarios for the Economic and Ethnic Futures of the Post-1965 American Immigrants." *Ethnic and Racial Studies* 15(2):173–92.

———. 2015. "The End of Late-Generation European Ethnicity in America?" *Ethnic and Racial Studies* 38(3):418–29.

García, Juan R. 1996. *Mexicans in the Midwest, 1900-1932*. Tucson: University of Arizona Press.

Gay, Claudine. 2006. "Seeing Difference: The Effect of Economic Disparity on Black Attitudes toward Latinos." *American Journal of Political Science* 50(4):982–97.

Gellner, Ernest. 1983. *Nations and Nationalism*. Ithaca, NY: Cornell University Press.

Gest, Justin. 2016. *White Working Class Politics in an Age of Immigration and Inequality*. New York: Oxford University Press.

Glazer, Nathan. 1997. *We Are All Multiculturalists Now*. Cambridge, MA: Harvard University Press.

Gleeson, Shannon, and Roberto G. Gonzales. 2012. "When Do Papers Matter? An Institutional Analysis of Undocumented Life in the United States." *International Migration* 50(4):1–19.

Golash-Boza, Tanya M. 2012. *Immigration Nation: Raids, Detentions, and Deportations in Post-9/11 America*. Boulder, CO: Paradigm Publishers.

Golway, Terry. 2014. *Machine Made: Tammany Hall and the Creation of Modern American Politics*. New York: Liveright Publishing.

Gonzales, Roberto G. 2015. *Lives in Limbo: Undocumented and Coming of Age in America*. Oakland: University of California Press.

Gonzalez-Barrera, Ana. 2015. "More Mexicans Leaving than Coming to the U.S." Washington, DC: Pew Research Center, November.

Gordon, Milton M. 1964. *Assimilation in American Life: The Role of Race, Religion, and National Origins.* New York: Oxford University Press.

Grusky, David, and Tamar Kricheli-Katz, eds. 2012. *The New Gilded Age: The Critical Inequality Debates of Our Time.* Stanford, CA: Stanford University Press.

Gulasekaram, Pratheepan, and S. Karthick Ramakrishnan. 2015. *The New Immigration Federalism.* New York: Cambridge University Press.

Gutiérrez, David. 1995. *Walls and Mirrors: Mexican Americans, Mexican Immigrants, and the Politics of Ethnicity.* Berkeley: University of California Press.

Hainmueller, Jens, and Daniel J. Hopkins. 2014. "Public Attitudes toward Immigration." *Annual Review of Political Science* 17: 225–249.

Hall, Matthew, Audrey Singer, Gordon F. De Jong, and Deborah Roempke Graefe. 2011. "The Geography of Immigrant Skills: Educational Profiles of Metropolitan Areas." Metropolitan Policy Program at Brookings, June 2011. www.brookings.edu/wp-content/uploads/2016/06/06_immigrants_singer .pdf.

Haller, William, Alejandro Portes, and Scott M. Lynch. 2011. "Dreams Fulfilled, Dreams Shattered: Determinants of Segmented Assimilation in the Second Generation." *Social Forces* 89(3):733–62.

Handley, John. 1997. *Toward the Golden Mountain: The History of the Chinese in the Santa Clara Valley.* Cupertino, CA: The Cupertino Historical Society.

Handron, Caitlin. 2014. "Immigration Changes the Meaning and Experience of Whiteness." Berkeley/Stanford Immigration Conference, December 12, Berkeley, CA.

Haney-López, Ian. 1996. *White by Law: The Legal Construction of Race.* New York: New York University Press.

Hannah, Seth D. 2011. "Clinical Care in Environments of Hyperdiversity." In *Shattering Culture: American Medicine Responds to Cultural Diversity,* edited by Mary-Jo D. Good, Sarah S. Willen, Seth D. Hannah, Ken Vickery, and Lawrence Taeseng Park, 35–69. New York: Russell Sage Foundation.

Handlin, Oscar. 1951. *The Uprooted: The Epic Story of the Great Migrations That Made the American People.* New York: Grosset and Dunlap.Hansen, Marcus L. 1952. "The Third Generation in America." *Commentary* 14(5):492–500.

Hartigan Jr., John. 1999. *Racial Situations: Class Predicaments of Whiteness in Detroit.* Princeton, NJ: Princeton University Press.

Hernández-León, Rubén, and Sarah M. Lakhani. 2013. "Gender, Bilingualism, and the Early Occupational Careers of Second-Generation Mexicans in the South." *Social Forces* 92(1):59–80.

Higham, John. 1955. *Strangers in the Land: Patterns of American Nativism, 1860–1925*. New Brunswick, NJ: Rutgers University Press.

Hobsbawm, Eric J. 1990. *Nations and Nationalism since 1780: Programme, Myth, Reality*. New York: Cambridge University Press.

Hochschild, Jennifer L. 1995. *Facing Up to the American Dream: Race, Class, and the Soul of the Nation*. Princeton, NJ: Princeton University Press.

Hochschild, Jennifer L., Vesla M. Weaver, and Traci R. Burch. 2012. *Creating a New Racial Order: How Immigration, Multiracialism, Genomics, and the Young can Remake Race in America*. Princeton, NJ: Princeton University Press.

Hondagneu-Sotelo, Pierrette. 1994. *Gendered Transitions: Mexican Experiences of Immigration*. Berkeley: University of California Press.

Hooghe, Marc, Tim Reeskens, Dietlind Stolle, and Ann Trappers. 2009. "Ethnic Diversity and Generalized Trust in Europe." *Comparative Political Studies* 42(2):198–223.

Hoover, Mary E. R. 1992. "The Nairobi Day School: An African American Independent School, 1966–1984." *The Journal of Negro Education* 61(2):201–10.

Hopkins, Daniel J. 2010. "Politicized Places: Explaining Where and When Immigrants Provoke Local Opposition." *American Political Science Review* 104(1):40–60.

Horowitz, Adam Luis. 2016. "Obviousness: The Unexpected Benefit of Phenotypic Dissimilarity." *Ethnic and Racial Studies*. Available at www.tandfonline.com/doi/abs/10.1080/01419870.2016.1211303.

Horton, John. 1995. *The Politics of Diversity: Immigration, Resistance, and Change in Monterey Park, California*. Philadelphia: Temple University Press.

HoSang, Daniel. 2010. *Racial Propositions: Ballot Initiatives and the Making of Postwar California*. Berkeley: University of California Press.

Hsin, Amy, and Yu Xie. 2014. "Explaining Asian Americans' Academic Advantage over Whites." *Proceedings of the National Academy of Sciences* 111(23):8416–21.

Huntington, Samuel P. 2004. *Who Are We? The Challenges to America's National Identity*. New York: Simon and Schuster.

Hutchings, Vincent L. 2009. "Change or More of the Same? Evaluating Racial Attitudes in the Obama Era." *Public Opinion Quarterly* 73(5):917–42.

Hutchings, Vincent L., and Cara Wong. 2014. "Racism, Group Position, and Attitudes about Immigration among Blacks and Whites." *Du Bois Review: Social Science Research on Race* 11(2):419–42.

Iceland, John. 2009. *Where We Live Now: Immigration and Race in the United States*. Berkeley: University of California Press.

Ignatiev, Noel. 1995. *How the Irish Became White*. New York: Routledge.

Jackman, Mary R. 1994. *The Velvet Glove: Paternalism and Conflict in Gender, Class, and Race Relations.* Berkeley: University of California Press.

Jackson, John L. 2005. *Real Black: Adventures in Racial Sincerity.* Chicago: University of Chicago Press.

Jacobson, Matthew F. 2002. *Special Sorrows: The Diasporic Imagination of Irish, Polish, and Jewish Immigrants in the United States.* Berkeley: University of California Press.

———. 2006. *Roots Too: White Ethnic Revival in Post-Civil Rights America.* Cambridge, MA: Harvard University Press.

Jerolmack, Colin, and Shamus Khan. 2014. "Talk Is Cheap: Ethnography and the Attitudinal Fallacy." *Sociological Methods and Research:*42(2): 178–209.

Jiménez, Tomás R. 2008. "Mexican-Immigrant Replenishment and the Continuing Significance of Ethnicity and Race." *American Journal of Sociology* 113(6):1527–67.

———. 2010a. *Replenished Ethnicity: Mexican Americans, Immigration, and Identity.* Berkeley: University of California Press.

———. 2010b. "Affiliative Ethnic Identity: A More Elastic Link between Ethnic Ancestry and Culture." *Ethnic and Racial Studies* 33(10):1756–75.

———. 2016. "Fade to Black: Multiple Symbolic Boundaries in 'Black/Brown' Contact." *Du Bois Review: Social Science Research on Race* 13(1):159–80.

Jiménez, Tomás R., Corey Fields, and Ariela Schachter. 2015. "How Ethnoraciality Matters: Looking inside Ethnoracial Groups." *Social Currents* 2(2):107–15.

Jiménez, Tomás R., and Adam L. Horowitz. 2013. "When White Is Just Alright: How Immigrants Redefine Achievement and Reconfigure the Ethnoracial Hierarchy." *American Sociological Review* 78(5):849–71.

Jiménez, Tomás R., Julie Park, and Juan Pedroza. Forthcoming. "The New Third Generation: Post-1965 Immigration and the Next Stage in the Long March of Assimilation." *International Migration Review.*

Jones-Correa, Michael. 2011. "All Immigration Is Local: Receiving Communities and their Role in Successful Immigrant Integration." *Progress 2050,* Center for American Progress, September 20. www.americanprogress.org/issues/immigration/reports/2011/09/20/10342/all-immigration-is-local/.

Joppke, Christian. 1998. "Immigration Challenges the Nation-State." In *Challenge to the Nation-State: Immigration in Western Europe and the United States,* edited by Christian Joppke, 3–46. New York: Oxford University Press.

Joppke, Christian, and John Torpey. 2013. *Legal Integration of Islam: A Transatlantic Comparison.* Cambridge, MA: Harvard University Press.

Karabel, Jerome. 2005. *The Chosen: The Hidden History of Admission and Exclusion at Harvard, Yale, and Princeton.* Boston: Houghton Mifflin.

Kasinitz, Philip, John Mollenkopf, and Mary C. Waters. 2002. "Becoming American/Becoming New Yorkers: Immigrant Incorporation in a Majority Minority City." *International Migration Review* 36(4):1020–36.

Kasinitz, Phillip, John H. Mollenkopf, Mary C. Waters, and Jennifer Holdaway. 2008. *Inheriting the City: The Second Generation Comes of Age.* Cambridge, MA and New York: Harvard University Press and Russell Sage Foundation.

Katznelson, Ira. 1981. *City Trenches: Urban Politics and the Patterning of Class in the United States.* Chicago: University of Chicago Press.

———. 2005. *When Affirmative Action Was White: An Untold History of Racial Inequality in Twentieth-Century America.* New York: W. W. Norton.

Keister, Lisa A., Jody Agius Vallejo, and Brian Aronson. 2016. "Chinese Immigrant Wealth: Heterogeneity in Adaptation." PLOS ONE 11(12): e0168043.

Keller, Morton, and Phyllis Keller. 2001. *Making Harvard Modern: The Rise of America's University.* New York: Oxford University Press.

Kennedy, John F. 1964. *A Nation of Immigrants.* New York: Harper-Collins.

Kesler, Cristel, and Irene Bloemraad. 2010. "Does Immigration Erode Social Capital? The Conditional Effects of Immigration-Generated Diversity on Trust, Membership, and Participation Across 19 Countries, 1981–2000." *Canadian Journal of Political Science* 43(2):319–47.

Kim, Claire J. 1999. "The Racial Triangulation of Asian Americans." *Politics and Society* 27(1):105–38.

Kim, Su Y., Yijie Wang, Diana Orozco-Lapray, Yishan Shen, and Mohammed Murtuza. 2013. "Does 'Tiger Parenting' Exist? Parenting Profiles of Chinese Americans and Adolescent Developmental Outcomes." *Asian American Journal of Psychology* 4(1):7–18.

Kopan, Tal, and Jennifer Agiesta. 2017. "CNN/ORC Poll: Americans Break with Trump on Immigration Policy." CNN.com. www.cnn.com/2017/03/17/politics /poll-oppose-trump-deportation-immigration-policy/.

Krikorian, Mark. 2008. *The New Case against Immigration: Both Legal and Illegal.* New York: Penguin.

Kukreja, Charu, and Matthew Green. 2016. "MAP: Why Black Women Out-number Black Men in the Bay Area and Beyond." KQED Radio News, July 6. https://ww2.kqed.org/lowdown/2016/07/06/why-black-women-significantly-outnumber-black-men-in-the-bay-area/.

Kymlicka, Will. 1998. "Multicultural Citizenship." In *The Citizenship Debates: A Reader,* edited by Gershon Shafir, 167–88. Minneapolis: University of Minnesota Press.

Lacy, Karyn. 2007. *Blue-Chip Black: Division and Unity in the Black Middle Class.* Berkeley: University of California Press.

Lai, James S. 2011. *Asian American Political Action: Suburban Transformations.* Boulder, CO: Lynne Rienner Publishers.

Lamont, Michèle, and Virág Molnár. 2002. "The Study of Boundaries in the Social Sciences." *Annual Review of Sociology* 28:167–95.

Lareau, Annette. 2003. *Unequal Childhoods: Class, Race, and Family Life.* Berkeley: University of California Press.

Lawrence, Sarah, and Gregory Shapiro. 2010. "Crime Trends in the City of East Palo Alto." Berkeley Center for Criminal Justice. www.law.berkeley.edu/files /EPA_Main_Report_Final.pdf.

Lay, J. Celeste. 2012. *A Midwestern Mosaic: Immigration and Political Socialization in Rural America.* Philadelphia: Temple University Press.

Lee, Jennifer. 2002. *Civility in the City: Blacks, Jews, and Koreans in Urban America.* Cambridge, MA: Harvard University Press.

Lee, Jennifer, and Frank D. Bean. 2010. *The Diversity Paradox: Immigration and the Color Line in Twenty-First Century America.* New York: Russell Sage Foundation.

Lee, Jennifer, and Min Zhou. 2015. *The Asian American Achievement Paradox.* New York: Russell Sage Foundation.

Lemann, Nicholas. 1991. *The Promised Land: The Great Black Migration and How It Changed America.* New York: Vintage Books.

Letki, Natalia. 2008. "Does Diversity Erode Social Cohesion? Social Capital and Race in British Neighbourhoods." *Political Studies* 56(1):99–126.

Levin, Michael, and Nancy Brink. 1996. "Dreams of a City: Creating East Palo Alto." (film). Academic Software Development/Stanford University Libraries and Stanford Committee on Black Performing Arts.

LeVine, Marianne. 2014. "East Palo Alto City Council Passes New Tenant Protections." *NewsFix: KQED's Bay Area New Blog,* April 4. https:// ww2.kqed.org/news/2014/03/11/east-palo-altos-biggest-landlord-opposes-proposed-tenant-protection-law/

Lewin, Ellen. 2009. *Gay Fatherhood: Narratives of Family and Citizenship in America.* Chicago: University of Chicago Press.

Li, Wei. 2009. *Ethnoburb: The New Ethnic Community in Urban America.* Honolulu: University of Hawaii Press.

Li, Wei, and Edward J. W. Park. 2006. "Asian Americans in Silicon Valley: High-Technology Industry Development and Community Transformation." In *From Urban Enclave to Ethnic Suburb: New Asian Communities in Pacific Rim Countries,* edited by W. Li, 119–33. Honolulu: University of Hawai'i Press.

Lichter, Daniel T., Julie H. Carmalt, and Zhenchao Qian. 2011. "Immigration and Intermarriage among Hispanics: Crossing Racial and Generational Boundaries." *Sociological Forum* 26(2):241–64.

Lichter, Daniel T., Domenico Parisi, Michael C. Taquino, and Steven M. Grice. 2010. "Residential Segregation in New Hispanic Destinations: Cities, Suburbs, and Rural Communities Compared." *Social Science Research* 39(2):215–30.

Lieberson, Stanley. 1961. "A Societal Theory of Race and Ethnic Relations." *American Sociological Review* 26(6): 902–10.

Linton, April. 2007. "Spanish-English Immersion in the Wake of California Proposition 227: Five Cases." *Intercultural Education* 18(2):111–28.

Linton, April, and Tomás R. Jiménez. 2009. "Contexts for Bilingualism among U.S.-Born Latinos." *Ethnic and Racial Studies* 32(6):967–95.

Logan, John R., and Wenquan Zhang. 2011. "Global Neighborhoods: New Evidence from Census 2010." *US2010: Discover America in a New Century*, November 2011. https://s4.ad.brown.edu/Projects/Diversity/Data/Report /globalfinal2.pdf.

López-Sanders, Laura. 2009. "Trapped at the Bottom: Racialized and Gendered Labor Queues in New Immigrant Destinations." Center for Comparative Immigration Studies Working Paper, University of California, San Diego.

———. 2012. "Bible Belt Immigrants: Latino Religious Incorporation in New Immigrant Destinations." *Latino Studies* 10(1–2):128–54.

Los Angeles Times. 2013. "California Schools Guide: Top Average SAT Scores." Retrieved June 14, 2013, http://schools.latimes.com/.

Luttmer, Ezro F. P. 2001. "Group Loyalty and the Taste for Redistribution." *Journal of Political Economy* 109(3):500–28.

Marrow, Helen B. 2009. "New Immigrant Destinations and the American Colour Line." *Ethnic and Racial Studies* 32(6):1037–57.

———. 2011. *New Destination Dreaming: Immigration, Race, and Legal Status in the Rural American South*. Stanford, CA: Stanford University Press.

Marx, Anthony W. 1998. *Making Race and Nation: A Comparison of South Africa, the United States, and Brazil*. New York: Cambridge University Press.

Massey, Douglas. 1985. "Ethnic Residential Segregation: A Theoretical Synthesis and Empirical Review." *Sociology and Social Research* 69:315–50.

———. 2007. *Categorically Unequal: The American Stratification System*. New York: Russell Sage Foundation.

Massey, Douglas S., and Nancy A. Denton. 1993. *American Apartheid: Segregation and the Making of the Underclass*. Cambridge, MA: Harvard University Press.

Massey, Douglas S., Jorge Durand, and Nolan J. Malone. 2002. *Beyond Smoke and Mirrors: Mexican Immigration in an Era of Free Trade*. New York: Russell Sage Foundation.

Massey, Douglas S., and Magaly R. Sánchez. 2010. *Brokered Boundaries: Creating Immigrant Identity in Anti-Immigrant Times*. New York: Russell Sage Foundation.

Masuoka, Natalie, and Jane Junn. 2013. *The Politics of Belonging: Race, Public Opinion, and Immigration*. Chicago: The University of Chicago Press.

McDermott, Monica. 2006. *Working-Class White: The Making and Unmaking of Race Relations*. Berkeley: University of California Press.

———. 2011. "Black Attitudes and Hispanic Immigrants in South Carolina." In *Just Neighbors? Research on African American and Latino Relations in the United States*, edited by E. E. Telles, M. Q. Sawyer, and G. Rivera-Salgado, 242–63. New York: Russell Sage Foundation.

McDermott, Monica, and Frank L. Samson. 2005. "White Racial and Ethnic Identity in the United States." *Annual Review of Sociology* 31:245–61.

Menjívar, Cecilia, and Leisy J. Abrego. 2012. "Legal Violence: Immigration Law and the Lives of Central American Immigrants." *American Journal of Sociology* 117(5):1380–421.

Meyer, J. W., P. Bromley, and F. O. Ramirez. 2010. "Human Rights in Social Science Textbooks." *Sociology of Education* 83(2):111–34.

———. 2015. "Profile of the Unauthorized Population: Santa Clara County, CA." Migration Data Hub, retrieved June 19, 2015. www.migrationpolicy.org /data/unauthorized-immigrant-population/county/6085.

Mindiola, Tatcho, Yolanda F. Niemann, and Néstor Rodriguez. 2002. *Black-Brown Relations and Stereotypes*. Austin: University of Texas Press.

Morning, Ann. 2014. "And You Thought We Had Moved Beyond All That: Biological Race Returns to the Social Sciences." *Ethnic and Racial Studies* 37(10):1676–85.

Motomura, Hiroshi. 2006. *Americans in Waiting: The Lost Story of Immigration and Citizenship in the United States*. New York: Oxford University Press.

Myers, Dowell, and John Pitkin. 2009. "Demographic Forces and Turning Points in the American City, 1950–2040." *The Annals of the American Academy of Political and Social Science* 626(1):91–111.

Nakano Glenn, Evelyn. 2009. *Unequal Freedom: How Race and Gender Shaped American Citizenship and Labor*. Cambridge, MA: Harvard University Press.

National Academies of Sciences, Engineering, and Medicine. 2015. *The Integration of Immigrants into American Society: Panel on the Integration of Immigrants into American Society*, edited by Mary C. Waters and Marisa Gerstein Pineau. Washington, DC: The National Academies Press.

Newman, Katherine S. 2012. *The Accordion Family: Boomerang Kids, Anxious Parents, and the Private Toll of Global Competition*. Boston: Beacon Press.

Newport, Frank, and Joy Wilke. 2013. "Immigration Reform Proposals Garner Broad Support in U.S. Democrats, Republicans Agree on Many Potential Immigration Measures." Gallup, June 19. www.gallup.com/poll/163169 /immigration-reform-proposals-garner-broad-support.aspx.

Newton, Lina Y. 2000. "Why Some Latinos Supported Proposition 187: Testing Economic Threat and Cultural Identity Hypotheses." *Social Science Quarterly* 81(1):180–93.

Ngai, Mae M. 2004. *Impossible Subjects: Illegal Aliens and the Making of Modern America*. Princeton, NJ: Princeton University Press.

Ochoa, Gilda. 2004. *Becoming Neighbors in a Mexican American Community: Power, Conflict and Solidarity.* Austin: University of Texas Press.

Olewe, Dickens. 2015. "Nairobi, California, USA?" *The Fifth Floor* (radio), BBC, July 24. www.bbc.co.uk/programmes/p02xy8j9.

Omi, Michael, and Howard Winant. 2014. *Racial Formation in the United States,* 3rd ed. New York: Routledge.

O'Neil, Molly. 1992. "New Mainstream: Hot Dogs, Apple Pie and Salsa." *The New York Times,* March 11.

Orum, Anthony M. 2005. "Circles of Influence and Chains of Command: The Social Processes Whereby Ethnic Communities Influence Host Societies." *Social Forces* 84(2): 921–39.

Pager, Devah. 2003. "The Mark of a Criminal Record." *American Journal of Sociology* 108(5):937–75.

Parigi, Paolo, and Warner Henson II. 2014. "Social Isolation in America." *Annual Review of Sociology* 40:153–71.

Park, Julie, and Dowell Myers. 2010. "Intergenerational Mobility in the Post-1965 Immigration Era: Estimates by an Immigrant Generation Cohort Method." *Demography* 47(2):369–92.

Park, Julie, Dowell Myers, and Tomás R. Jiménez. 2014. "Intergenerational Mobility of the Mexican–Origin Population in California and Texas Relative to a Changing Regional Mainstream." *International Migration Review* 48(2):442–81.

Park, Robert Ezra. 1950. *Race and Culture.* Glencoe, IL: Free Press.

Park, Robert E., and Ernest W. Burgess. 1969 [1921]. *Introduction to the Science of Sociology.* Chicago: University of Chicago Press.

Park, Robert E., Ernest W. Burgess, and Roderick D. McKenzie. 1925. *The City.* Chicago: University of Chicago Press.

Passel, Jeffrey, and D'Vera Cohn. 2011. "Unauthorized Immigrant Population: National and State Trends, 2010." Pew Hispanic Research Center, February.

Passel, Jeffrey S., D'Vera Cohn, Jens Manuel Krogstad, and Ana Gonzalez-Barrera. 2014. "As Growth Stalls, Unauthorized Immigrant Population Becomes More Settled." Pew Research Center's Hispanic Trends Project, September.

Patterson, Orlando. 1998. *The Ordeal of Integration: Progress and Resentment in America's "Racial" Crisis.* New York: Basic Civitas Books.

Pattillo, Mary. 2007. *Black on the Block: The Politics of Race and Class in the City.* Chicago: University of Chicago Press.

Pellow, David N., and Lisa S. Park. 2002. *The Silicon Valley of Dreams: Environmental Injustice, Immigrant Workers, and the High-Tech Global Economy.* New York: New York University Press.

Pew Research Center. 2013. "The Rise of Asian Americans." Washington, DC, April 4.

———. 2015a. "Modern Immigration Wave Brings 59 Million to U.S., Driving Population Growth and Change through 2065: Views of Immigration's Impact on U.S. Society Mixed." Washington, DC, September.

———. 2015b. "On Immigration Policy, Wider Partisan Divide over Border Fence than Path to Legal Status." Washington, DC, October.

Pitti, Stephen J. 2003. *The Devil in Silicon Valley: Northern California, Race, and Mexican Americans.* Princeton, NJ: Princeton University Press.

Portes, Alejandro, and Robert L. Bach. 1985. *Latin Journey: Cuban and Mexican Immigrants in the United States.* Berkeley: University of California Press.

Portes, Alejandro, and Patricia Fernández-Kelly. 2008. "No Margin for Error: Educational and Occupational Achievement among Disadvantaged Children of Immigrants." *The Annals of the American Academy of Political and Social Science* 620(1):12–36.

Portes, Alejandro, and Rubén G. Rumbaut. 2001. *Legacies: The Story of the Immigrant Second Generation.* Berkeley and New York: University of California Press and Russell Sage Foundation.

———. 2006. *Immigrant America: A Portrait.* Berkeley: University of California Press.

Portes, Alejandro, and Erik Vickstrom. 2011. "Diversity, Social Capital, and Cohesion." *Annual Review of Sociology* 37:461–79.

Portes, Alejandro, and Min Zhou. 1993. "The New Second Generation: Segmented Assimilation and its Variants." *Annals of the American Academy of Political and Social Science* 530(1):74–96.

Poterba, James M. 1997. "Demographic Structure and the Political Economy of Public Education." *Journal of Policy Analysis and Management* 16(1):48–66.

Putnam, Robert D. 2000. *Bowling Alone: The Collapse and Revival of American Community.* New York: Simon and Schuster.

———. 2007. "E Pluribus Unum: Diversity and Community in the Twenty-First Century: The 2006 Johan Skytte Prize Lecture." *Scandinavian Political Studies* 30(2):137–74.

Ramakrishnan, S. Karthick, and Allan Colbern. 2015. "The 'California Package' of Immigrant Integration and the Evolving Nature of State Citizenship." *Policy Matters* 6(3):1–19.

Ribas, Vanesa. 2016. *On the Line: Slaughterhouse Lives and the Making of the New South.* Oakland: University of California Press.

Robitaille, Stephen. 1989. "E. Palo Alto Coming of Age—Painfully: City's History a Saga of Unfulfilled Promise." *San Jose Mercury News*, February 12.

Roediger, David R. 1991. *The Wages of Whiteness: Race and the Making of the American Working Class.* New York: Verso.

———. 2005. *Working toward Whiteness: How America's Immigrants Become White: The Strange Journey from Ellis Island to the Suburbs*. New York: Basic Books.

Ruhs, Martin. 2013. *The Price of Rights: Regulating International Labor Migration*. Princeton, NJ: Princeton University Press.

Rumbaut, Rubén G. 2005. "Turning Points in the Transition to Adulthood: Determinants of Educational Attainment, Incarceration, and Early Child-bearing among Children of Immigrants." *Ethnic and Racial Studies* 28(6):1041–86.

Rumbaut, Rubén G., Douglas S. Massey, and Frank D. Bean. 2006. "Linguistic Life Expectancies: Immigrant Language Retention in Southern California." *Population and Development Review* 32(3):447–60.

Saad, Lydia. 2014. "One in Six Say Immigration Most Important U.S. Problem: Immigration Concerns Surged in July, While Economic Mentions Ebbed." Gallup, July 16. www.gallup.com/poll/173306/one-six-say-immigration-important-problem.aspx.

Salter, Phia S., Kelly A. Hirsch, Rebecca J. Schlegel, and Luyen T. Thai. 2015. "Who Needs Individual Responsibility? Audience Race and Message Content Influence Third-Party Evaluations of Political Messages." *Social Psychological and Personality Science* 7(1):29–36.

Sampson, Robert J., Jeffrey D. Morenoff, and Felton Earls. 1999. "Beyond Social Capital: Spatial Dynamics of Collective Efficacy for Children." *American Sociological Review* 64(5):633.

Samson, Frank L. 2013. "Multiple Group Threat and Malleable White Attitudes towards Academic Merit." *Du Bois Review* 10(1):233–60.

Sánchez, George J. 1997. "Face the Nation: Race, Immigration, and the Rise of Nativism in Late 20th Century." *International Migration Review* 31(4):1009–30.

Sanders, Jimy M. 2002. "Ethnic Boundaries and Identity in Plural Societies." *Annual Review of Sociology* 28:327–57.

Santa Clara County Planning Department. 1956. *A General Plan for Berryessa: A Community Chooses between Farm and City*. San Jose, CA: Santa Clara County Planning Department.

Sassen, Saskia. 1991. *The Global City: New York, London, Tokyo*. Princeton, NJ: Princeton University Press.

Saxenian, AnnaLee. 2006. *The New Argonauts: Regional Advantage in a Global Economy*. Cambridge, MA: Harvard University Press.

Schachter, Ariela. 2015. "A Change of Heart or Change of Address? The Geographic Sorting of White Americans' Attitudes towards Immigration." Paper presented at the Annual Meeting of the Population Association of America, San Diego, May 1.

————. 2016. "From 'Different' to 'Similar': An Experimental Approach to Understanding Assimilation." *American Sociological Review* 81(5): 981–1013

Schildkraut, Deborah J. 2005. *Press One for English: Language Policy, Public Opinion, and American Identity.* Princeton, NJ: Princeton University Press.

————. 2010. *Americanism in the Twenty-First Century: Public Opinion in the Age of Immigration.* New York: Cambridge University Press.

Sears, David O. 1993. "Symbolic Politics: A Socio-Psychological Theory." In *Explorations in Political Psychology,* edited by Shanto Iyengar and William J. McGuire, 113–49. Durham, NC: Duke University Press.

Shankar, Shalini. 2008. *Desi Land: Teen Culture, Class, and Success in Silicon Valley.* Durham, NC: Duke University Press.

Sharkey, Patrick. 2013. *Stuck in Place: Urban Neighborhoods and the End of Progress toward Racial Equality.* Chicago: University of Chicago Press.

Shin, Gi-Wook. 2006. *Ethnic Nationalism in Korea: Genealogy, Politics, and Legacy.* Stanford, CA: Stanford University Press.

Simmel, Georg. 1922 [1955]. *Conflict and Web of Group Affiliations.* Glencoe, IL: Free Press.

Singer, Audrey, Susan W. Hardwick, and Caroline Brettell. 2008. *Twenty-First-Century Gateways: Immigrant Incorporation in Suburban America.* Washington, DC: Brookings Institution Press.

Skrentny, John D. 2002. *The Minority Rights Revolution.* Cambridge, MA: Harvard University Press.

————. 2014. *After Civil Rights: Racial Realism in the New American Work-place.* Princeton, NJ: Princeton University Press.

Small, Mario L. 2002. "Culture, Cohorts, and Social Organization Theory: Understanding Local Participation in a Latino Housing Project." *American Journal of Sociology* 108(1):1–54.

————. 2004. *Villa Victoria: The Transformation of Social Capital in a Boston Barrio.* Chicago: University of Chicago Press.

————. 2009. *Unanticipated Gains: Origins of Network Inequality in Everyday Life.* New York: Oxford University Press.

Small, Mario L., David J. Harding, and Michèle Lamont. 2010. "Reconsidering Culture and Poverty." *The Annals of the American Academy of Political and Social Science* 629(1):6–27.

Smith, Robert C. 2005. *Mexican New York: The Transnational Lives of New Immigrants.* Berkeley: University of California Press.

————. 2014. "Black Mexicans, Conjunctural Ethnicity, and Operating Identities Long-Term Ethnographic Analysis." *American Sociological Review* 79(3):517–48.

Smith, Rogers M. 1997. *Civic Ideals: Conflicting Visions of Citizenship in U.S. History.* New Haven, CT: Yale University Press.

South, Scott J., Kyle Crowder, and Erick Chavez. 2005. "Migration and Spatial Assimilation among U.S. Latinos: Classical Versus Segmented Trajectories." *Demography* 42(3):497–521.

Soysal, Yasemin N. 1994. *Limits of Citizenship: Migrants and Postnational Membership in Europe*. Chicago: University of Chicago Press.

Spencer, Kyle. 2015. "New Jersey School District Eases Pressure on Students, Baring an Ethnic Divide." *The New York Times*, December 25. www.nytimes .com/2015/12/26/nyregion/reforms-to-ease-students-stress-divide-a-new-jersey-school-district.html.

Stack, Carol B. 1997 [1970]. *All Our Kin: Strategies for Survival in a Black Community*. New York: Basic Books.

Stevens, Leonard A. 1976. *Equal! The Case of Integration vs. Jim Crow*. New York: Coward, McCann & Geoghegan.

Stinchcombe, Arthur L. 2005. *The Logic of Social Research*. Chicago: University of Chicago Press.

Stocklmeir, Louis. 1975. "Monta Vista: A Small Piece of Paradise." In *Cupertino Chronicle*, edited by Seonaid McArthur and David W. Fuller, vol. 19, 120–35. Cupertino, CA: California History Center, De Anza College.

Telles, Edward E., and Vilma Ortiz. 2008. *Generations of Exclusion: Mexican Americans, Assimilation, and Race*. New York: Russell Sage Foundation.

Telles, Edward E., Mark Q. Sawyer, and Gaspar Rivera-Salgado. 2011. *Just Neighbors? Research on African American and Latino Relations in the United States*. New York: Russell Sage Foundation.

Theiss-Morse, Elizabeth. 2009. *Who Counts as an American? The Boundaries of National Identity*. New York: Cambridge University Press.

Tocqueville, Alexis de. [1840] 1994. *Democracy in America*. New York: Knopf.

Tran, Van C. 2015. "More than Just Black: Cultural Perils and Opportunities in Inner-City Neighborhoods." In *The Cultural Matrix: Understanding Black Youth*, edited by Orlando Patterson, 252–80. Cambridge, MA: Harvard University Press.

Tran, Van C., and Nicol M. Valdez. 2015. "Second-Generation Decline or Advantage? Latino Assimilation in the Aftermath of the Great Recession." *International Migration Review* 51(1):155–90.

Tsuda, Takeyuki. 2003. *Strangers in the Ethnic Homeland: Japanese Brazilian Return Migration in Transnational Perspective*. New York: Columbia University Press.

———. 2016. *Japanese American Ethnicity: In Search of Heritage and Home-land across Generations*. New York: New York University Press.

Tuan, Mia. 1998. *Forever Foreigners or Honorary Whites? The Asian Ethnic Experience Today*. New Brunswick, NJ: Rutgers University Press.

Tyson, Karolyn, William Darity, and Domini R. Castellino. 2005. "It's Not 'a Black Thing'": Understanding the Burden of Acting White and Other

Dilemmas of High Achievement." *American Sociological Review* 70(4):582–605.

U.S. Census Bureau. 2012. "2012 National Population Projections." www.census .gov/population/projections/data/national/2012.html.

———. 2013. "American Community Survey (5-Year Estimates)." Prepared by Social Explorer. www.socialexplorer.com/tables/ACS2013_5yr/R11371538.

Varsanyi, Monica W., Paul G. Lewis, Doris Marie Provine, and Scott Decker. 2012. "A Multilayered Jurisdictional Patchwork: Immigration Federalism in the United States." *Law and Policy* 34(2):138–58.

Vasquez, Jessica M. 2011. *Mexican Americans across Generations: Immigrant Families, Racial Realities.* New York: New York University Press.

Vasquez-Tokos, Jessica. 2017. *Marriage Vows and Racial Choices.* New York: Russell Sage Foundation.

Vertovec, Steven. 2007. "Super-Diversity and its Implications." *Ethnic and Racial Studies* 30:1024–54.

Vigdor, Jacob L. 2004. "Community Composition and Collective Action: Analyzing Initial Mail Response to the 2000 Census." *Review of Economics and Statistics* 86(1):303–12.

Voss, Kim, and Irene Bloemraad. 2011. *Rallying for Immigrant Rights: The Fight for Inclusion in Twenty-First-Century America.* Berkeley: University of California Press.

Voyer, Andrea. 2011. "Disciplined to Diversity: Learning the Language of Multiculturalism." *Ethnic and Racial Studies* 34(11):1874–93.

Wadhwa, Vivek, AnnaLee Saxenian, and F. D. Siciliano. 2012. "Then and Now: America's New Immigrant Entrepreneurs, Part IV." Ewing Marion Kauffman Foundation.

Waldinger, Roger D. 1996. *Still the Promised City? African-Americans and New Immigrants in Postindustrial New York.* Cambridge, MA: Harvard University Press.

———. 2007. "The Bounded Community: Turning Foreigners into Americans in Twenty-First Century LA." *Ethnic and Racial Studies* 30(3):341–74.

Waldinger, Roger, and Michael Lichter. 1996. "Anglos: Beyond Ethnicity?" In *Ethnic Los Angeles,* edited by R. Waldinger and M. Bozorgmehr, 413–41. New York: Russell Sage Foundation.

Wang, Wendy. 2012. "The Rise of Intermarriage Rates, Characteristics Vary by Race and Gender." Pew Research Center, February 16.

Warikoo, Natasha. 2004. "Cosmopolitan Ethnicity: Second Generation Indo-Caribbean Identities." In *Becoming New Yorkers: Ethnographies of the New Second Generation,* edited by Philip Kasinitz, John Mollenkopf, and Mary C. Waters, 361–91. New York: Russell Sage Foundation.

———. 2011. *Balancing Acts: Youth Culture in the Global City.* Berkeley: University of California Press.

Warikoo, Natasha, and Irene Bloemraad. 2015. "'Opportunities to Succeed' or 'Money and More Rights': Social Location and Young People's Views on American Identity." Unpublished paper.

Warner, W. L. and Leo Srole. 1945. *The Social Systems of American Ethnic Groups.* New Haven, CT: Yale University Press.

Warren, Jennifer. 1993. "E. Palo Alto Murder Rate Worst in U.S.; Drug Wars Blamed." *Los Angeles Times,* January 5,http://articles.latimes.com/1993–01–05/local/me-833_1_east-palo-alto.

Waters, Mary C. 1990. *Ethnic Options: Choosing Identities in America.* Berkeley: University of California Press.

———. 1999. *Black Identities: West Indian Immigrant Dreams and American Realities.* New York and Cambridge, MA: Russell Sage Foundation and Harvard University Press.

Waters, Mary C., and Tomás R. Jiménez. 2005. "Assessing Immigrant Assimilation: New Empirical and Theoretical Challenges." *Annual Review of Sociology* 31:105–25.

Waters, Mary C., and Philip Kasinitz. 2015. "The War on Crime and the War on Immigrants: Racial and Legal Exclusion in the Twenty-First-Century United States." In *Anxiety and National Identity: Immigration and Belonging in North America and Europe,* edited by N. Foner and P. Simon, 115–43. New York: Russell Sage Foundation.

Watson, Sophie, and Anamik Saha. 2013. "Suburban Drifts: Mundane Multiculturalism in Outer London." *Ethnic and Racial Studies* 36(12): 2016–34.

Weber, Eugene. 1976. *Peasants into Frenchmen: The Modernization of Rural France, 1870–1914.* Stanford, CA: Stanford University Press.

Weber, Max. 1978 [1922]. *Economy and Society: An Outline of Interpretive Sociology.* Berkeley: University of California Press.

Weis, Lois, Kristin Cipollone, and Heather Jenkins. 2014. *Class Warfare: Class, Race, and College Admissions in Top-Tier Secondary Schools.* Chicago: University of Chicago Press.

Western, Bruce. 2006. *Punishment and Inequality in America.* New York: Russell Sage Foundation.

Wimmer, Andreas. 2004. "Does Ethnicity Matter? Everyday Group Formation in Three Swiss Immigrant Neighbourhoods." *Ethnic and Racial Studies* 27(1):1–36.

———. 2013. *Ethnic Boundary Making: Institutions, Power, Networks.* New York: Oxford University Press.

———. 2015. "Race-Centrism: A Critique and a Research Agenda." *Ethnic and Racial Studies* 38(13):2186–205.

Winant, Howard. 2015. "Race, Ethnicity and Social Science." *Ethnic and Racial Studies* 38(13):2176–85.

Winders, Jamie. 2013. *Nashville in the New Millennium: Immigrant Settlement, Urban Transformation, and Social Belonging*. New York: Russell Sage Foundation.

Wise, Amanda, and Selvaraj Velayutham. 2009. *Everyday Multiculturalism*. New York: Palgrave Macmillan.

Woldoff, Rachael A. 2011. *White Flight/Black Flight: The Dynamics of Racial Change in an American Neighborhood*. Ithaca, NY: Cornell University Press.

Wong, Janelle, S. K. Ramakrishnan, Taeku Lee, and Jane Junn. 2011. *Asian American Political Participation: Emerging Constituents and their Political Identities*. New York: Russell Sage Foundation.

Zhang, Wenquan, and John R. Logan. 2016. "Global Neighborhoods: Beyond the Multiethnic Metropolis." *Demography* 53(6):1933–53.

Zhou, Min. 1992. *Chinatown: The Socioeconomic Potential of an Urban Enclave*. Philadelphia: Temple University Press.

Zhou, Min, and Carl L. Bankston. 1998. *Growing up American: How Vietnamese Children Adapt to Life in the United States*. New York: Russell Sage Foundation.

Zlolniski, Christian. 2006. *Janitors, Street Vendors, and Activists: The Lives of Mexican Immigrants in Silicon Valley*. Berkeley: University of California Press.

Zolberg, Aristide R. 2006. *A Nation by Design: Immigration Policy in the Fashioning of America*. New York: Russell Sage Foundation.

Index

Figures and tables are represented by italic locators, e.g., *15*.

269